AGAINST THE GRAIN

Southern
Radicals
and
Prophets

1929-1959

AGAINST THE GRAIN

Southern

Radicals

and

Prophets

1929-1959

Anthony P. Dunbar

University Press of Virginia

Charlottesville

THE UNIVERSITY PRESS OF VIRGINIA
Copyright © 1981 by the Rector and Visitors
of the University of Virginia

First published 1981
Second printing 1982

Title page: Ralph Tefferteller, staff member of the Highlander Folk School,
recording the experiences of East Tennessee miners, 1937 (promotional
photograph for *People of the Cumberland*, a Frontier Film Production, courtesy
of Highlander Research and Education Center).
Endpapers: Photo © Pat Goudvis 1974.

Library of Congress Cataloging in Publication Data
Dunbar, Anthony P.
  Against the grain.

  Bibliography: p. 263
  Includes index.
  1. Radicalism—Southern States—History. 2. Trade-unions—Southern
States—History. 3. Afro-Americans—Civil rights—Southern States. 4.
Southern States—Economic conditions—1918–   I. Title.
HN79.A133R33   322.4′4′0975   81–1782
ISBN 0–8139–0892–2   AACR2

Printed in the United States of America

For Penny

Preface

Best remembered of all southern protest movements are the Populist campaigns of the 1890s and the civil rights struggle that began in the 1950s. The former was basically an economic protest, and it incorporated the idea of black political equality only as a logical necessity. The expressed goal of the later freedom rides was simply the attainment of equal rights for blacks. Between these two popular movements came a period of widespread dissent and confrontation over much the same issues, fueled by the miseries of the Great Depression, and that is the subject of this book. It was a radical "movement" with many leaders but no messiah, related closely in time to the civil rights uprising but more nearly akin to Populism in the breadth of its economic and social critique.

Among its distinguishing features, the southern radicalism of the 1930s had a basis in Christianity. Many of its articulators were Protestant seminary graduates. Their theology sprang generically from the Social Gospel, but so unabashedly revolutionary was its theme that I refer to it as the "radical gospel." Its impact upon the established church was minimal, but it gave spiritual meaning to many far-flung rebellions of farm and mill workers in the South.

At the time when most of these radical gospel activists came of age, around 1930, progressivism was defined in the South as the belief that race relations must be gradually and moderately improved. The Commission on Interracial Cooperation, founded in 1919 by the Methodist minister Will W. Alexander, expressed this philosophy best. It abhorred lynching, held that blacks must be given greater educational and vocational opportunities, but did not take issue either with systemic economic injustice or with legally imposed racial segregation. By comparison, the visionaries discussed in this book attacked segregation head on and linked all injustice to the inherent oppressiveness of the economic order. Many of them lived to see the civil rights movement renounce their approach, isolate segregation as the central problem, and march to victory on that issue.

This book does not purport to contain the entire history of radical thought and political action in the South during the years concerned. No single work could record all that happened in the mines and factories, all that was attempted by women's organizations, or all that resulted from the dissatisfaction of blacks and the poor in little towns without number. What is offered here is a piece of the history, an account of people native to the region, grounded in its traditions, whose unorthodox views caused them to play a conspicuous and sometimes dangerous role in campaigns aimed at changing the old order of the South.

Most of the material presented here is drawn from manuscript collections and from the recollections of some of the principal figures involved. Both sources have their shortcomings. It is an inescapable tendency to devote more space to topics that are well documented. The papers left by the Southern Tenant Farmers' Union and by Howard Anderson Kester are so extensive and rich that they may tempt a researcher to ignore other pockets of historical evidence. It would be useful to know more about the "other side" of certain political disagreements mentioned in this book, but the record is incomplete. Specifically, one must regret the destruction by fire of large document collections preserved by two ministers, Don West and Claude Williams.

Oral history has been relied upon here to supplement the written word. Personal recollection often provides invaluable insights into the meaning of events, but it must be carefully sifted in this case because angry and emotional differences arose among several of the important figures. The Marxist Claude Williams, for example, could remember very little that was good in the record of the Socialist Howard Kester. Williams professed admiration for the Socialist H. L. Mitchell; yet in another conversation he accused Mitchell of plotting to have him killed when he tried to preach the funeral of an Arkansas sharecropper. Finally, several characters in this book were harmed by the anti-Communist probes of government, and they developed from this experience a habit of being uninformative whenever questions concerning personal political beliefs or activities are asked.

I wish to express my gratitude to Albert Wells, Patricia Hewitt, and Will D. Campbell for providing me with the opportunity to begin this study. I am indebted to Harmon Wray, Cliff Kuhn, Charles H. Martin, Sue Thrasher, John Egerton, Bob Hall, Robert Amberg, and Elizabeth M. Kester for both their interest and their assistance as this work was in progress. Finally the preparation of this volume would have been far less enjoyable were it not for the patience and ability of several fine librarians, including Carolyn A. Wallace, Richard Shrader, and the staff of the Southern Historical Collection and the North Carolina Collection at the University of North Carolina and, especially, Nancy Braun and Clarise DeQuasie at the Vanderbilt University Divinity School Library.

Contents

AGAINST
THE
GRAIN

Southern
Radicals
and
Prophets

1929-1959

I The First Encounter : Wilder

Today one drives past the vine-covered Wilder sign on Tennessee's twisting State Route 85 and discovers that there is no town left at all. But in 1932 Wilder was a busy coal-mining village in the midst of a mountain wilderness interrupted only by tiny farms and steep cow pastures. It was linked to the world outside by a spur line from the Tennessee Central Railroad running fifteen miles through the narrow gorge of the Obey River. Coal by the millions of tons traveled to the distant markets of Chattanooga and Nashville along these rails, and back into Wilder trickled a small supply of dry goods and cash to buy them with.

From rickety bathhouse to squared-off steeple Wilder was owned by the Fentress Coal and Coke Company, and only company employees, a category that included the town's doctor, preacher, constable, and teacher, could live there. The miners' pay was small even by Depression standards: $2 for a sixteen-hour shift. But little of the money ever reached the men's pockets because they were always in debt for all the "extras," like rent on the company house, electricity, burial insurance, doctor's fees, and bathhouse privileges, that the company docked from their checks. The miners also had to furnish their own picks, shovels, drills, and detonators and had to buy their blasting powder from the commissary that commanded the crook in the road that was Wilder's "downtown."

Groceries at this store were expensive. Bacon sold for 15¢ a pound in larger towns cost 40¢ in Wilder. Miners who could not heat their homes sufficiently with the small bags of coal their children scavenged from the railroad tracks had to buy the "blue diamonds" from Fentress for $1.05 a ton — three times more than they had been paid to dig it out of the rocky mountainside. The bitter joke that the miners seemed to be paying the company for the privilege of working very nearly expressed the hard facts of the situation.

Wages were cut twice after the stock market crash of 1929, and a third reduction was scheduled for 1931. In secret, the Wilder miners organized a local of the United Mine Workers, swiftly threatened to strike, and to their surprise quickly won a contract holding wages steady for the time being. But when the contract expired on June 8, 1932, the Fentress Company started firing active union members and announced that wages were going down by 20 percent. The Wilder union, representing about 200 miners, ordered the men to lay down their picks. The strike quickly spread to include about 75 workers at the nearby Davidson Mining Company and 100 more men at the Brier Hill Collieries in the neighboring communities of Twinton and Crawford. It was the first Depression-era conflict for the UMWA in the East Tennessee coalfields, but the international only authorized the strike after the fact, not because it thought it could win.[1]

A few days later Fentress Coal and Coke announced that it was reopening its shafts. The company began recruiting workers from distant mountain communities and bringing them into the mines behind a cordon of hired "deputies." There was no federal law then giving workers the right to organize, compelling employers to bargain in good faith, or governing the conduct of a strike. Coal production was negligible, however, until late in October when a substantial minority of the strikers, facing winter with empty larders, caved in and returned to work. The holdouts reacted with violence. They, or someone, burned down several strikebreakers' barns and fired shots from wooded ambushes at men traveling to work. The company tipple in Davidson was set afire, and, in broad daylight, two power substations of the Fentress Company were dynamited with the company's own powder. The concussion was so great, a local paper reported, that books "rocked off their shelves" at the home of mine superintendent L. L. Shivers. The union claimed that some of these acts were perpetrated by the company to provoke state intervention.[2]

The Wilder saga began to share the front pages of Tennessee newspapers with the repeal of Prohibition, the Japanese invasion of Manchuria, and a hunger march on Washington. A UMWA attorney, Hal Clements, went to court to obstruct temporarily the coal company's attempt to evict the strikers, and Fentress retaliated by sending a petition bearing 250 signatures to Governor Henry H. Horton asking for troops to restore order. Along with this petition came the news that a bridge on the Tennessee Central spur line had been blown up late on the night of November 16. This made the governor act, and he sent a troop of 17 cavalrymen from Cookeville to the strike scene to guard railroad and company property. When a second trestle was dynamited on November 23, not fifteen minutes after soldiers had ridden past the spot on a railroad trolley, 160 more guardsmen were moved to Wilder. Two more bridges were burned on the day they arrived.[3]

The troopers brought little peace to the erupting town. They searched miners' homes without reason or warrants, consumed much moonshine liquor, and were given to firing their automatic weapons at nothing in particular. Wilder's Sunday school teacher, Waymon D. Jones, protested to an influential Nashville pastor that "on last Saturday night, Dec the 10th at about midnight When the miners Their wives & children were in bed Sound asleep they were awaken by the plattering of The machine guns   no one was dynamiting burning up Company's property . . . no one was stealing or doing anything. they have got no case Whatsoever   people at home quiet and peacefull with their condition   Then the

National guards out Shooting Around it's a Shame to the name of the Great State of Tennessee."[4]

Sympathizers with the miners' cause now began to drift into Wilder. Not all of them had previous experience with labor conflicts, but they were strongly motivated by socialist and religious ideas. The Wilder battles helped these educated radicals to jell into the nucleus of a southern protest movement that effectively advanced the causes of civil rights and organized labor during and beyond the remainder of the decade.

One of the first of these labor supporters to venture into the community was twenty-seven-year-old Myles Horton. Bespectacled and always courteous, he would have been taken for a college professor by the miners except that his mannerisms were "country" (he used words like "roo-cus" to mean disturbance). Horton was the educational director of the newly formed Highlander Folk School located some ninety miles south near Monteagle, Tennessee. It was a small establishment created to train leaders for the South's emerging labor movement, and Horton hoped to find a few prospective students at Wilder. He was invited to sit down to a Thanksgiving Day meal of turnips and sweet potato pie at the home of Barney Graham, the local union president. Their small supper, Horton noticed, used up the last flour in the house.

The teacher was waiting for a bus out of town the next morning when he was arrested by Captain Hubert Crawford of the 109th Cavalry "in connection with recent disturbances." The officer, Horton said, accused him of loafing around the sector with the intention of "obtaining information which he would teach in his school." Horton was taken to the home of the mine superintendent, which served as militia headquarters, and was held overnight while his case was discussed. In the morning the adjutant general released him with instructions to leave town.[5]

Horton rode the bus to Crossville to tell his story at the church of the Reverend Abram Nightingale, a liberal Congregational minister. A reporter from Knoxville covered the sermon for his paper, and the upshot, according to Don West, chief organizer on the Highlander staff, was to "stir up a lot of hell" and provoke accusations that Horton was an outside agitator using his school as a cover for Communist subversion. These charges would be repeated so often in the years to come by politicians and hostile editors that they became accepted as the truth by the majority of Tennesseans who heard about Highlander.[6]

Four days after Horton's arrest Fentress Coal and Coke won an injunction against the union prohibiting picketing, meetings, and just about any action normally associated with a labor dispute. For all practical purposes, the Wilder strike was broken. About seventy-five families stuck with the union, however, hoping that the tide might be turned after Franklin Roosevelt and Tennessee's New Deal governor, Hill McAlister, were sworn in.

Governor Horton thought the strike was finished, and he withdrew the troops three days before Christmas. Within the next two weeks, however, a mine guard and two strikebreakers were shot, workers at the Davidson mine were driven from the pits by a mob of union men, and another bridge on the Tennessee Railroad was demolished. The union claimed that a lot of this violence was being orchestrated by the company, but the governor sent troops back in to patrol the "holler." They were withdrawn for good after McAlister's inauguration.[7]

A systematic effort to bring relief to the now destitute families began on November 27, 1932, just as winter was closing in, when about twenty people were convened in Nashville by Howard Kester, southern secretary of the New York-based Fellowship of Reconciliation and a leading figure in the South's tiny interracial movement. The group elected an emissary, Albert Barnett, a Methodist minister and professor at Scarritt College, to visit Wilder to see if reconciliation between the company and the union were possible.

Barnett began his visit at the headquarters of the Fentress Company, where he was told that the strike was broken and that there was nothing left to talk about. He then met with the strike leaders, who explained how desperate their situation was. Only a small monthly allowance from the UMWA permitted them to obtain a ration of lard and meal, and scores of children had been taken out of school because they had no clothes to wear. Measles, pellagra, and pneumonia were rampant, and the company doctor, who had lost his job after siding with the strikers, was out of medicine. Barnett carried the word to Nashville that "men and their families are hungry and cold, and abundant relief in the form of clothing and food must be supplied." Barnett also noted that the strikers had heard it rumored that their recent visitor, Myles Horton, was a "red," and they did not want any "reds" in their midst. "They were greatly relieved on being assured that Mr. Horton was not a 'Red' and that they could regard him as a good friend," Barnett reported.[8]

The outgrowth of Barnett's visit was the Wilder Emergency Relief Committee. Howard Kester and his wife, Alice, were charged with distributing such supplies as the committee could scavenge from donors who were themselves hard-pressed by the national crisis. Several hundred cans of food were collected by Julius Mark, rabbi of the Nashville synagogue, and the Kesters borrowed a truck to deliver these a few days before Christmas.[9] "Barefooted and in rags," Howard Kester reported, "strong mountain men and women walked in the slush and snow to the relief station which was established by the WERC. . . . Children were brought wrapped in blankets with no body clothes about them. Beans, coffee, sugar, meal and meat were distributed to all. There was candy, apples and toys for the children of the strikers. On

Christmas eve there was warmth and cheer in Wilder for the first time in months."[10]

The Kesters took up residence in Wilder and distributed the supplies which began trickling in from two politically left-wing national organizations: the Emergency Committee for Strikers' Relief and the Church Emergency Relief Committee. The former was chaired by Norman Thomas, leader of the Socialist party, and directed by his aide, Jack Herling. The latter was chaired by Alva W. Taylor, a Disciples of Christ minister and professor of social ethics at the Vanderbilt University School of Religion, and directed by the Reverend James Myers, industrial secretary of the Federal Council of Churches. Myers had been a church liaison to the labor movement for several years and had preached the funeral service for the six cotton mill workers killed in the Marion, North Carolina, strike of 1929.

At first the Kesters, who were both Socialist party members and strong union supporters, gave food only to the families on strike. But they soon bowed to pressure from Taylor, who said of the strikebreakers: "Their kids bellies hurt when they are empty and my book tells me to feed even the enemy." "When we go socialist we will want a few *living* miners to dig the coal even if it is more idealistic to let them starve for the sake of propaganda," Taylor added. This Vanderbilt professor was an enthusiastic New Deal Democrat and wrote that "I am for these ardent young radicals [like Myles Horton and the Kesters] heart and soul, but must object to the apostolic zeal that makes socialism and every other good thing synonomous." He had taught Howard Kester (nicknamed "Buck") in seminary and remarked that, "Buck is the salt of the earth and one of my favorite of all my students. I gave him a suit of clothes the other day. *But* on the explicit promise that he wear it and not give it to the first socialist that came along in need."[11]

Alice Kester passed out lemons to treat measles and yeast

and vegetables to treat pellagra. Barney Graham, the union leader who kept the strike alive, was completely penniless, and he turned his children over to the Kesters to be cared for in Nashville. The girl, Birtha, was malnourished but soon recovered; her brother, Barney Junior, was kept at Vanderbilt Hospital until his emaciated condition was tracked to an allergy. The Kesters returned the children to Wilder reluctantly because their mother had acute pellagra and epilepsy and was barely able to function. During this period the Kesters were living on $5 per week and donating whatever else they raised to the relief fund. Alice developed a chronic condition which she would afterwards describe as a nervous disorder. It could not have been incapacitating at the time, however, for according to her log the relief committee distributed 14,000 items of clothing and between five and six tons of food by the end of July 1933.[12]

Norman Thomas visited Wilder on March 5, between engagements in Asheville and Atlanta. He gave a morale-boosting speech about the mission of organized labor, but the union had little chance to build upon the enthusiasm he aroused. On Saturday, April 29, Myers and Taylor accompanied Kester to Wilder to pick up Barney Graham for a trip to the Red Cross office at the county seat. Along the way Kester asked Graham if he would like to make a trip to Washington, D.C., four days later to speak before a Continental Congress on Economic Reconstruction sponsored by the Socialist party and several unions. Graham promised, "If I'm here on Thursday I'll go with you." But by the end of the next day Barney Graham was dead.[13]

He had gone out after dark to find some medicine for his wife. Graham walked down Wilder's main street and must have passed the church where late services were in progress. Lounging outside the company store was a group of mine guards, some of whom wore deputy's badges. No impartial observer was on the scene to record what was said between

Graham and the deputies, but it was reported that suddenly the street became "a bedlam of roaring firearms." As the deputies told it, Graham walked up brandishing a pistol and started insulting them. Mine guard Jack "Shorty" Green, a Fentress County native who most recently had been a company gunman in the coalfields of Illinois, "commanded peace"; but Graham raised his gun and fired twice. Green returned the fire and emptied his gun into the body of the union president. Deputy "Doc" Thompson swore he had seen the whole thing and that Green had only pulled the trigger in self-defense.

These were the official accounts, and the coal miners believed none of them. By the time they had poured from their houses and the church, Barney Graham was lying dead in the middle of the street, his body riddled by ten bullets. Four of the slugs, according to a newspaper's account of the statement of the examining physician, had hit Graham in the back. The mine police set a machine gun astraddle the union president's body and camped there, holding all onlookers at bay until orders came to turn the slain leader over to his friends.[14]

Alice and Howard Kester stayed at the Graham home that night to try to comfort the widow and her three children. Howard would later write of this sorrowful vigil: "There was not a crumb of food in the house except for the groceries we had brought. Furniture was scarce and no beds were available so we spent the night in two straight back chairs. The only light available came from a cotton string wick inserted in a Coca Cola bottle partially filled with kerosene. It was an awesome and terrible night as sobs of grief came from Mrs. Graham and the children. There were tears coming from all eyes including our own, and when morning broke neighbors began to bring in such food as they could spare from their own meagre supply."[15]

Graham's murder had been anticipated well in advance. A week before the shooting Green had been pointed out to

Horton as a "hired assassin" imported from Illinois to kill the union president. Horton had taken a snapshot of Green standing in front of the company store showing off his three pistols, and he had gone to Nashville with Myers, Taylor, and Albert Barnett to try to show the photograph to the governor. They got only as far as the commissioner of labor, and the trip produced no results. A few days later it was too late.[16]

Graham was buried on Tuesday afternoon in the village cemetery. The body was carried home from a funeral parlor in Livingston, and as the hearse reached the top of the mountain overlooking Wilder, the coal-laden crest that had set this war into motion, seven hundred miners and their families joined the processional. Following an American flag, they marched two-by-two down the winding highway to Wilder where they somberly circled the spot on which Graham had died and went then to the cemetery where several hundred more awaited. Mrs. Graham was too ill, either from pellagra or grief, to leave the automobile that had carried her to the graveside.

The Reverend H. S. Johnson, a miner, performed the service with Kester, who said simply, "I knew Barney Graham intimately. I had no better friend." William Turnblazer, president of the UMWA district, said at the graveside that Barney Graham would be "enshrined in the hearts of workers all over America." But all in all the UMWA had done little to aid the strike. After Graham's murder Kester wrote to John L. Lewis, president of the international union, to ask for help in prosecuting Green. Lewis promised $500 to hire a lawyer, and he may have sent the money to Turnblazer, but it never reached Wilder. Kester personally offered to pay the union's attorney $300 if he would act as a special prosecutor at Green's trial, held in Jamestown on September 6, 1933, but the lawyer failed to show up in court. The state's prosecution was anything but vigorous, and Green was acquitted upon his plea of self-defense.[17]

The Kesters drove to Washington, D.C., on the weekend following Graham's death to attend the Continental Congress on Economic Reconstruction. Instead of Barney Graham, they took his eldest child, twelve-year-old Della Mae Graham. Outfitted in new clothes, she gave a short, stumbling speech about the strike and her father's death. Little money was raised, but many people learned for the first time what had happened at Wilder.

There were other shootings and outbreaks of violence at Wilder, but with the death of Graham the strike was hopelessly broken. Green and his lawyer were fired at, but not hit, one day as they drove from Jamestown to Wilder. Two strikebreakers were attacked late in May, and one of them was injured so severely that he died on the way to the hospital. Ten union men were arrested for this crime. Kester's efforts to link the Graham killing to high officials in the Fentress Company marked him in some quarters as a dangerous man, and the armed guard that surrounded him whenever he was in the coal country was increased.[18]

The relief committee brought two community workers to Wilder. One was Margaret S. Lehman, a German Baptist who had studied nursing in London and had first come to the United States to care for the children of Walter Rauschenbusch, the prophet of the Social Gospel movement. The other was Eleanor Kellogg, a Mississippi woman who had studied at the Brookwood Labor College founded by A. J. Muste. Kellogg lived in Wilder with the Delta Rigsby family, and in their home she came to know the life of the poor. "Never have I seen people in a more wretched, distressing state than these people up here," she wrote to Taylor. "Barefooted, ragged, sick and above all hungry. There is nothing in the way of food, medicine, and clothing that they don't need. Babies are dying of bloody flux to the right and to the left. People are ill with pellagra on every side . . . there is no telling how many have hookworm, venereal diseases, malaria, and goodness knows what else. I am no nurse . . . but I would to God I were when some desperate mother tells of her baby dying of the bloody flux." Kellogg organized clubs for boys and girls of various ages and kept them active with crafts, music, carpentry, and lessons about labor unions. Della Mae Graham was in the older girls' club, and it was likely for one of its programs that she wrote "The Ballad of Barney Graham."

On April the thirtieth
In 1933,
Upon the streets of Wilder
They shot him, brave and free.

They shot my darling father
He fell upon the ground;
'Twas in the back they shot him;
The blood came streaming down.

They took the pistol handles
And beat him on the head;
The hired gunmen beat him
Till he was cold and dead.

When he left home that morning
I thought he'd soon return;
But for my darling father
My heart shall ever yearn.

We carried him to the graveyard
And there we lay him down;
To sleep in death for many a year
In the cold and sodden ground.

Although he left the union

He tried so hard to build,
His blood was spilled for justice
And justice guides us still.

Within a year Della Mae was married, at the age of thirteen, to a coal miner named Jess Smith. Graham's widow, Barney Junior, and Birtha soon moved in, and Smith became a second father to the younger children. He mined coal until 1951, contracted black lung, then moved the family to Dayton, Ohio, where he found a job in a sheet metal factory.[19]

Six weeks after Graham's death, Congress passed the National Industrial Recovery Act. This triumph for organized labor capped Roosevelt's famed "One Hundred Days," which had already seen the president declare a national bank holiday to keep the country solvent, congressional passage of a resolution to repeal Prohibition and legalization of 3.2 beer to lift the nation's spirits, the appropriation of $500 million for relief to the jobless, vast appropriations for state highways and shipbuilding, and the establishment of the Tennessee Valley Authority. It was the NIRA that reached the farthest for it guaranteed the right of employees to organize unions "free from the interference, restraint, or coercion of employers of labor." United Mine Workers President John L. Lewis compared it to the Emancipation Proclamation, and labor's chieftains immediately launched an organizing campaign which brought hundreds of thousands of new members into the American Federation of Labor. The UMWA emerged from this drive as the largest and richest union in the AFL.

The NIRA was no help to the Wilder miners who had had to wage their strike as a guerilla war. While workers elsewhere were being signed up en masse in the summer of 1933 by a new wave of tough-talking and combative union organizers, Wilder's blacklisted miners sank deeper into idleness and drunkenness. A few joined clandestine gangs that stuck up grocery trucks on the highway for food.[20] It was the fall of

1934, after the last bitter holdouts had been evicted from their company houses, when some real help finally came their way. Due to Horton's pestering, Arthur E. Morgan, chairman of the fledgling Tennessee Valley Authority, agreed to give the Wilder miners preference in hiring for TVA jobs. At Kester's request Morgan also arranged for Dagnall F. Folger to venture into the Wilder countryside to begin selecting residents for the Cumberland Homesteads. This was an early project of the New Deal's Resettlement Administration designed to relocate some of the poorest rural families to new farms which, in time, they would own. Folger, a Clemson University engineer who subsequently selected "human engineering" as his vocation, was responsible for seeing that the first residents of these homesteads, located just south of Crossville, Tennessee, were the exhausted and defeated remnants of the Wilder local.[21]

The Wilder strike, however costly it was to its participants, was a beginning of sorts for a new radical movement in the South. In the midst of the outbreaks of violence and disease the Kesters, Don West, and Myles Horton saw close at hand the callous and wasteful exploitation of muscle and sweat and the bareknuckled ferocity of class conflict. Their careers after Wilder place them squarely within the southern tradition of agrarian radicalism, except that they were not farmers, though born on the farm, but educated ministers.

Howard Kester and Don West had studied under Alva Taylor at the Vanderbilt School of Religion. Alice Kester was a committed YWCA worker, and Myles Horton had been trained by Reinhold Niebuhr and Harry Ward at Union Theological Seminary in New York City. They, and most of the other dissidents who formed the core of the South's radical movement in the 1930s, saw the church as a critically important instrument of change. Some even thought it would play a daring and prophetic role as the vanguard of a cataclysmic class struggle that would bring forth the Kingdom of God on

Earth. Their ideas about changing society were further affected by the debates about socialism arising in northern cities and in Europe, by the expanding power of industrial
unions, and by the commitment of the national administration, however cautious, to reforming the South.

Their movement was, in a sense, born at Wilder. It would
reach beyond the coalfields to assail the structures of Jim
Crow, take on the plantation overseers, challenge the church,
expand the acceptable boundaries of southern liberalism,
and, as it joined the broader political current, alter state and
national policy on race and rural development. One of the
individuals who tried to do all of these things, in a career of
activism that lasted from the 1920s to the 1960s, was Howard
Anderson Kester, a Virginian who was proud to say that the
divided strands of his family represented both abolitionism
and the Old Confederacy.

Fellowship of Reconciliation Conference, LeMoyne College, Memphis, Tennessee, March 1932. Middle row, from left, W. R. Amberson (2d), Alice Kester (6th); front row, from left, Guy Sarvis (2d), Howard Kester (4th), Claude Williams

(5th). The poster held by the latter reads: "War The World's Enemy." (*Howard A. Kester Papers, Southern Historical Collection, UNC, Chapel Hill*)

The
II Early Days

Howard Kester was born on July 21, 1904, in Martinsville, Virginia, a foothills town of 2,500. It was divided into white and black sections by the "Dick and Willie Railroad," as the Danville & Western line was then known. Howard's father, William, was a Pennsylvanian, a master tailor, and nominally a Quaker. Earlier ancestors, family tradition had it, had signed the first declaration against slavery in America. William had married Nannie Holt, the daughter of a Virginia plantation overseer, whose youth had been spent surrounded by relatives lamenting the collapse of the Confederate cause. She cherished the family silver that her forebears had hidden from Yankee cavalrymen in the banks of the James River because it was a last memento of her clan's former place in society. Nannie's own childhood had been spent in proud poverty, and she hoped that her last son, Howard, would enjoy educational opportunities denied to her generation. To underscore her wishes she had it announced at Howard's baptism that his life would be devoted to the Christian ministry.[1]

Like most southern towns Martinsville was given to reliving past tragedies. The War Between the States was grandly and frequently commemorated. Though the last two Confederate generals—Longstreet and Gordon — had died in the year of Howard's birth, aged veterans still held court on the downtown street corners and assembled for annual parades. Segregation codes were strictly enforced, and lynchings were not uncommon. William Kester was a Ku Klux Klansman, but his uniform was seldom seen. Howard's more vivid memory was his horror at watching a black traveler being beaten almost to death for some minor social error. At home the Kester children were forbidden to say the word "nigger."[2]

The family moved to Beckley, West Virginia, in 1916 to capitalize on the wartime boom in coal production. Playing on the line for the Woodrow Wilson High football team, Howard picked up the nickname "Buck." Almost no one who later met him in the sharecroppers' union, at secret interracial gatherings, or in the church referred to the spunky, muscular young man as Howard; it was always "Buck." He won a ministerial scholarship from the Presbyterian church and in 1921 returned to Virginia to attend Lynchburg College. Here he was active in sports and the Young Men's Christian Association, and he pledged to carry the gospel to African jungles as a member of the Student Volunteer Movement.[3]

But his attention soon was turned to social problems in the United States, ironically, by his participation in the YMCA's 1923 American Pilgrimage of Friendship to Europe. Kester and fifteen fellow students were guided through eight countries to acquaint them with the wreckage wrought by war, and indeed they were shocked at the political unrest still rocking the continent four years after the Treaty of Versailles. A government fell while they were in Germany, and a meal that had cost 100,000 marks when they arrived cost 5,000,000 six days later. They talked to White Russian refugees in Prague who were plotting to overthrow the Soviets, and in once stately Vienna they found the sidewalks lined with tubercular beggars and maimed soldiers. But it was a tour through the Jewish ghettos of Krakow and Warsaw that startled Kester the most—not just their "filth, poverty, and stench," but the massive chains that until a few years before had been drawn across the stone gates each evening to seal the Jews within. Kester was horrified by these steel links, which he described like a Virginian as a "tremendous log chain." He suddenly realized, as he later recalled, that "this is exactly what we do to Negroes in the United States."

20

Channing Tobias, the foremost black in the American YMCA, talked to Kester soon after he returned from Europe and then nominated him for a job as southern representative of the YMCA's European Student Relief project. In this work Kester, still a student, traveled across the South from Richmond to New Orleans speaking on white and black campuses and taking donations of money and textbooks to send to European students. In the town of Lynchburg he organized an interracial fellowship of young people from the black Lynchburg Seminary, Randolph Macon Women's College, and his own school. The group was made up of the more serious members of each college's YMCA or YWCA, and, however small, it was one of the first racially mixed collegiate organizations in the South. Its community activity was to put on gospel singings and Bible readings, and the members also integrated the larger assemblies of Christian students in Virginia. Kester was stricken from the list of candidates for the Presbyterian ministry at about this time because his church elders heard him call for higher coal miners' wages from a pulpit in Thurmond, West Virginia. They subjected him to an interrogation, and he was dismissed for failing to affirm the Virgin Birth and other matters of doctrine.[4]

In their senior year at Lynchburg, John C. Crighton, Harriet K. Cutter, Francis A. Henson, and Kester, all of whom ran the college newspaper and were considered radical, put out an issue under the banner headline: "THE YOUTH OF THE WORLD ARE TIRED OF WAR." Kester wrote the main essay, in which he condemned war as "an utter denial of the Jesus way of life" and called on Christians to refuse to serve in the army. In defense of the charge that this was cowardly, Kester asked, "How much strength, courage, conviction . . . does it take to suffer social ostracism, to be called a yellow cur, to be subject to open persecution and probably imprisonment or death for your belief in Jesus?" A group of angry students burst into the newspaper office, carted off the entire pressrun, and burned

it; but the college president, John T. Hundley, soon apprehended the guilty ones and forced them to make restitution.[5]

In spite of his unpopular views, Howard "Buck" Kester cut
an awesome figure at Lynchburg. Always at the center of
heated dicussions, rushing to catch a train, or scurrying across
campus to attend an important meeting, he was plainly out to
make a mark on life. A fellow student, a freshman when Kester was a senior, years later remarked, "We would watch him
striding across the yard, and though we did not know exactly
what he was doing, we were sure it had a deep significance."[6]
In 1925 the college yearbook gave this farewell to the departing senior: "A bright student, a hard worker, a leader, warm
and sincere. A brother to all. Fearless. An idealist with revolutionary tendencies, and with a code that brooks no compromise. A keen student of national and international affairs.
'Buck' is a man who demands the respect, admiration, and
love of all who know him. Such qualities have made his influence felt, not only on campus and in Virginia, but throughout
the South. His wide activities indicate that he is destined to
occupy a place of importance in world affairs."[7]

Kester attended Princeton Theological Seminary briefly in
1925, but was repelled by its conservative intellectual climate. He returned to Virginia to continue his YMCA work.
During the previous summer he and several other students
had begun to lobby the southern YMCA and YWCA chapters
to desegregate the all-white leadership conferences held at
Blue Ridge Assembly in North Carolina. All the Student
Christian Leadership meetings were then segregated: whites
met at Blue Ridge and blacks went either to Kings Mountain,
North Carolina, or to Waveland, Mississippi. The student liberals presented a resolution to erase this color barrier at the
1925 policy meeting of the southern YMCA, but it was defeated. They won permission, however, to invite Mary Mc-
Leod Bethune, founder of Bethune-Cookman College, and
George Washington Carver, the leading scientist of Tuskegee

Institute and, possibly, the South, to address the whites at Blue Ridge Assembly in 1926.[8]

Kester joined those making plans for the appearance of the dignitaries. Bethune planned only a quick stopover at the conference, but Carver made it clear that he wanted to spend several days at Blue Ridge. The rub was that the director of the Assembly grounds, the Reverend W. D. Weatherford, a noted southern liberal, insisted that by state law the retreat's hotel and dining hall were off limits to the Negro no matter how famous he was. Since there was no Negro hotel nearby, the Lynchburg delegates rented a cottage on the Blue Ridge grounds, and here they hosted Carver and brought his meals from the dining room in covered trays.[9]

Carver's speech was on "The Potential of Southern Agriculture," and though YMCA officials had been apprehensive about the talk for months, it was well received. Some of the student listeners, including the entire delegations from Florida and Louisiana, had threatened to walk out, but they were kept in their seats by the persuasive remarks of the presiding officer, the Reverend Will W. Alexander of the Commission on Interracial Cooperation. In the end, the entire audience gave Carver a standing ovation.

Carver and Kester began a warm friendship that week. Both were early risers, and they walked the Blue Ridge trails together. When the conference ended, Carver invited Kester to visit Tuskegee later in the summer. Kester also met Alice Harriet Harris at Blue Ridge. She had just finished her fifth semester at Wesleyan College in Macon, Georgia, and she was a liberal YWCA member. She accompanied him to a sunrise prayer service on High Top Mountain and selected him as her escort on the hike back down. Three weeks later they were engaged, and in eight months they were married.

Kester was the first white southerner to be a "fraternal delegate" to the black YMCA conference at Kings Mountain that summer. He met people there, including Mordecai Johnson, Herbert King, H. W. Pope, Howard Thurman, Sue Bailey, John Dillingham, and Benjamin E. Mays, who were emerging as religious and political leaders. Alice Kester also became a regular participant at these black assemblies in later years. The simple fact that she was a white southern woman made her presence significant. After the 1930 Kings Mountain conference, its director, Benjamin Mays, told her that "you made a finer contribution to racial understanding than you can ever possibly comprehend."[10]

Neither Howard's nor Alice's parents could tolerate the new racial attitudes their children were exploring. William Kester expelled Howard from the family home, an exile which continued for two years until William signified that he had forgiven his son by giving him a $10 gold piece. Howard went to Tuskegee nevertheless, stopping only to visit his fiancée at her home in Decatur, Georgia. Alice was the fourth of the six children of Herman L. and Ruby Nancy Slappey Harris. She had been born in 1904 on a large plantation in Warren County, Georgia, managed by her father. Her mother died when Alice was quite young, and the Harris family moved to the outskirts of Atlanta. Herman Harris was outspoken on the subject of white supremacy. A devout Methodist, he had written according to family tradition, some of the popular antiblack speeches given by the Reverend Horace Mallard Dubose who was installed as Methodist bishop of Tennessee in 1925.

Herman would not sanction his daughter's marriage to a man who claimed friendship with George Washington Carver. He made life so miserable for Alice that she left home and moved in with an elder sister, Bulah, in Atlanta. The couple were married in this house in a small ceremony which none of the parents could bear to attend. Alice never saw her father again, for Herman Harris's various business ventures went sour, and he committed suicide in 1928 in Atlanta's Piedmont Park.

Howard Kester stayed two months at Tuskegee during the summer of 1926. He lived in Carver's home and spent most of his time in the scientist's laboratory compiling a scrapbook of Alabama herbs. The unlikely pair attended church together, and once, on the way to vespers, Carver displayed what Kester thought were mystical powers. Carver was a tidy dresser and in the habit of wearing a flower or sprig of herbs in the lapel of his coat. He came to pick up Kester for chapel service one Sunday and brought with him two roses. One was for Kester to wear; the other for himself. The day was "hot enough to boil an egg right out in the open," and before long the petals of Kester's rose fell away. Yet that evening when the pair met Carver's flower was still fresh and bright. How could it be so well preserved, the student asked. Carver replied, "It is because the rose knows that I love it."[11]

One of the letters Howard wrote to Alice that summer reveals a little about what the steamy Alabama nights and the strange surroundings were stirring inside him. "My Dearest Alice," he wrote:

I wish you were here with me tonight for two reasons. First because I need you and secondly because you would see a part of me you have not yet known directly, and I wish you to know me from all angles. My brow is . . . drawn and across my forehead reach two long wrinkles as I sit and look out upon the world. I see all the sorrow, all the pain, all the suffering. I look past the superficial lives, the unreal lives of countless men and women and see in their heart of hearts a deep flowing desire for reality: I look out and see men, rich men, honorable men, capable men leaning over tables planning wreck and ruin to countless thousands yet unborn; I look out and see boys and girls walking leisurely down the road that leads to disaster and ruin; I see old men and women broken in the wheels of industry, crying and in great bitterness; I look out and see Negroes pushed aside, Hindoos driven away, Chinese maltreated because their skin is not white. I see the misery and poverty in countless cities and hear the cry of little children for bread, and I grow weary and downcast.

What is to be done? How am I to use my life, are questions I have asked myself thousands of times. Tonight they beat against my head until it feels as if it will split. . . . How difficult it is to forget self in this thing and abandon ones self to God.[12]

The Kesters moved to Nashville in 1926 where Howard enrolled at the Vanderbilt University School of Religion. At first they found the atmosphere congenial. An impressive collection of white and black intellectuals met for lunch each Saturday at the Negro Baptist Publishing House, including the sociologist Charles S. Johnson and his brother James Weldon Johnson; J. B. Matthews and Albert Barnett, both left-leaning Scarritt College professors; and liberal white students like Louise Young and Wilson Newman. Alice tried to overcome her youthful conditioning at one of these meetings by eating her first meal at the same table with blacks, but she could not keep her food down. She ran back to Vanderbilt in tears.[13]

The episode completed a change in Alice, however, and she thereafter fraternized naturally with blacks. She became the chairwoman of the Nashville YWCA's Industrial Committee, and as such was involved in the Y's programs for women factory workers. In these days before the unions came to middle Tennessee, these nighttime meetings of boot makers, textile workers, bookbinders, and bag makers gave women laborers a rare opportunity to articulate their discontents.[14]

The Kesters got into hot water fast by helping to organize a meeting protesting the intervention of the Western powers in China in 1927. China at that time was divided between antagonistic warlords, each of whom made separate pacts granting trade monopolies to Britain, France, Italy, and the United States. General Chiang Kai-shek and his nationalist forces were disrupting this lucrative arrangement, and they had their enemies bottled up in Shanghai in the early months

25

of 1927. Amid clamorings for a Marine expedition to China to exact reparations for lost American property, the Nashville students made their demonstration. It was organized by the interracial group that met at the Publishing House and held in Wesley Chapel on March 29. About half of the two hundred students who showed up to denounce United States militarism were black. The crowd was addressed by J. B. Matthews, who spoke to international issues as a socialist and a former missionary to Java; Malcolm Nurse, a Fisk student from Trinidad; and J. H. H. Berckmann, a China missionary who had barely escaped Nanking before the British bombed that city. Warmed by the speeches, the group composed a cable to the State Department asking the government to withdraw its soldiers from China. They sent another telegram to the Student Christian Associations in China saying, "We sympathize with Chinese students in their aspirations for national unity and sovereignty." According to the *Evening Tennessean*, Uncle Sam was "held up to scorn."[15]

Vanderbilt's chancellor, James H. Kirkland, was widely admired for his liberal views, but he did not bother to conceal his anger after he read the newspapers. He summoned the presidents of the city's colleges to a closed-door meeting at which he said, according to the campus grapevine, "I don't mind the jackasses braying. I just don't want them braying on my campus." Kester was fired from his job as assistant secretary of the university YMCA, and, left with no means of financing his education, he accepted a post as youth secretary of the pacifist Fellowship of Reconciliation in New York City. The Kesters soon moved to Manhattan, and then to Leonia, New Jersey, when the city noises became too much for them. Another Nashvillian followed them to New York. Under fire for speaking at the China protest meeting and for his interracial activities, J. B. Matthews resigned from Scarritt College and, on Kester's recommendation, he was hired as co-director of the FOR. Matthews soon became one of the most popular orators at leftist political events in the country.[16]

Kester's job was to make the rounds of college towns in the South and Midwest speaking on such topics as the perils of United States military involvement in Nicaragua. It became his custom to ride in the black "Jim Crow" cars when going by rail although this was an illegal act for a white person. He was roughly handled more than once by angry train conductors, but he was never arrested. In November 1928 he spoke at Jackson State College and wrote Alice: "Jackson is a city of shanties, colored and white. Some are the worst I have ever seen. I passed through portions of the city solely inhabited by Negroes and it was positively awful. I don't see how people could live in some of the houses and right in the heart of Jackson behind the *State Capital*. The odor was terrific. I do not blame the poor Negroes, but I do blame these lilly white Mississippians who allow such conditions to exist. . . .This city is a stain on the record of human progress and enlightenment." And he added, "I am staying at the Edwards Hotel which is the best hotel in Jackson. Whiskey and Women are all the go. Three times yesterday I was asked if I didn't want either or both."[17]

Kester persuaded the FOR to create the part-time position of southern secretary for him, and he and Alice moved back to Nashville in the summer of 1929. He again enrolled at Vanderbilt's School of Religion, although he knew that some there thought him "radical, red and crazy."[18] The notable intellectual force on campus then emanated from a group of professors, including John Crowe Ransom, Donald Davidson, and Allen Tate, who became known as the Nashville Agrarians. In 1930, along with nine other southerners, they published *I'll Take My Stand*, a collection of essays lauding the "classical" agricultural civilization of the South. Kester attended one of Ransom's lectures but found nothing of value in it. Where, he wondered, was any concern for the welfare of black southerners? It was "utterly irrational," he concluded, to find virtue in the "magnolias, mocking birds, and moonlight" of a dying rural culture based upon isolation and racism. The future of the South, he thought, must be linked to socialized industry, to modern agricultural practices, and to large-scale cooperative farming. Kester was fortunate to find a professor at the School of Religion, Alva Wilmot Taylor, who shared these beliefs and who could express them in a Christian context.[19]

Born in 1871, Taylor was a Disciples of Christ minister and a leading exponent in that church of the Social Gospel. The Social Gospel may be described most simply as a minority viewpoint in American Protestantism, spawned by the prevalent optimism and faith in science at the turn of the century, which held that people should, and could, reform society along Christian lines. Nearly all of the shifting currents of the Social Gospel movement were depicted in Taylor's career, and he believed in its principles throughout his life. For example, in 1914 Taylor insisted, like many of his educated contemporaries, that the white man's burden was "to civilize and enlighten all other peoples."[20] Five years later he was in the forefront of the Interchurch World Movement, a grandiose scheme aimed at the "complete evangelization of all life" at a proposed cost of one billion dollars, which its promoters intended to raise from wealthy financiers. But this majestic project was sidetracked into investigating the 1919 strike at United States Steel that idled 300,000 workers. Taylor was one of the authors of the report that told of the exploitation of workers in the industry, criticized the twelve-hour day, and exposed the vicious strikebreaking tactics of the steel barons. The reading public was outraged, and as a result the workday in steel was shortened. Corporate contributions to the Interchurch World Movement vanished, however, and the gaudy balloon fell back to earth.

During the 1920s Taylor fought for Prohibition as the director of the Disciples' only social action organization, the Board of Temperance and Social Welfare. This gained him a substan- tial reputation in the church, and he came to Vanderbilt in 1928 to teach social ethics, a novel and suspect course to be offered by a southern seminary in that period. He was quickly identified as the radical in the School of Religion though he himself would comment that "the average radical is a dogmatist and dont agree very long with anyone but himself." In a 1931 essay Taylor wrote, "When science gives the technique and the Church gives the social passion, we will possess power to make the world over into the kingdom of God." No more succinct statement of the Social Gospel principle exists.[21]

The aging professor advised his students to become involved in social problems, and he demonstrated what he meant by chairing the Church Emergency Relief Committee. The CERC, founded in 1930 by liberal Protestant ministers like William B. Spofford, James Myers, Charles Webber, Jerome Davis, Winifred Chappell, and Reinhold Niebuhr, performed tasks too controversial for the Federal Council of Churches, such as foraging for food and clothing for the Wilder strikers. Taylor himself administered relief at strikes in Marion, North Carolina, at Danville, Virginia, and in the Kanawha Valley of West Virginia.[22]

Taylor's classroom was an oasis of social concern in what many inquiring students and pastors viewed as Vanderbilt's wasteland of interminable biblical debate. In his lecture hall Howard Kester, Don West, Ward Rodgers, and Claude Williams came to know one another for the first time. When they left the university, all except Williams bearing a degree earned under Taylor's supervision, they formed the leadership of a new spirited challenge to the southern establishment.

First there was Don West, a tall and handsome Georgia boy with artistic inclinations who came to Vanderbilt in 1930 from tiny Lincoln Memorial University in the Cumberland Gap. He had been born in 1906, fifteen miles by creek road from the little mountain town of Elijay. His parents were poor farmers, and only by dint of native intelligence and athletic ability did West earn admission to the Berry School, a private boarding academy in Rome, Georgia, sponsored by many benefactors, including Henry Ford.

Critical from the first of Berry's prim and proper administration, West was expelled in his senior year, but this did not prevent his being admitted to Lincoln Memorial. He worked his way through by milking cows, sweeping floors, and washing clothes, and he again got expelled—this time for fomenting a strike against the campus parietal rules—but he managed to get reinstated in time for graduation. While at Lincoln, West met and married Constance Adams, a mountain girl from Corbin, Kentucky.

West liked to compose poetry that extolled the working people of the mountains. He wanted to be a preacher, also, and he spent his summers teaching Sunday school and visiting backcountry churches in Kentucky's Poor Fork Valley. After his graduation from Lincoln, he was drawn to Vanderbilt seminary and Alva Taylor, who, in comparison to West's other teachers, was "the greatest of all."[23]

Though he interrupted his course of study at Vanderbilt to teach briefly, with Constance, at the Hindman Settlement School in Kentucky, and again for a trip to Denmark, West left Vanderbilt in 1932 with degrees in both education and religion. His divinity thesis, "Knott County, Kentucky: A Study," was supervised by Taylor and bore testimony to the unorthodoxy Taylor encouraged in his students. Among the many generalities set forth by West in an attempt to convey the character and enduring strengths of the Appalachian people were several which represented avenues of study not normally a part of the Vanderbilt seminary curriculum. For example, he forthrightly stated: "Of course there is much that

is unlovely in the marital relations of these pioneer people.
The women become passive and disappointed with sex life
and experiences. The men know nothing other than the
physical satisfaction of their own desires. They have never
been taught better, perhaps a few learn, but the great mass
go on torturing their wives and leaving them unsatisfied and
longing for a real experience." West examined the power
structure of this mountain country closely and concluded: "It
is easy for us in America to say that there is opportunity for
everyone who has ambition and ability, but it is not easy for
even those to come into any form of success unless they are
lined up with the capitalist powers that be."[24]

The paper ended with a poem, "Mountain Boy":

> *You are more than a dirty child*
> *In patched overalls.*
> *You mountain boy. . . . . !*
> *The hills are yours,*
> *The fragrant forests,*
> *The silver rivers*
> *Are your heritage.*
>
> *Dreamers. Thinkers.*
>
> *Rise up, young hillmen*
> *Sing your ballads,*
> *Dream your future,*
> *Up and down the valleys,*
> *Over the ridge-roads,*
> *Climb your jagged mountains.*
> *Gaze into blue space. . . . .*
> *Turn your thoughts free*
> *Nourish your imagination.*

Another in the youthful group that formed around Taylor
was Ward Rodgers, who later earned the sobriquet "Storm

32

Center Rodgers" for his habit of turning up in the center of controversy. He was born in Combes, Texas, and had graduated from Oklahoma State Teachers College before coming to Vanderbilt in 1930. His divinity thesis, also prepared under Taylor, described the rising tide of nationalism around the world, but especially in the United States where the people were "peculiarly gullible, ignorant, and emotional." It was the role of the church, he thought, to train ministers who could channel nationalist feeling toward international peace and justice. He carried these beliefs with him to his first pulpit in the Methodist church of Winona, Missouri. [25]

And there was steely-eyed Claude Closey Williams, the oldest of Taylor's students, who had been preaching for eight years before he came to Vanderbilt. Born in 1895 to a farm family barely scratching a living from the rocky hills of Weakley County, Tennessee, Williams was a Great War veteran who had risen to the rank of first sergeant before he got a call to the ministry. He left the service and went to Bethel College in McKenzie, Tennessee, a little school maintained by the Cumberland Presbyterian Church. Here he met and married Joyce King, a missionary student. At graduation Williams asked the rival Presbyterian Church, U.S.A., the "northern" branch of Presbyterianism, for a pastorate, and it gave him three—Lebanon, Auburntown, and Watertown, a cluster of middle Tennessee communities each with its own small flock of Presbyterians. In the age-worn tradition that "God said it, Jesus did it, and I believe it," Williams preached with great success for several years.

He chanced upon Harry Emerson Fosdick's *The Modern Use of the Bible*, a book which justified glossing over scientific inaccuracies in the Bible and called bringing men into a more abundant life the central, revolutionary theme of Christianity. It conjured up such unrest in Williams's mind that he took leave from his congregations to attend the Rural Church School at Vanderbilt. Here he met Taylor and Kester, who guided Williams to meetings of the Interracial Student Committee. Kester also persuaded Williams to go along to a black YMCA conference in Waveland, Mississippi, though Williams agreed only on condition that he not be expected to share a room with a black man.[26]

But that night Ned Pope, a Negro student YMCA secretary, arrived from Atlanta and moved into bed with the sleeping Williams. The Tennessee preacher had experienced difficulty earlier in even swallowing his food while seated next to blacks in the dining room, and it was a great shock to him to discover in the morning that he had survived the night with a black roommate. "It was a brand new experience for Claude," Kester said happily, "but he made it through all right." Williams's former race perspective was shattered, and in less than a year he uprooted his family and moved to Paris, Arkansas, to found a "Working Man's Church." Of his professor he wrote, "Dr. Taylor is doing more to effect the transition from Medievalism and Southern revivalism to an ethical conception of religion and the Social Gospel of the Nazarene than any man I know."[27]

Kester earned a bachelor of divinity degree under Taylor by writing "A Study of the Negro Ministers of Nashville." Taylor undoubtedly passed him because he was impressed with Kester's achievements in other areas. In February 1931, for example, Kester staged a public interracial conference in Birmingham, Alabama, under the auspices of the FOR. The eighty-five blacks and whites who participated talked of peace and racism, and they "slept, ate, socialized and thought together." It was certainly one of the first meetings of this nature ever held in Birmingham. In May, Kester organized a similar retreat at Paine College in Augusta, Georgia, for the purpose of studying "the assets and liabilities of capitalistic society and the technique for the realization of the Kingdom of Right Relations."[28]

He returned to Alabama that summer to appraise the trials

34

of the "Scottsboro Boys" for Walter White, executive secretary of the NAACP. These nine black youths were accused of raping two white millworkers in the boxcar of a train southbound from Chattanooga. They chose to be represented by attorneys from the Communist party's International Labor Defense rather than by Arthur Garfield Hays and Clarence Darrow of the NAACP. Kester was one of those who thought the defendants had made a mistake. "The Communists are making every effort to capture the Negro," he reported.

It is certain that more Negroes know what Communism is than before the Scottsboro case and it is also certain that more know what the Communists are talking about then ever before. I am convinced, however, that the Communists are hurting themselves, hurting the Negroes, and hurting those of us who are trying to build interracial goodwill and cooperation. . . .The tactics of the Communists are the tactics of a crazy man. They are trying to bulldoze the state and to turn the Negroes against everyone who is not lined up with them. . . .It seems to me that the Communists are more interested in proving the necessity of class warfare to the Negroes than they are in freeing the nine boys.

As if struck suddenly with the notion, he wrote in capital letters that "IT IS NOT THE ECONOMICS OF COMMUNISM THAT FRIGHTENS THE WHITE SOUTHERNER; IT IS THE RACIALISM OF COMMUNISM THAT FRIGHTENS HIM. One can talk about the economics of the Five Year Plan and find positive interest in it on the part of many Alabamians, and Southerners in general, but at the mention of a classless society . . . they fly into a RED rage."[29]

White also asked Kester, in August 1931, to go to Union City, Tennessee, to investigate the lynching of George Smith, a twenty-year-old black accused of entering the bedroom of a white woman. His death by hanging had been witnessed by an estimated two thousand people. Kester pretended to be a traveling salesman as he made the rounds of Union City, talking to various participants in the event, but his charade was

Easter Sunday Has Not Come for the Nine Lads in the
SHADOW OF DEATH

CIVIC MEETING
ON THE
Scottsboro Case

Introduction: A. Johnston, 1st Bapt. Church, Graymont

Chairman: Dr. BENJ. B. GOLDSTEIN
Rabbi, Temple Beth-Or, Montgomery

SPEAKERS
BISHOP B. G. SHAW

DR. HOWARD KESTER
Southern Director, Fellowship of Reconciliation

ADA WRIGHT
Mother of Two of the Scottsboro Boys

BRIEF TALKS BY—

P. D. DAVIS, President, Birmingham Civic Association
BROOKS FULMER, Student, Birmingham-Southern College
MISS JANE SPEED, Member, International Labor Defense
ERNEST SHELL, Student, Miles College; Editor, "The Milean"

White Citizens Are Invited

At 1st Baptist Church, Graymont
Weaver Street & 8th Avenue, West

SUNDAY, APRIL 16, at 3:00 P. M.

Auspices: CITIZENS SCOTTSBORO AID COMMITTEE
of Birmingham, Alabama

Easter Sunday, 1933, in Birmingham (*Howard A. Kester
Papers, Southern Historical Collection, UNC, Chapel Hill*)

utterly unconvincing. While having a shave in the town bar-bershop, he was confronted by a United States marshall who announced to the room that "there is a young fellow in town investigating the alleged lynching of a Negro boy. If this man has any brains he will be out of town before sundown." As quickly as he could get out from under the razor Kester checked out of the Palace Hotel and got away in his Model-T Ford.[30]

To be involved intimately in the South's interracial movement meant to share in its tragedies. The Kesters tried to make their apartment in Nashville a social and intellectual gathering spot for people of both races. It happened that on November 5, 1931, they had three good friends for dinner, J. B. Matthews, H. W. Pope, and Juliette Derricote, a national student secretary for the YWCA. Derricote left the next morning for Atlanta with three students. Thirty miles south of Chattanooga their car collided with a wagon driven by white people. Derricote and one of the students were badly injured, and they were rushed to a nearby hospital in Dalton, Georgia. But the hospital refused to admit them because they were not white, and an ambulance was summoned to take them to Waldron Hospital in Chattanooga. The student, Nina Johnson, died on the way, and Derricote succumbed soon after her arrival because her wounds had not been attended in time. Kester mourned this as "the most tragic and eternally unforgiveable incident in the history of segregation."[31]

The knowledge of these and similar calamities gave new depth to the seminary experience just as the times themselves summoned Taylor's students onto untraditional paths of ministry. The familiar range of churchly good works appeared to them less and less adequate once the stock market crash of 1929 propelled the United States into the center of the worldwide economic crisis. Millions of people quickly lost their jobs, and the blow upon the South was particularly severe. Cotton prices plummeted, and a host of peripheral manufacturing firms that had been trying to get a toehold in the region simply closed their doors. By the last days of the Hoover administration key elements of "southern civilization" like the plantation system had been wounded in ways that would ultimately prove fatal, and another of the agonizing migrations of rural people to city ghettos had begun. The revolutionary feeling in the air was as strong in the South as anywhere else, and, at Vanderbilt, Alva Taylor was trying to interpret it in a religious context when he lectured his students that they must labor to "Christianize" industrial relationships else "the machine may prove a Frankenstein turning to destroy what it has helped to create."[32]

Other radical political messages were filtering down to southern campuses. One that had a special appeal was the kind of socialism represented by Norman Thomas. It was easy for a seminarian to be drawn to Thomas the man, because he came from a Presbyterian background and had been a pastor of both rich and slum churches before he abandoned the parish for political action, and he was a thrillingly articulate speaker. Though Thomas had gotten a smaller vote in his first run for the presidency in 1928, the pre-Depression apex of complacency, than any candidate in the history of the Socialist party, his style made socialism an acceptable topic for dinner-table conversation, and the onslaught of the Depression made it a thinkable alternative to the two old capitalist parties. Thomas was also active in the FOR and was chairman of the socialist League for Industrial Democracy; through the campus chapters of these organizations his reputation and influence were spread among the young. Thomas seemed particularly touched by the abysmal poverty of the South and intrigued by the region's political conservatism. He made it a point to become personally acquainted with the radical and reform leaders who emerged there during the Depression.

Kester, for one, was powerfully drawn to Thomas. He

dined with the Socialist leader in October 1931 while in New York attending FOR meetings, and he wrote home to Alice that he had joined the Socialist party. She was already a member. Howard told her that they must cut their budget some more (he was then earning $2,100 a year) because "I've simply got to have some magazines and newspapers. . . .I never felt so 'backward' in all of my life. I have a real inferiority complex." Four months later, after listening to an inspiring talk by the nationally prominent Socialist Alfred Baker Lewis, the Kesters and five others applied for a charter as the Nashville local of the Socialist party. Kester gave his views on the southern racial situation in a speech at Scarritt College a few weeks after this; his pessimistic conclusion was that "we are much nearer a civil war than most people realize."[33]

Kester threw his hat into the 1932 congressional race in Nashville as the Socialist candidate. Norman Thomas was in the race for president, and all signs pointed to an excellent showing by the 25,000-member third party. Herbert Hoover's candidacy was undercut by his administration's inability to halt the economic decline, and there was cause to think that the jaunty Franklin Roosevelt was too much of an aristocrat to touch the voters' hearts. Of the three, the Socialist party promised the most decisive action to reverse the Depression. Its platform called for the nationalization of basic industries, unemployment insurance, old-age pensions, and end to child labor, more jobs through public works, higher taxes for the rich and corporations, and a shorter work week. With considerable evidence Norman Thomas could charge that the two old parties were "merely glass bottles with different labels, and both of them empty of any medicine for the sickness of our times."[34]

In Nashville, Kester campaigned on the basis of his ten years of work (he exaggerated a little) aimed at "revolutionizing present-day institutions." In the one and only newspaper interview he was afforded during the campaign, he asserted that "unemployment and war are inevitable under a capitalistic society" and that "capitalism has failed modern man because it has produced the most gigantic war in human history and has filled the world with millions of unemployed men and women." Kester also let it be known that he was a "wet," since for millions of Americans the decisive issue of the year was repealing Prohibition. This in itself was a major departure from his Presbyterian upbringing.[35]

The outcome of the 1932 election was less than encouraging for the Socialist party. The Democrats won by a landslide: Roosevelt captured forty-two of the forty-eight states and nearly 23 million votes. Norman Thomas's total was 884,649; it was three times as many votes as he had gotten in his first race for the presidency, but a far smaller percentage of the total than Socialist candidate Eugene V. Debs had won in the banner years of 1912 and 1920. No Socialist was elected to Congress. Howard Kester was one of those who lost badly. While the incumbent Democrat received over 23,000 votes, against 2,405 for the Republican challenger, Howard received just 677. At least he outpolled the party leader in his district; only 297 people voted for Thomas.[36]

Communism, too, was becoming a force to be reckoned with in the South. It had found scattered converts among the coal miners of Kentucky, the sharecroppers and millworkers of Alabama and North Carolina, and the unemployed of Atlanta and other large cities mainly through the efforts of organizers from the "outside." Though there had always been an element of class theory in the Social Gospel movement, communist thought gained its greatest influence over southern Protestant activists after several highly esteemed theologians, including Harry Emerson Fosdick, Harry F. Ward, and Reinhold Niebuhr, began publicly to embrace certain Marxist principles. The ideas of these last two men were of particular importance to the development of the South's radical movement not only because they were read widely by students, including those of Alva Taylor, but also because Ward and Niebuhr were the teachers of another group of southern seminarians who had assembled at Union Theological Seminary in New York. Among these students, who returned south in the early 1930s to promote civil rights and union causes, were Myles Horton, John Thompson, and James Dombrowski.

Ward was the older man and more of a leftist, in the traditional sense, than Niebuhr. Since 1907 he had been a leading figure in the Methodist Federation for Social Service, whose members sought to address the problems of twentieth-century America with the same militance that the abolitionists had once brought to the fight against slavery. The modern problem, as Ward first perceived it in his pulpit near the Chicago stockyards, was wage slavery. He published a popular book in 1929 called *Our Economic Morality* in which he found that there existed in capitalism "an irreconcilable antagonism to the ethic of Jesus." Claude Williams and James Dombrowski both claimed Ward as a pivotal influence in their lives. [37]

Reinhold Niebuhr was the little-known pastor of a Reformed church in Detroit when Howard Kester first met him at a YMCA conference. Shortly afterwards Niebuhr was brought to Union Theological Seminary by the YMCA evangelist Sherwood Eddy, and there he rapidly won a measure of fame with the publication in 1932 of *Moral Man and Immoral Society*. Many Christian thinkers traced their theological awakening to reading in these pages the liberating announcement that man is by nature sinful. Niebuhr flatly rejected the Social Gospel premise that man's goodness would usher in a godly kingdom on Earth. Instead, he held that men were inescapably children of nature whose defects would be exaggerated by any social system they constructed. People should stop chasing utopias, he argued, and work to create the most just society possible.

Niebuhr was a Socialist, having joined that party and other

left-leaning groups like the League for Independent Political Action shortly after coming to New York in 1928, and he thought that imperialism was the foremost manifestation of sin in society. He was attracted to Marxism, though he delighted in pointing out its weaknesses, because he felt it was the weapon that the poor and downtrodden would most likely use to slay capitalism. Niebuhr was no pacifist, nor did he believe in Christian evangelism as the route to man's salvation. He anticipated violent revolution, and he foresaw that he might have to play a role in it.

Niebuhr lent his name and energy to dozens of the causes and letterhead committees of the thirties, and he gave great service to the integrationist, socialist, and union-building movements that would be launched by southern activists. The New York theologian became an invaluable fund raiser and adviser, and without his inspiration and practical assistance these movements might not have existed or succeeded to the extent that they did.

One of the first of the southern radicals to come under Niebuhr's wing was Myles Horton. He had been born on July 9, 1905, in a log house by Paulk's Grist Mill, near the riverboat town of Savannah, Tennessee. His parents, Perry and Elsie Falls Horton, were schoolteachers and sharecroppers; an ancestor, Joshua Haughton, had in 1775 received the first land grant in the Watauga settlement, the original white outpost in what later became Tennessee.[38] Horton attended Cumberland University in Lebanon, Tennessee, and spent his summers organizing vacation Bible schools for the Presbyterian church in the eastern mountain counties. While traveling between the isolated rural communities, Horton met an inspirational figure, the Reverend Abram Nightingale, Congregational minister at Crossville. Though he had been trained at the fundamentalist Moody Bible Institute in Chicago, Nightingale practiced a ministry aimed at reaching, as he termed it, the whole of man's existence, not just the spiritual. He spent more time advising farmers on agricultural techniques than he did preparing his Sunday sermons, which, as a consequence, were dry but thankfully short. Nightingale led privy-building campaigns in his community, and his manse was a common stopover for hoboes. After treating strangers to one of the few bathtubs on the Cumberland plateau, Nightingale would provide them with a clean pair of socks. Horton called this man "as near a saint as anyone I ever knew."[39]

Under Nightingale's direction Horton began an adult education program in the hamlet of Ozone, and he awoke here to the ability of people to contribute to the solution of their problems by sharing experiences. The idea of opening a more permanent school had taken root in his mind when Nightingale persuaded him to apply to Union Theological Seminary. Horton arrived there in 1929 and became a student of both Ward and Niebuhr. Oddly, he acquired a reputation as something of a mystic among his seminary classmates. He did not show much interest in "the rational search for a god," but thought enough of Niebuhr's advice that "the madness of Jesus should be followed" to jot it down and preserve it.[40]

After a year in New York, Horton went to the University of Chicago where, searching for educational models, he paid frequent visits to Jane Addams's Hull House. He then traveled to Denmark to examine its world-renowned system of folk schools, and he returned to the states ready to open a folk school of his own in the South. Like the Danish version, the program of Horton's school would contain a strong religious element, but, unlike the model, his school would be designed to promote social change by bringing black and white farmers and factory workers together to discuss and solve their problems. "My job is to organize a school just well enough to get teachers and pupils together," Horton wrote, "and to see that it gets no better organized."[41]

Reinhold Niebuhr wrote a fund-raising letter for the

school, and Sherwood Eddy made a first contribution of $100. Niebuhr's appeal stated: "The Southern mountaineers who are being drawn into the coal and textile industries are completely lacking in understanding of the problems of industry and the necessities of labor organization. We believe that neither A. F. of L. nor Communist leadership is adequate to their needs. Our hope is to train *radical* labor leaders who will understand the need of both political and union strategy." With this appeal serving as something of a charter for the new school, Horton headed south with Eddy's check in his pocket.[42]

In Atlanta he paid a courtesy call on Will W. Alexander, head of the Commission on Interracial Cooperation, who introduced him to Don West, just out of Vanderbilt. The two young men joined forces. Since they had little to start with but high hopes, they were fortunate to stumble upon an elderly woman who had a school, of sorts, and wished to give it up. Lillian Wyckoff Johnson's school, or community center, was located in Summerfield, two miles from Monteagle, Tennessee. Johnson was the daughter of a Memphis banker, but she had spurned the life-style of a southern-belle and instead had gone to college. She studied under John Dewey at the University of Michigan, made a career of teaching, and became president of Western College for Women. Woodrow Wilson appointed her to a government panel which was sent to Europe to study rural cooperatives, and upon returning she settled on the Cumberland plateau in 1915 with dreams of creating a cooperative community.

Johnson turned her new home into a community attraction; she started potato- and tomato-growing clubs and a cooperative cannery and crocheting club among the mountain women. She introduced community Christmas parties to the area, and she held "sacred music" services around her Victrola on Sunday mornings. She brought in college-educated teachers to school the children (May Justus, author of many children's books, was the first) and founded the first credit union in Tennessee and the first county fair on the plateau. This woman of boundless energy called her association "KinCo," which to her was short for "Friendship and Cooperation." "What I desire above all things," she said, "is just to be a good neighbor, to live the fullest country life possible and to let my home radiate the spirit of love and co-operation."[43]

Age had caught up with her by 1932, and Johnson was looking for someone to take charge of her life's greatest work. When she met Horton and West, who bore vouchers of good character from the Reverend Mr. Nightingale and the Reverend Fred P. Ensminger, both Tennessee Congregationalists, she decided to take a chance and turn over to them all of her property in Summerfield, her home, and her goodwill for one year as an experiment. Johnson retired to her family's homeplace in Memphis where she kept a watchful and fretful eye on the two as they made friends among the poor and enemies among the powerful in Grundy County.

Horton and West began holding meetings in Johnson's spacious home, which they renamed the Highlander Folk School. From the beginning neighbors were welcome to visit the farm and attend the workshops where they heard a novel blend of sincere religious talk, discussion of agricultural problems, and intense criticism of the establishment. As the school developed it became, in the words of the historian George B. Tindall, a mecca for "a radical fringe that championed the proletarian causes of the 1930's." The Wilder strike was the most talked-about event on the plateau during that first summer, and Horton went there to recruit participants for a workshop on union organizing.[44]

The press coverage of Horton's arrest at Wilder gave Johnson her first inkling that the young men to whom she had entrusted her home and school were engaged in a different type of community program than she had envisioned. She

quickly advised Horton to stick to teaching "technical cooperation" and to forswear "theories and slogans that are divi-
sive." "Socialism is too closely connected with loose living,"
she cautioned. "It is the passing thing, dont you boys get
caught by it." But she defended the school in a lengthy letter
to the Chattanooga *Times* in which she emphatically stated
that West and Horton were not communistic but, instead,
"Christlike" in their devotion to the South's needy. Though
she continued to be plagued by misgivings, her support for
the school held firm.[45]

H. L. Mitchell (standing, with tie) and friends in front of his dry-cleaning business, Tyronza, Arkansas, 1933 (*Southern*

enant Farmers' Union Papers, Southern Historical
Collection, UNC, Chapel Hill)

III From Social Gospel to Radicalism

To a substantial number of ministers, trade unionists, and actors on the stage of politics, the Soviet Union had by 1933 arisen to pose a great moral and political challenge to the beleaguered capitalist system. The economy of the United States, the world's capitalist leader, lay in shambles, and the debacle of its stock market had triggered a global depression. The Soviet Union, on the other hand, completed the first of its Five-Year Plans in 1932 and had placed virtually the whole economy of its country under collective management (though what this had meant in terms of human suffering was not then known, or fully believed, outside of Russia). While the United States could not find export markets for its superior manufactured goods, the Soviets "dumped" many of their products throughout the West at prices too low for capitalist powers to beat. They lost money at it but kept their work force employed. America had Roosevelt, but while its allies floundered in search of leaders and objectives commensurate with the difficult times, the Russians boasted Stalin, whom Lenin had aptly described as a "Man of Steel." The Soviet colossus seemed to many to have risen from the ashes of serfdom, revolution, war, and famine at the same time that the Western capitalist democracies were failing. While Russia was not widely admired by the poor of America, it was keenly watched by those who cared about the poor: the ministers, intellectuals, artists, writers, and social workers. Not all looked forward to the dictatorship of the proletariat, but many thought it was inevitable.

All predictions were shadowed by the rise of Nazism in Europe, a force antithetical to everything socialists and democrats alike believed in. In the same month that Franklin Roosevelt enjoyed his inaugural parade in Washington, a triumphant Adolf Hitler was appointed chancellor of Germany after masterfully manipulating the tired leaders of the Weimar Republic. A self-styled "born revolutionary," Benito Mussolini, had created a fascist Italy a decade before, but the Nazification of Germany was infinitely more ominous. In the United States a new right wing was emerging with leaders like Father Charles Coughlin, a popular radio evangelist and anti-Semite. When Huey Long, the scrappy senator from Louisiana, revealed his presidential aspirations, many liberals feared that an American brand of fascism was at last being unveiled. Long was considered the enemy by southern leftists, in whose eyes the world was rapidly separating into reactionaries and allies of the revolutionary working class.

After the murder of Barney Graham, Howard Kester wrote: "That society which permits such tyranny and oppression must perish from the face of the earth." He still interpreted the turmoil of the world in biblical terms, but it is evident that he had come to believe in the working class as an avenging angel.[1] He was a delegate to the first United States Congress Against War held in New York City in October 1933. It was intended to be a "united front" affair, which meant that the Communist party was a highly visible participant. The second ingredient for a united front was the participation of the Socialist party, and on this occasion it was missing. Upset by derogatory article in the Communist *Daily Worker*, the Socialists officially pulled out of the conference. Kester, increasingly one of the most militant of Socialists, obviously did not feel bound by his party's boycott. He thought the congress was a "whale of a success"; especially the final meeting, which he said was attended by 30,000 people. Unanimously the delegates passed a resolution praising the Soviet Union as the one nation where "the basic cause of war

50

has been removed." The wording of this resolution skillfully blended the pacifist and martial philosophies that were vying for ascendancy among the intellectuals of the left. "The consistent peace policy of the Soviet Union," it read, "around which the anti-war struggles throughout the world must be rallied was made possible by the revolution which overthrew the capitalist system . . . and established a powerful government of workers and peasants. One cannot fight seriously against the war danger unless one fights against all attempts to weaken or destroy the Soviet Union."[2]

In his own bailiwick Kester got along well with the Communist party district organizer in Birmingham, Nat Ross, who was married to Don West's sister, Johnnye. At Ross's invitation Kester spoke to a packed church in Birmingham on Easter Sunday 1933 and gave a sermon condemning Alabama's persecution of the Scottsboro Boys. Outside the church uniformed police officers tried to take down the names of all those who entered. Kester also helped to investigate a lynching in Tuscaloosa as part of a group sponsored by the Communist-organized National Committee for the Defense of Political Prisoners.[3]

In the midst of it he dashed off a note to Alice telling her:

The strain has been terrific on all of us, being watched and spied upon at every turn has caused us to be quite jerky.

We have gotten some "hot stuff." . . . Much of our work has been on the surface but a lot has been underground and secret. We've had to be as careful as we could everywhere. Today I got in a jam and in the twinkling of an eye became a book salesman from the Methodist Pub. House. . . .

Since I have had such a pronounced Southern accent I've had to be the spokesman. I started with the Governor, Attorney General, Sheriff and others. Last night was my first night of sleep. We have had to see most of our people around midnight in various places. Life is hell, hell, hell! We are afraid there will be an epidemic of deaths among our informants after we get away.[4]

In his 1933 annual report to the Fellowship of Reconciliation, Kester laid his thoughts bare for all those in the organization who might yet have doubts about what it was he was
preaching. In doing so he distanced himself from southern
liberals. "The task of the Fellowship," he declared, "is that of
a revolutionary movement which must approach its work with
the abandon, enthusiasm, and realism of the revolutionary.
. . .To attempt to emancipate the mass of white and Negro
workers in the South . . . only through the methods of good-
will, moral suasion and education is to invite the continued
exploitation misery and suffering of generations yet unborn."
He had aligned himself, he said, "with those forces making
for a revolutionary change," and he was "helping to prepare
the bier of a dying civilization." In all of this, Kester said, he
was merely accepting the historical position of Jesus. However, these were exceptional words from the lips of one whose
entire training and experience had been in the Christian and
pacifist ministry.[5]

The rhetoric was too much for the FOR. Troubled by Kester's politics, and even more so by those of "united front" or-
ator J. B. Matthews, who was co-director of the organization,
the FOR governing body polled its membership in 1933 to
see where it stood in the cross fires of pacifism and class
struggle. Posing in essence the hypothetical question "how
far will you go to bring about a society free of exploitation,"
they allowed members to select from six answers, listed in
order of increasing militance. The "fifth" hypothetical position stated that in the event that factory owners turned their
guns on the workers, one might "consent to the use of armed
force if necessary to secure the advantage of the workers, but
regretfully and only while the necessity for it continues."
Some nine out of ten of the one thousand who responded
found this position to be too fierce to harmonize with the
spirit of pacifism. Unfortunately, it was this answer that secretaries Matthews and Kester chose.

On Saturday night, December 16, 1933, the FOR council met at Union Theological Seminary and voted 18 to 12 not to reappoint Matthews as executive secretary when his term expired in the coming February. The other three secretaries were reappointed, but in Kester's case, the reappointment was conditional upon his rejection of "position five." Kester wired from Nashville that he would not back down, and he thereby automatically lost his job. This telegram prompted the resignation of numerous FOR members, including Roger N. Baldwin, of the American Civil Liberties Union; Dorothy Detzer, of the Women's International League for Peace and Freedom; Francis Henson, Kester's Lynchburg College classmate who was now secretary of the American League Against War and Fascism; Reinhold Niebuhr; and Elisabeth Gilman, a prominent Baltimore Socialist whose father was the first president of Johns Hopkins University. All of them had by late 1933 come to believe that the realities of the class struggle were more compelling than simon-pure pacifism. In time, these renegades from the FOR would regroup to form the Committee on Economic and Racial Justice, which existed for the sole purpose of keeping Buck Kester in the field.[6]

Another of Alva Taylor's students, Don West, mixed his ministry with revolution when he returned to his native Georgia. West left the Highlander Folk School in April 1933 to move with Constance to a relative's farm near Kennesaw Mountain, Georgia. The couple wanted to start a program similar to Highlander, and they organized the Southern Folk School and Library, which their letterhead announced would "Arouse and Educate Southern Farmers and Workers for a Society of Justice, Freedom and Plenty." The idea was to spread a progressive message across the state by stocking a farmer's or worker's home with books about the hardships of southern living, like Grace Lumpkin's *To Make My Bread* or Erskine Caldwell's *Tobacco Road*, and leftist journals like

New Masses and to circulate these publications far and wide. It was taking the folk school to the folk, they said. They listed the "professional advisors" to their project as Howard Kester and Benjamin Davis, Jr., a black Atlanta attorney who was a member of the Communist party, and they collected many books through ads in political magazines. Before the year was out Constance claimed that eleven libraries had been established in Georgia.[7]

One of the Wests' associates in the library venture was Willis Sutton, Don's cousin, who was following in the family tradition as a student at the Berry School in Rome, Georgia. Like Don, Willis reacted against the Berry program, which he interpreted as taking the best of mountain youth, polishing off their highland heritage, and training them to pass in polite society. In Don West's words, "Helping a few tad poles to climb up out of and leave the slime doesn't mean the slime isn't still there with other tad poles wiggling around in it."[8]

Like all Berry students, Willis Sutton worked at the school in lieu of tuition; his pay was 12¢ an hour. He helped the other students to organize a "union," and they called a strike which broke up after two days when the administration persuaded many of the students to go back to work. Some of the more militant students wanted to try again and asked Sutton to help them get an organizer from the National Student League. The NSL was a Communist high school and college organization (competing with the socialist-oriented League for Industrial Democracy). It was a militant and rambunctious outfit, and its executive secretary, economics professor Donald Henderson, was fired from Columbia University in 1933 for his part in the group. One of his student colleagues, Clyde Johnson, wanted to see the South. In response to the request from Sutton, he hitched and rode freights from New York to Atlanta.

Astraddle the mighty Indian 85 motorcycle that was his trademark, Don West picked up Clyde Johnson and carried him to the home of one of West's relatives in Snow Springs, not far from the school. Johnson and Sutton went to a supposed rendezvous with the dissident students on the following night, but they were surprised by an armed body of school officials and hustled off to jail. They were released without charges, but the next morning Johnson was arrested again, carried into Rome, and threatened with hanging if he did not leave the area. He was set free a second time to hike home in the dark.[9]

That ended the Berry episode except that Don West wrote a letter to the *New Republic* describing the situation at the school. Under the heading "Sweatshops in the Schools," he wrote: "I am an alumnus of Berry and know too well the reality that lies behind their fine story of helping 'poor mountain boys and girls.' I think the public should be told the nature of this and other missionary institutions with which the South is cursed."[10]

Though West was right about the pay scale at the school, its founder, Martha Berry, denied that there had ever been a strike. She wrote indignant letters to the *New Republic* and to several influential liberals, like Will W. Alexander, whom she knew had previously supported West, and though some rushed to his defense, others were persuaded. She drew from Alva Taylor the comment that "Don has gone communist with all the trimmings. His letter to the New Republic sounds like he had gone blooie also."[11]

Whether or not West had then joined the Communist party is academic. He never identified himself publicly as a party member, and, in fact, he stated flatly on numerous occasions that he joined no political parties. But it is probable that he viewed himself as a part of an underground revolutionary movement in which the Communist party was the most dynamic force. He was, in the words of a poem he wrote at about this time, an agitator:

Listen, I'm An Agitator
"He stirreth up the people, teaching . . ."   55

Listen . . .

I am an agitator—
    They call me "Red",
The color of blood,
    And, "Bolshevik"!
But do you of the toiling south
    Know me?
Do you believe these things
    About me?
You croppers, factory hands—
    Negroes
Poor whites, and you youth
    Who look
Into a dark future,
    You who love
The south as I do—
    Do you understand?
Do you see that I am YOU,
    That I
The Agitator am
    YOU . . . ?
I am Don West, too,
    The poet—
A lover of peace and quiet places
    A working man
With rough hands that know how
    To work
When there is work.
    But the poet
Is a cry for justice,
    The Agitator

56

Is the restless soul of the
    Toiling millions—
Stirring, stumbling, groping
    Toward
A new world, a world of plenty
    And peace!
I am the son of my grandfather,
    Of old Kim Mulkey.
His blood burns my veins,
    And cries out for justice!
I am the poet who sings to a submerged south
    And she responds
With deep sobs of misery,
    She stirs
And anger sets on her lips.

As West saw it, the main problem facing Communists in the South was that too few of them knew much about the region or cared to learn. The party's primary policy toward the South, formulated in 1928, was contained in the slogan "Self Determination for the Black Belt," a hazy but far-reaching plan to provide blacks in the Old Confederacy with a state of their own. At a time when most blacks were concerned with putting food on the table, the party won few adherents to balance off the thousands of whites who were alienated by the idea. West was a thorn in the side of such doctrinaire Communists because he was attached to the southern mountains far more strongly than to the Soviet Union, and he was a caustic critic of "bohemian intellectuals" who "go proletarian" and theoreticians from New York and other "furriners." But West was certainly drawn to Communist causes, and one of these was Angelo Herndon's trial for subversion in Atlanta. [12]

Herndon was a nineteen-year-old black from coal country on the outskirts of Cincinnati, Ohio. He was arrested in Atlanta in 1932 on the charge of "inciting insurrection" after he was identified as a leader of demonstrations protesting unemployment. The statute under which the young man was charged had originated in slave days to prevent further Nat Turner–style uprisings, and it carried the death penalty. Herndon identified himself publicly as a member of the Communist party. He had joined it while a coal miner near Birmingham, Alabama. He became deeply involved in Communist activities among sharecroppers, miners, and the jobless, but he was forced out of Birmingham in 1931 by police harassment. Turning up in Atlanta, he jumped into the 1932 Communist presidential campaign (the vice-presidential candidate, James W. Ford, was black) and then began organizing interracial unemployment councils. A demonstration of these groups, demanding jobs or welfare, drew about a thousand people to the courthouse in Atlanta and resulted in Herndon's arrest. His trial began on January 16, 1933. The defense attorneys were John H. Geer and Benjamin Davis, Jr.

The trial, which resulted in Herndon's conviction, was splashed across the front pages of newspapers throughout the United States. Defense committees sprang up comprised of people with diverse political viewpoints, from the liberal Democrat C. Vann Woodward to the Socialist Mary Fox. The General Board of the Colored Methodist Episcopal Church urged its members to send contributions to the International Labor Defense on Herndon's behalf, and A. Philip Randolph got a resolution through the national AFL convention calling for Herndon's release.[13]

West began spending more time in Atlanta performing chores for the defense team and less in Kennesaw developing folk libraries. As a native white Georgian, a minister, and a good public speaker, his value to the cause was obvious. Before long he headed the Atlanta defense committee, and the Wests rented a small basement apartment on Georgia Avenue near Grant Park. From here they coordinated support activity for Herndon, lived on a salary of $5 a week, and fed fellow conspirators like Clyde Johnson.

The daily demonstrations of the unemployed, the very presence in Atlanta of Communists, and the Herndon trial raised tensions to the boiling point in the Georgia capital. The police banned all Communist literature and began arresting the street hawkers. They raided the homes of movement activists like Leah Washburn and Max Singer, and soon the state's attorney, John H. Hudson, issued warrants for West, Johnson, and several others, charging them, as he had Herndon, with inciting insurrection. It then became a game of hide-and-seek between the police and the agitators. West became "Dave Lee" and eluded police by hiding in the homes of black allies. On one occasion, a police search party arrived at the Georgia Avenue apartment just as Connie was putting the final touches to a fresh batch of handbills. Thinking fast, she stuffed the pamphlets deep into the garbage can, donned an apron, and pretended to be cooking as the agents breached the door. To keep their mimeograph machine and list of supporters from falling into the hands of the police, the defense committee secreted all that they had in the apartment of an Atlanta lawyer who had been one of West's classmates at Berry. It was an unfortunate choice, for the attorney was in league with the police, and he turned the names over to them.

West escaped Atlanta crouched in the back of a car driven by lawyer Davis. He was let out east of Decatur, and the twenty-eight-year-old fugitive flagged down a bus traveling toward the state line. After some drifting he next settled in Burlington, North Carolina, where, again under an alias, he was caught up in the defense of a band of union men convicted of dynamiting a cotton mill. [14]

The Supreme Court, over Justice Cardozo's strenuous dissent, dismissed Herndon's appeal in 1935. The case was heard again in the spring of 1937, and this time the Court granted Herndon's freedom by a vote of 5 to 4. Herndon then moved to Harlem where he remained active in the Communist party, and he settled finally in Chicago.

Taking Don West's place at the Highlander Folk School were James Dombrowski and Elizabeth Hawes. Dombrowski was the son of a Tampa jeweler, an Emory University graduate, an ordained Southern Methodist minister, and a Socialist. He had just finished his doctoral work at Columbia under the direction of Harry Ward, and his thesis, *The Early Days of Christian Socialism in America*, was published as a book after he came to Highlander as an instructor on religious topics. Elizabeth Hawes, who had been trained at the Brookwood Labor College, was also a Socialist. Soon after her arrival at Highlander she began organizing for the Amalgamated Clothing Workers of America. In the summer of 1933 she chartered the first ACWA local in the South: Shirtworkers Local no. 90, comprised of 13 women at the Liebovitz Shirt Factory in Knoxville. When the boss fired 6 of the women, more than 125 others went on strike. Their bargaining rights were now guaranteed by law, and Liebovitz recognized the union on the day after Labor Day.[15]

At the same time Myles Horton was helping local bugwood cutters (who chopped stumps to use for distilling wood alcohol) wage a strike against their pay of 75¢ a day. They halted bugwood cutting throughout Grundy County, but the industry was so depressed that the strike failed. Its lasting effect was to establish Highlander as an ally of local labor and to strengthen the conviction of Tennessee industrialists that the school was communist. Indeed, some political propaganda was going on; the first Socialist Summer School was held there in June 1933.[16]

Dombrowski's first major project at Highlander was to organize the Conference of Younger Churchmen of the South, an effort, as he described it, to involve "liberal and progres-

60

sive young ministers" like himself in social struggle. An invitation went out in April 1934 to hear Reinhold Niebuhr speak on the topic "Religion and the New Social Order," and some 180 people responded that they were interested in joining the new organization. Only about 40, however, were able to attend the meeting at Monteagle Assembly Grounds at the end of May 1934.[17]

Kester was one of the participants, and he described Niebuhr's contribution this way:

When the meeting got underway, Dr. Niebuhr lost no time in unbuckling his flaming sword against . . . the denial of the basic teachings of Christianity as found in the New Testament — the Sermon on the Mount — and in the Old Testament — Isaiah, Amos, Micah, etc. He analyzed the state of the nation with penetrating insight and spoke tellingly of the abysmal failure of the churches to deal with the desperate sickness of a sick society. This failure, said Niebuhr, was a heinous and grievous sin not only against the Lord Jesus Christ but God and the whole of His creation. Most, if not all of us, were thunderstruck by the depth of his knowledge about man's sinfulness and man's inability to cope with the evils of his own creation. . . .As the time for adjournment drew near T. B. "Scotty" Cowan summed up our feelings by saying, "Reinie", as he was affectionately known to thousands, "is Judgement Day in britches." The idea stuck, and he was not unfrequently spoken of in this manner.[18]

The published "findings" of the conference reveal something about what was on the minds of progressive young pastors and seminarians of the day as they witnessed the evident collapse of the old economic order. They had good words to say about the New Deal—at least its attempts to abolish poverty and child labor, to secure bargaining rights for workers, and to move the United States toward a planned economy. They found, however, that relief for the unemployed was inadequate, the industrial codes were little enforced, sharecroppers were being displaced by government policy, and the nation was following an imperialist road to war. All of these shortcomings, they concluded, were "inherent in the capital-ist system."

Their strongest words were reserved for the race issue: "We condemn the manifest injustices to the Negro, as evidenced in discrimination by employers and trade unions in the mat-ter of wages, in the exclusion from skilled trades and in the courts, in the disproportionate sums expended for education, in restricting the right of suffrage, in the operation of Jim Crow laws, and the inadequacy of housing, recreation, and health facilities. We call upon church groups to make the principle of brotherhood concrete in the relationships be-tween the races, especially in the economic area."

They also wanted a "radical political party of all races" with a socialistic program except that the farmer would retain pos-session of the land he used. "Such a party should recognize the revolutionary tradition of America," they wrote, "and the higher values of patriotism and religion." It was a strong state-ment for southern clergymen to make, and it illustrated how widespread was the disillusionment with capitalism.[19] Kester, whose job as a free agent of the Committee on Economic and Racial Justice granted him considerable flexibility, was elected the ongoing secretary of the conference. His task was to ex-pand the organization before its next meeting, scheduled a year hence, and to establish it as the boldly prophetic voice of the church in the South.

Kester and Dombrowski believed the prophecy that a vio-lent revolution was close at hand. Along with Elizabeth Hawes and J. B. Matthews they signed *An Appeal to the Membership of the Socialist Party* which was published in the spring of 1934 by the extreme left wing of the party, known as the Revolutionary Policy Committee. The RPC called So-cialists to a hard-nosed course of action in light of recent world events, particularly Hitler's rise to power and the suppression of the world's largest Social Democratic party in

62

Austria by the fascist Chancellor Engelbert Dollfuss. "There is no longer a middle road," the RPC announced; the Socialist party must become a "militant working class party." It must realize that "it is necessary to acquire possession of the state power so as to transform capitalist society into socialist society by means of the dictatorship of the proletariat." In choosing its tactics the party must make "no fetish of legality." Capitalism would react violently to prevent the establishment of a workers' republic, and the better organized the masses were, the quicker it would all be over. Once in power the Socialists must arm the workers. They also gave an endorsement to the Soviet Union, described as "preeminent, unique among the nations of the world. There, only, are the workers in power and constructing a Socialist society. The danger of attack by imperialist nations upon the Soviet Union is increasing. The Socialist Party must pledge itself to defend the victories for Socialism which have been achieved in the U.S.S.R."[20]

Sentiments such as these placed the RPC almost too far to the left to be in the Socialist party, where power was divided between the "Old Guard," representing mainly New York's needle trades, and the "Militants," who were generally younger and more aggressive activists clustered around Norman Thomas. The differences largely centered on how friendly with the Communists and ready to bear arms against the government Socialists should be. The gap ultimately became too wide to bridge, and the Old Guard leadership, which was strictly democratic and opposed to any endorsement of a violent class struggle, was unceremoniously ousted at the Socialist convention in Detroit in June 1934. They deserted the party altogether, robbing it of much needed finances and a large part of its union membership in New York.

The southern militants also seemed radical now in comparison to another old organization, the National Association for the Advancement of Colored People. After his ouster from the FOR, Kester was rejected for membership on the

NAACP board of directors because, he thought, Walter White believed he was "too radical." Francis Henson organized an interracial conference at Shaw University in November 1934 to discuss the possibility of creating an aggressive alternative to the NAACP, and Kester was one of the featured white speakers. The idea was dropped only when it seemed to Kester and Henson that the NAACP was becoming interested in real and risky fights like the struggle of sharecroppers to build a union.[21]

In April 1934 Alice Kester gave birth to a baby who was christened Nancy Alice. Before the birth, which was extremely difficult, Howard referred to the child as their "coming comrade and friend." After she was born he wrote to Alice that "When Nancy begins school both of us will have to be on our toes to keep up with her. She is going to be a grand student, revolutionary and comrade of man and woman just as her mother is." Parenthood did nothing to dampen Howard Kester's revolutionary ardor though it did much to distract Alice from the movement. On a fearfully hot July day in Nashville, while the young couple strove to keep their infant cool with electric fans and big cakes of ice, Howard sat down to write a letter to a woman he had met during a brief visit to Austria in 1932 to attend an FOR conference:

You have doubless watched with care the drift of events in America. I am personally convinced that each day brings us nearer to the dreaded Fascist dictatorship. I rather feel that those of us who work in the South will feel its strength first. With the South's background of violence, deep-seated race prejudice and attendant evils the world may be provided with horror of which we have scarcely dreamed. Terrorism against revolutionary groups has already begun in many southern states, particulary in the Deep South. One of my former classmates at Vanderbilt with whom I worked in Atlanta last winter has been driven out by the police [Don West]. He is wanted by the state dead or alive. Numerous individuals have been arrested, murdered, or forced to flee.

Howard Kester, Executive Sec'y.
Reinhold Niebuhr, Chairman
Elisabeth Gilman, Treasurer
Adelaide Case, Secretary

COMMITTEE ON ECO
FOR THE SUPPORT OF HO

WHO'S WHO OF
HOWARD KESTER

Native of Martinsville, Va.

A. B. Lynchburg College; graduate study **Princeton Seminary**; B. D. Vanderbilt University.

Served on state, regional and national **Council of Student** Christian Movement.

Director European Student Relief in South.

Secretary, Fellowship of Reconciliation, 1926-34.

Visited Europe twice and travelled extensively in the United State on speaking tours.

Investigated numerous lynchings and riots, participated in many strikes and labor conflicts in the South.

Mentioned in The Nation's Honor Roll of 1935.

Author: "Lynching of Claude Neal" and "Revolt Among the Sharecroppers."

NOMIC AND RACIAL JUSTICE
WARD KESTER'S WORK IN THE SOUTH

Committee on Economic and Racial Justice literature, 1936
(*Howard A. Kester Papers, Southern Historical Collection, UNC, Chapel Hill*)

While America's toiling masses, he feared, were still wedded to "the myth of a capitalistic revival or they are deeply indoctrinated with the idea that their lot has been ordained of God," Kester still believed that "the period of disillusionment is beginning to set in and as it increases the master's will tighten the chains about the feet of the slaves." And thus might come the revolution.[22]

All of Kester's strongest public statements calling for the overthrow of capitalism were made in 1934 before dozens of black and white audiences across the South. In October he addressed the Women's International League for Peace and Freedom in Roanoke. After opening with a poem of his own creation, "I See America," which was filled with visions of grimy streets, industrial sweatshops, prostitutes, and prisons, he told the women that "the capitalist system . . . has served its day and time." So long as workers were enslaved by capitalism, whether "in the gold mines of S. Africa or on a plantation in Georgia," there could be no peace or racial harmony. The New Deal, he said, was merely "a new shuffle in an ancient game the ruling class has practiced . . . from time immemorial." The entire administration was "conceived in the womb of a senile, frightened, decaying, half dead ruling class. The Chamber of Commerce . . . served as midwife and the Manufacturers' Association, employers organizations, bankers and financiers have served as nursemaids."[23]

In making these statements, Kester knew he was not protected by any strong local tradition of free speech. Nor was he in any sense the provocative "guest lecturer," secure in the knowledge that he would soon be on his way home and out of earshot of any protests he may have aroused. In Roanoke, Kester was home, or nearly so. Many of the people in the audience had known him from childhood, his college days at Lynchburg, or his work with the Student Volunteers and the Virginia YMCA. Within the span of five years Kester's message had gone half circle from gentle persuasion to world revolution. It would be interesting to know if his audience found this surprising or if they had made the circuit too.

As complete as this transformation had been, it was not so extreme as that undergone by another of Alva Taylor's students, Claude C. Williams. He had been a new man ever since his first experience of mixing socially with blacks at Waveland, and his middle Tennessee parishioners soon tired of hearing regular sermons about race prejudice. By the summer of 1930 Williams was ready to try new ground. He accepted a call from a twenty-member Presbyterian congregation in the west Arkansas town of Paris.

The main figures in the church were businessmen or supervisors from the local coal mines, but Williams sought to change that by bringing in miners and mendicants from across the tracks. He hung out at the town pool hall and then went into competition with it by installing a pool table in an unused wing of the church. He and his wife, Joyce, invited the young people in to discuss topics ranging from current events to sex. The couple's own view on these subjects was increasingly socialist and more than a little "bohemian." With students from as far away as the College of the Ozarks in Clarksville they went on overnight spiritual retreats to the top of Magazine Mountain. They opened their church-owned home to young people for Saturday night dances and provided them with stimulating artistic and political journals, including, the gossips said, some that portrayed nudity.[24]

When the mine workers went on strike in 1931, Williams accepted invitations to speak at union meetings. He got the idled men to help him lay the foundation of a church he had envisioned, a "Proletarian Church and Labor Temple." The work site was decorated with a giant wooden cross from which a banner proclaimed, "That They Might Have Life, And Have It More Abundantly." Under the cornerstone they laid a time capsule which Williams thought would indicate the state of the world in 1931. It contained a list of those lynched that year, the names of those states with Jim Crow laws and no workmens' compensation or social security, a list of the numerous Christian sects and denominations, the proceedings of the Scopes "monkey trial," and a sample of a yellow-dog contract by which workers pledged not to join a union. About this time, also, the elders of the Presbyterian church stopped paying Williams his salary.

The coal miners won a contract and a daily wage of $4, but the contract did not cover the mines where the United Mine Workers were weak. The men who had struck these mines were left out in the cold. Williams and many of the union miners called it a sellout. They blamed the district union boss, David Fowler, who, like all the important officials of the UMW, was appointed directly by John L. Lewis. Fowler had also refused to include in the contract a provision desired by several locals which would have required small weekly check-offs from the miners' paychecks to finance Williams's Labor Temple, and, thus, it was never finished. Williams supported the dissident miners who tried unsuccessfully to form an autonomous union outside of Fowler's control, thereby estranging himself from the labor hierarchy in the state.[25]

Adding to the list of unpopular causes he espoused, Williams became very attracted to Marxism. He was greatly influenced in this by his new friends among the student body and faculty at Commonwealth College, a labor school in nearby Mena, Arkansas. This unusual institution was an offshoot of the Llano Cooperative Colony established in Vernon Parish, Louisiana, in 1917 by a group of California socialists under the leadership of Job Harriman, a former labor lawyer and vice-presidential candidate beside Eugene V. Debs. At its peak this colony, which bragged that it discarded theory as soon as it was found impractical and that it had neither jail, saloon, nor church, housed six hundred residents on twenty thousand acres. They lived, farmed, and worked in a communal setting and developed a number of successful businesses including a sawmill, an icehouse, a cannery, a fertilizer plant, and a publishing house. William Edward Zeuch came to Llano in 1923; he had taught at the University of Illinois and had previously tried to develop a labor education program at Ruskin College in Florida. That venture had failed, but the Llano Colonists were receptive to Zeuch's plans, and they set aside forty acres in the center of their town as the campus of Commonwealth College. The goal of the school, in one writer's view, was "to recruit and train leaders for unconventional roles in a new and radically different society — one in which the workers would have power and would need responsible leadership."[26]

The college faculty soon had disagreements with the colony managers, however, and the school was moved to Mena, Arkansas, in 1925. The first students lived in army tents, but contributions from liberal friends and from the American Fund for Public Service—better known as the Garland Fund for its benefactor, Charles Garland—provided for the construction of several dormitories, stores, and faculty cottages. Most of Commonwealth's students were from northern urban areas. They were taught subjects very uncommon in southern schools, such as Marxism and labor organizing. The director when Claude Williams first became acquainted with the school was Lucien Koch.[27]

Williams's failure to keep his beliefs to himself brought him into direct conflict with his ruling elders, who petitioned the Fort Smith Presbytery to remove him on the grounds that he had neglected his congregation, that he had espoused Communism, and that he had preached beliefs not recognized by the church. After a cursory investigation, the presbytery took away Williams's pulpit. He appealed the decision to the Judicial Commission of the Presbyterian General Assembly; Howard Kester and Willard Uphaus testified on their friend's behalf, but to no avail.[28]

An example of the kind of things Williams had done to

alienate his church is contained in a letter he wrote to the Kesters in May 1934. He first asked Howard to send a Negro speaker to Paris who would lodge with the Williamses. The value of this would be to arouse the small black community and, of course, shock the whites. Williams boasted that he had helped to organize a sixty-member Socialist party local; he said he was trying to start an Arkansas Folk School with the help of Ward Rodgers, and that he was organizing four "Worker and Youth Churches" in the coalfields. Williams wrote in conclusion that "hell is popping," and he signed himself "Revolutionary Bill."[29]

Ward Rodgers, the Vanderbilt classmate of Kester, Williams, and West, came back into the picture when he left a parish in Winona, Missouri, in 1933 to take over three Methodist churches clustered about Pumpkin Center, on the slopes of Magazine Mountain. He spent five months there, but he became "very discouraged because nobody had any money. Even the money that they were able to scrape up for me, I didn't like taking it from them." So he quit his tiny church and moved in with Joyce and Claude Williams in Paris.[30] He made himself immediately useful by helping the Williamses arrange a conference on "Religion and the Revolution" on August 25, 1934, which was attended by students from Commonwealth, local labor leaders, and travelers from afar like Myles Horton and Willard Uphaus of the National Religion and Labor Foundation. The meeting was one of the Williamses' last in Paris. Evicted from their home, Claude and Joyce moved to Fort Smith, where they hoped to organize a religion and labor school. Joyce also by this time was caring for their two daughters.[31]

In Fort Smith they encountered a citywide strike of WPA workers who were angry because their 30¢ per hour wage was about to be chopped a dime to keep it in line with the pay at the mines. Daily demonstrations were being led by a Communist organizer, Horace Bryan, until he was arrested. Ray-

mond Koch, the brother of the director of Commonwealth
College, came from Mena to help and was promptly arrested
too.

While they were in jail, Williams took over as march
leader. He led a demonstration at the courthouse which so
intimidated the judge that he released Bryan and Koch on
bail. These three men joined hands a few days later to lead a
procession across Fort Smith in defiance of the mayor's orders. Their column was broken up by a club-wielding police
squad, and the leading trio (plus George Edwards, Jr., a
League for Industrial Democracy lecturer who had come to
Fort Smith out of curiosity) were wrestled into a paddy wagon
and hauled back to jail. Deputies ransacked the Williamses'
home and carted off a trunk of radical literature deposited
there by Ward Rodgers.[32]

The arrests got outside attention when Edwards was permitted to send a telegram to Norman Thomas which read,
succinctly, "Am in jail. Please wire instructions." Francis
Henson began trying to raise money in New York for the legal
defense, and Jack Herling, head of the Emergency Committee for Strikers' Relief, tried to raise $600 for Williams's bail.
But Williams's most energetic supporter was the Reverend
Willard E. Uphaus, secretary of the New Haven-based National Religion and Labor Foundation. Until then the NRLF
had concerned itself mainly with harmless projects like sending a "Social Action Questionnaire" to 100,000 religious leaders to determine their views on the Bible, the New Deal, and
the class struggle. Now, through Uphaus, it became a source
of funds for the organizational and educational work of Claude
Williams.[33]

Initially Williams and Uphaus were quite far apart in their
thinking. Kester undoubtedly spoke for Williams when he
said of Uphaus that "these cockeyed people who go about
talking of love and good-will in the midst of all this oppression
and hell make me pretty tired. We won't love people into the

Kingdom, we've got to bust this damn society to hell before love can find a place in it." But Williams went on a fund-raising trip to New York City immediately before moving to Fort Smith, and, according to his biographer, Cedric Belfrage, he found "that Uphaus was now moving rapidly away from his emotional liberalism towards the logical conclusion of accepting the class struggle." (While in New York, Williams also visited Earl Browder, secretary of the Communist party, who gave him $20 for his fare back to Arkansas.) Uphaus formed a steadfast attachment to the ornery Tennessee preacher, and he launched a National Committee for the Support of the Reverend Claude C. Williams.[34]

The court came down hard on the three prisoners. They were found guilty of "barratry," a charge usually reserved for lawyers who stir up trouble to enrich themselves, and sentenced to ninety days and $100 fines. They appealed, and Edwards was bailed out by his father. Williams and Bryan, however, remained in jail eighteen days before bond was arranged.[35] The conditions of their confinement were gruesome and extremely depressing for Williams. After two weeks in the jail, he arranged for the following pencil-scrawled note to be mailed to Kester:

> February 25, 1935
> In Ft. Smith Jail

Dear "Buck"

I have never made this request in writing though I have intended to do so for two years because both of my health and my activities which are very hazardous. The request is this: If I should "86" and it is likely I know—Sentiment is high—I ask, since I have given all for humanity, that the Church, the liberals, the workers, and those of even a more radical hue care for my "little girlies" (god how I love them) and not let them suffer.

I would not want them to be victimized by my "leaving".

And it seems to me a small (pittance) remuneration which Society would be glad to give to ask that they are educated and cultured without too great a hardship on their parts.

I am writing this to you and through you to the *World*. I hope I succeed in getting it out.

We need outside help desperately! The situation is extremely serious.

Respectfully yours in the cause of a world more nearly like that for which the Nazarene dreamed and worked.

Claude C. Williams[36]

Williams survived what he called this "post-graduate course in the pain of the despised and rejected." He moved from Fort Smith, where his family had been evicted from its home, to Little Rock. Here he once again set about trying to establish his New Era School, which was now conceived as a place where grass-roots labor leaders and evangelists could be taught the connection between the teachings of Jesus and the teachings of Marx.

What could be called a "radical gospel" movement, which conceived that the world might be redeemed not through man's good works but through the rising up of the poor, had now found a place for itself in the forefront of southern progressivism. Its participants may only occasionally have thought of themselves as part of a single movement, since their political strategies differed, but the latter-day observer cannot help but be impressed by the many things they had in common— their background, their age, their resistance to racial and economic injustices, their religious calling, and the style of life it imposed upon them. There was no written agenda for this movement, but it was primarily active in three fields. It sought to help the South's neediest—sharecroppers, textile workers, and the unemployed—through community and union organizing and through education. Second, it hammered away at Jim Crowism and tried to make liberals stand

74

and fight on this issue. And third, it sought to express a biblical message of human liberation and to draw the body of the church in the South into struggles for social justice.

As it turned out, this third task was the most difficult. The Conference of Younger Churchmen was the vehicle designed for the job by Kester, Dombrowski, and Horton, but not the least of the many obstacles it faced was the poverty of its members, which prevented them from regularly attending meetings. Despite the fact that Kester expected an "epoch making" event and mailed out several hundred invitations, only about thirty ministers showed up for the second conference on December 4, 1934. It convened at the Third Presbyterian Church of Chattanooga, pastored by the Reverend Thomas B. "Scotty" Cowan. None of the featured participants had the drawing power of Reinhold Niebuhr, but they included George Streator of the League for Industrial Democracy; Louise McLaren, director of the Southern Summer School for Women Workers in Asheville; and Francis Henson.

The group adopted a powerful Statement of Principles which was written mainly by the Reverend Eugene W. Sutherland, a Unitarian minister from Kentucky. It read, in part:

Whereas our present competitive profit-seeking economy shows itself to be increasingly self-destructive, and

Whereas, it depends for its existence upon exploitation of one group by another, creates industrial and civic strife and international war . . . and progressively curtails the cultural and educational opportunities of our people, thus destroying human values . . .

Be it resolved that: We set ourselves to work toward:

The abolition of the system responsible for these destructive elements in our common life, by eliminating the system's incentives and habits, the legal forms which sustain it, and the moral ideas which justify it.

The inauguration of a genuinely co-operative social economy democratically planned . . . , eliminat[ing] private ownership of the means of production and distribution wherever such ownership interferes with social good.

The conference heard from Frank Ward and Fred Held, officials of a striking American Federation of Hosiery Workers local in Rome, Georgia, and it sent a telegram to Governor Eugene Talmadge asking him not to send troops to break the strike. After sending a resolution to the Presbyterian church of Paris, Arkansas, asking it to reinstate Claude Williams, the conference elected Williams to its executive committee and asked Kester to serve another term as secretary. One result of this interracial gathering and the telegram to Talmadge was that twenty-two members of Cowan's church resigned in a protest that ultimately cost him his pulpit. He was soon called to a more liberal church in the new town, called Norris, Tennessee, being created to house the builders and managers of the first gigantic TVA dam.[37]

The task of publicizing the southern racial situation also had its dangers. In the midst of organizing the Chattanooga conference, Kester was asked by Walter White to investigate a particularly gruesome lynching that had taken place in Marianna, Florida, on October 26, 1934. Marianna is a small town in the northern part of the state, just inland from the Gulf, and Kester drove there in November to get a clear account of what had happened.

The story he pieced together was that on the afternoon of October 18, a white, twenty-year-old farmer's daughter named Lola Cannidy had disappeared from her home near the town of Greenwood. Her parents launched a search, and early the next morning the girl's body was discovered beneath a brush pile a short walk from the Cannidy home. She had been strangled. Sheriff W. F. Chambliss began scouring the community for suspects. One of the first houses searched belonged to a black field hand, Annie Smith, mother of Claude Neal. Here, the sheriff said, he found some bloody garments. More damning than these were rumors told by frightened black neighbors that Lola and Claude Neal had been having an affair.[38]

Neal was caught on Friday, October 19, at a nearby peanut farm, and his mother and aunt, Annie and Sallie Smith, were picked up as accomplices. Under persistent "interrogation" Neal confessed that he had murdered Lola Cannidy. Sheriff Chambliss, aware that tempers were running high among Jackson County whites, ordered that Neal be concealed in the jail of the small town of Chipley rather than at the courthouse in Marianna, but a mob of angry whites formed to pursue and lynch the suspect. When they appeared in Chipley, Neal was spirited away by lawmen to Panama City, forty-five miles south. The mob got wind of this, but their caravan of cars reached the Panama City jail twenty minutes after Neal had been taken away on a boat said to be bound for Pensacola. When the would-be lynchers got to Pensacola, they were told by the sheriff that Neal was gone again because the jailers would not have him. Over the weekend and into the next week roving gangs of white toughs searched jails throughout west Florida for Neal.

Some of the whites had hoped to use Neal's mother and aunt as substitutes, but their trail was lost to the mob also. On Saturday night 350 men stormed the Washington County Jail at Chipley looking for the women, but Sheriff John Harrell stood them off. The mob returned in a more determined frame of mind on Sunday, but by then the women had been taken elsewhere, probably to Fort Barrancas at Pensacola.

There was nothing secretive about the manhunt. The newspapers, and even the radios, were full of the story of the mob's relentless pursuit of the black prisoner. The papers also printed explosive interviews with the slain girl's relatives and other outraged citizens. The Saturday edition of the Marianna *Daily Times-Courier*, for example, carried the headline: "I WISH EVERY RESIDENT OF JACKSON COUNTY COULD SEE THE BODY OF LOLA, SAYS SISTER OF SLAIN GIRL," followed by the statement that:

When I viewed the body of my sister I was horrified.

Whoever killed her—well I don't believe any form of punishment could fit the crime. . . . I know that there has never been anything in Jackson County that was as brutal. I'd just like to see the man who did this just once. . . . To think that Claude Neal, who has been raised with my sister and me and worked for us all his life, could do such a thing—it is unbelievable. I only wish that every resident of Jackson County could view the body of my sister. If they could, they wouldn't rest until the murderer was caught and justice meted out.[39]

Many of the Negroes in Jackson County (the population was about 45 percent black) were afraid of retaliation against their community, and some tried to put as much distance as possible between themselves and Neal. The Marianna paper carried a resolution written by eight "leading colored citizens" deploring the death of Miss Cannidy at the hands of a colored man and praying for a return to "that friendly and mutual relationship that has so long existed among the white and colored citizens of our fair county." In the same edition, there was a letter from John Curry "To The White Citizens of Jackson County." It read:

Just a few lines to let you all know that we good colored citizens of Jackson County don't feel no sympathy toward the nigger that —— the white lady and killed her. No! We haven't felt that he did right because he should stay in his place, and since he did such as he did, we are not feeling that we have a right to plead to you all for mercy. . . .

But I am writing to let you all know that we leave it to you all to do what you see fit to do with him. But still asking you all not to be hard on your good servants that have been honest and faithful. . . . Because we good colored people want to thank you all for the favors and the chance that you all have given us to let us have schools for our children and teachers to teach them and jobs for us to work and to get bread for them that they can have a chance.[40]

Almost a week after Neal was arrested, word leaked out that he had been secretly held all the time in Pensacola. One step ahead of the mob, Claude Neal was moved again; this time it was across the state line to Brewton, Alabama, where almost no provision was made for his defense. According to Kester the transfer of Neal to this isolated county seat "was equivalent to handing him over to the mob."

Just after midnight on Friday, October 26, about one hundred white men broke into the Brewton jail, shouldered the turnkey aside, and dragged Neal screaming and crying into the first of a line of cars. Their intention, one of the mob informed the jailer, was to take Neal back to Marianna and let Lola Cannidy's father do what he wanted to with him. Word was spread by printed handbills and even radio announcements across the Florida panhandle and southern Alabama that Neal had been captured and would be lynched later that day at the Cannidy's farm in Greenwood. Thousands of people poured into Greenwood to take part in the execution; in fact, the news was carried all over the United States by wire services, and people almost everywhere could read that a Negro, held by a mob, was to be lynched on Friday afternoon in Jackson County, Florida.

Claude Neal was evidently tortured by his abductors throughout the day as they carried him by a roundabout route back to Marianna. At some point the lynchers decided to kill Neal before returning him to the Cannidy farm in order to prevent a chaotic execution in which someone else might accidentally get hurt. They took him into the woods by the Chipola River and subjected him to grotesque degradations. Finally he was killed.

Neal's body was dragged behind an automobile to the Cannidy home where a crowd estimated to number somewhere between three thousand and seven thousand people from eleven southern states awaited his arrival. A woman ran from the Cannidy house and drove a butcher knife into Neal's heart. Then the mob pushed in to kick the corpse. Some even drove their cars over it. In the dark hours of early morning, Neal's body was carried to Marianna and hung from the courthouse tree. A long procession of people followed the body to town, and on the way they burned the home of Neal's mother to the ground. Sheriff Chambliss cut Neal down at daybreak and laid him in the jail. Hundreds of people lined up to view the remains. Some of them then went on a rampage through the Negro neighborhood of Marianna, beating people indiscriminately. The mayor sent a plea for help to the governor, and late that afternoon a contingent of National Guardsmen arrived from Apalachicola. It took several days before order was restored enough for blacks to walk the streets again in safety.[41]

Howard Kester arrived in Marianna about a week after these events had taken place. He stopped first at a nearby Negro college where he expected some assistance from the faculty. Walter White had sent a confidential note to the school's president telling him that Kester was on his way. The president, however, wanted no part of the affair, and he ordered his faculty to keep quiet. One teacher did introduce Kester to a Negro pastor who agreed to bring some parishioners to their church in Marianna on Sunday, eight days hence, to tell what they knew. During the intervening week Kester scouted about Marianna gathering facts and hearsay about the lynching and riot. Then on Sunday night he went to the church.[42]

Exercising caution, he did not drive but walked "as if on a fresh air journey." No one was at the church, so Kester prudently withdrew to the shadows outside the building. Suddenly a dozen cars drove up, and men with flashlights got out and started searching the church; by their voices, Kester could tell they were whites. His only escape was down a ravine which led to Marianna. He made his way slowly through the brush and briers to the side entrance to his hotel and silently climbed the stairs to his room. With the help of a black porter, he washed and changed clothes quickly, then appeared in the lobby and took a seat as if nothing was amiss.

The next morning Kester checked out, stopping only to buy gas at a Gulf station. The attendant told Kester to leave town immediately because people were beginning to think he was

Don West, on his Indian Chief, in Georgia, 1933 (*courtesy of Don and Constance West*)

investigating the lynching. Before departing, Kester purchased from the man a photograph of Neal hanging from a limb in the woods by the river.[43]

He filed his report of the Marianna affair with the NAACP, which published several thousand copies of the document under the title *The Lynching of Claude Neal*, but Kester was not identified as the author. Instead, Walter White prefaced the report by calling the investigator "a southern white university professor." White went on to say that "this report is published with the hope that its sheer sadism and abnormal cruelty may stir thoughtful Americans to action." The report was quoted by newspapers in the United States and other countries. The New York *Post* editorialized that "nothing in the annals of German, Italian and Balkan dictatorship is worse than the story revealed in the report on this lynching."[44]

The NAACP used the report to dramatize the need for federal antilynching legislation, and it called Kester to Washington to testify for the passage of the Costigan-Wagner bill which would have made a sheriff's failure to halt a lynching a federal crime. The bill went down to defeat, but it resurfaced in 1937 when another of Kester's lynching reports brought it to the brink of passage.

Active as he was, Kester was hardly the only southerner working to put a stop to lynchings. A number of NAACP leaders including Walter White, who could pass for a Caucasian, had risked their lives investigating mob violence. White had even written a book about it, *The Fire in the Flint*, in 1924. The Commission on Interracial Cooperation had probed and lamented these crimes since its inception in 1919, and the Association of Southern Women for the Prevention of Lynching, led by Jessie Daniel Ames and Dorothy Tilly, long agitated against Judge Lynch. But the radicals were distinguished by their desire to organize the group victimized by these crimes, the poor, and the largest and most effective organization they helped to create was the Southern Tenant Farmers' Union.

IV Sharecroppers Organize

The attention of most American radicals was drawn in February 1934 to the political disruptions of Germany and Austria, where fascist militias were methodically eliminating their left-wing opponents. A tiny gathering of Socialists at a lodge hall in Tyronza, Arkansas, went entirely unnoticed, but it brought together Ward Rodgers, Joyce Williams, H. L. Mitchell, J. R. Butler, and Charles ("Uncle Charlie") McCoy, the future leaders of a farm workers' revolt. Their primary concern was a local one—the deteriorating situation of the sharecroppers and tenants on the cotton plantations of eastern Arkansas.[1]

One of the most striking of the group was Harry Leland Mitchell, a handsome young man with penetrating eyes who ran a small dry-cleaning business in Tyronza. He had been born on June 14, 1906, near Halls, Tennessee, just seventy-five miles from the birthplace of Claude Williams and a little farther from that of Myles Horton. His grandfather was a Baptist preacher; his father, James Young Mitchell, was an odd-job man—a farmer, house painter, barber, and, eventually, a Baptist evangelist—who married Maude Ella Stanfield. The couple spent the first years of their marriage in the Reverend Mr. Mitchell's parsonage, and Maude here developed a cynical disdain for men of the cloth which she impressed upon her firstborn, Harry Leland.[2]

The family moved frequently during Mitchell's youth. He later estimated that he had lived in ninety-seven different places by the time he reached the age of thirty-six. He made his first sharecrop at the age of fourteen on the Marshall plantation near Ruleville, Mississippi. The year was 1919, and the boy farmer made $35—not enough to buy the new suit he wanted to date a young girl down the road. She was the sister of James O. Eastland, who, after his election to the United States Senate in 1943, would oppose everything that men like Mitchell, Horton, and the students of Alva Taylor stood for.

H. L. Mitchell grew up a rebel. He favored the Darwinists in the Tennessee "monkey trial," read the *Little Blue Books* published by the atheistic socialist E. Haldeman-Julius in Kansas, and passed out leaflets on the streets of Halls for the presidential ticket of Robert La Follette. He was married, at nineteen, to Lyndell Carmack, the daughter of the mail carrier in Curve, Tennessee, and that summer he sharecropped while she taught school. The jobs hardly paid, and Mitchell accepted his father's invitation to come to Tyronza, Arkansas, to operate some dry-cleaning equipment gathering dust in the back room of the elder Mitchell's barber shop. Surprisingly, the business thrived. Mitchell delivered, and his face was soon familiar to most of the white and black farmers in the area.

He became friends with the proprietor of a Tyronza gas station, Clay East, and, after lengthy debate, he converted East to socialism. East joined the party after he was elected town constable in 1932, and the two then campaigned for Norman Thomas in the presidential election. They had the satisfaction of seeing the Socialists outpoll the Republicans in their county, though, of course, the Democratic ticket swamped all comers.

Mitchell wished to learn more about the larger Socialist movement, and he drove to Washington, D.C., for the Continental Congress for Economic Reconstruction, which opened on May 6, 1933, under the auspices of the Socialist party, several railway unions, and the National Farmers' Union. His first stop along the way was in Memphis where he met a number of local Socialists including William Amberson, a professor of physiology at the University of Tennessee Medical School, and Willie Sue Blagden, the radical member of a prominent local family. Blagden went with him to Nashville to spend the night with the Kesters, who lived on the top floor of an Episcopal rectory at 1700 Edgehill Avenue. The Committee on Economic and Racial Justice paid the rent for this apartment, and Howard justified its relatively high cost on the grounds that the landlord allowed them to entertain Negro guests. This was the first meeting between the Kesters and Mitchell. Della Mae Graham, whose father, Barney, had been killed and buried that week at Wilder, was staying with the Kesters at this time, and she planned to speak in her father's place at the Continental Congress.

The party set off for Washington to join four thousand or more Socialists, farmers, and union members who were angry enough about world events to want to repeat the Congress that had sparked the American Revolution. They had much to be alarmed about: Hitler was defying the Treaty of Versailles and conscripting German youth into the army; Japan and China were at war in Manchuria; and, closer to home, much of Iowa had been declared a "war area" by the press as National Guardsmen confronted armed members of the Farm Holiday Association who were urging their neighbors to "stay at home, buy nothing, sell nothing" until market prices went up.

This hectic meeting opened with an address by Norman Thomas, who demanded an end to capitalism. The delegates drafted a program calling for a thirty-hour week, a huge public works program, old age and unemployment insurance, public ownership of all basic industries and vital resources, and the confiscation of all annual incomes in excess of $25,000. Some of the delegates were in favor of marching on the Capitol and taking over the government that very weekend, but a more moderate leadership was in control.[3]

The closest they came to taking their demands into the

streets was when the New York delegation, which included A. Philip Randolph and several other blacks, was refused rooms at the Cairo Hotel. Norman Thomas led a demonstration of about five hundred people to the hotel and made a speech from its steps on the evil of segregation—that those who cooked and cleaned for the establishment were not allowed to sleep there. The Cairo appeased the demonstrators by refunding all of the money paid in advance by the New Yorkers, and it is probable that the most lasting impact of this demonstration was upon the mind of H. L. Mitchell. Thomas's speech was the first that Mitchell had ever heard condemning segregation. "It had never occurred to me it was wrong," Mitchell said later. "Negroes had their place, and we had ours."[4]

Two Socialist party organizers, Edward and Martha Johnson, visited Tyronza six months after Mitchell returned from Washington. They were much impressed with "the boys," as they referred to Mitchell and East. The pair showed every evidence of taking their socialism so seriously that it overshadowed whatever segregationist views they may once have had; they had organized a predominantly black protest organization of unemployed men and women who wanted public works jobs. Moreover, they possessed boundless energy and envisioned a vast socialist movement, led by sharecroppers growing from the Arkansas cotton fields. The Johnsons also acclaimed the farm workers they met. "Here you will find the true proletariat," wrote Martha Johnson; "here you will find inarticulate men moving irresistably toward revolution and no less. Remember, these people are politically impotent. They can not vote out the poll tax, since they can't pay a poll tax to vote. . . . The communists, if they ever learn to use southern leaders, would sweep these bottom lands like wildfire." She urged Norman Thomas to visit Arkansas, saying "a day spent here will put the Socialist Party on a higher plane than ever in the past." The patrician Socialist agreed to make a stop in Tyronza part of his upcoming southern tour (promoted as a challenge to Huey Long) early in 1934.[5]

Visitors were a rarity on the plantations. Though most of the Arkansas farms were less than thirty years old, the life of the field worker was the same as it had been throughout the South for one hundred and fifty years. The men wore kneepads, and as long as there was light they "walked" on their knees down the long rows of cotton. The women's dresses prevented them from doing this, so they worked bent from the waist. Everyone's hands swelled at the start of the season; when they shrank again, the skin and fingers cracked, and stayed cracked until the harvest was over. Children missed three or four months of school, where there was school, and hardly anyone could read or understand the foreman's arithmetic. Wages rose over time; they had reached 40¢ to 80¢ a day for cotton field workers in Arkansas in 1934. Sharecroppers were lucky if they finished the year free of debt.

With Mitchell and East as his guides, Thomas visited the plantation shacks of several white and black sharecroppers and heard firsthand the troubles of a people facing starvation and eviction. During lunch at East's home Thomas noted that since the sharecroppers were prevented from voting by racial custom and poll taxes their political needs could best be met by organizing a union. It undoubtedly did not escape Thomas that the farm tenants owed nothing to the New Deal and, in fact, blamed much of their current misery on Roosevelt's agricultural policies. These workers were a disenfranchised mass who might well rise to power in the revolutionary days ahead, and the Communist party, except for an underground organization in Alabama, had not yet come on the scene.

Upon returning to New York, Thomas arranged for the League for Industrial Democracy to finance a study of conditions among the sharecroppers conducted by William Amberson. The Memphis physiologist's scathing report on the effects of New Deal negligence in administering its farm programs became a large part of Thomas's *The Plight of the Sharecropper*, published in 1934.

The problem highlighted by this book was quite obvious to anyone who looked at southern agriculture. In the face of forced government restrictions on production (though the cotton and tobacco programs were called "voluntary," taxes for nonparticipation made them coercive), farm owners naturally cut back their work force or else reduced the parcels of land allotted to each tenant. Thousands of families who had abided by the sharecropper system were cut adrift to search for day-by-day wage work on the big farms. Under the Agricultural Adjustment Administration contract signed by each farm owner, landlords were required to "endeavor in good faith" to preserve the status of their sharecroppers and were bound to give all tenants their rightful share of the government subsidy payment proportional to the number of acres each had been forced to take out of production. But by various ruses such as minipulating their tenants' indebtedness, or by outright fraud, many, and probably most, of the affected plantation owners managed to keep all of the subsidy payment for themselves. The sharecroppers knew they were being cheated and were ready to organize to fight back.[6]

In the spring of 1934 Hiram Norcross, the owner of a 5,000-acre plantation near Tyronza, precipitated the confrontation in Arkansas by evicting 23 of his 248 tenant families to avoid loaning them money to get through the planting season. Eleven white and seven black men from among these ousted families called a meeting with Mitchell and East in the Sunnyside Schoolhouse near the Norcross place. The idea that whites and blacks be joined together in the one organization was much discussed. In everyone's mind were memories of the "Elaine Massacre" of 1919 where between 25 and 100 sharecroppers in Phillips County, Arkansas, were killed by white mobs for taking part in the Progressive Farmers and Householders Union of America, a strictly black association.

Twelve blacks were sentenced to death in the aftermath of the riot, and 80 more went to prison for terms ranging from one to twenty years. Walter White, reporting the affair for the NAACP, had narrowly escaped lynching. Nevertheless, the group voted to create an interracial organization to resist the evictions.[7]

After the Sunnyside meeting Mitchell sent out a call to everyone he knew in the Socialist party asking them to come to Tyronza to help get the union started. The first to answer was Ward Rodgers, who had been boarding with Claude and Joyce Williams. Then came J. R. Butler, an Ozarks sawmill hand, who hitchhiked down from White County. The three of them wrote a constitution for the Southern Tenant Farmers' Union and got the organization legally chartered. The dramatic struggle of this union over the next four years would mark the high point of agricultural unionism in the South and provide an example of the races working together which would not be repeated until the civil rights movement emerged two decades later. The STFU drew more heavily upon political ideology than did the later civil rights organizations, but it was propelled just as strongly by religious faith as were the future lunch-counter sit-ins and freedom rides.

The union's first test came when C. H. Smith, a black minister and farmer, was arrested with Ward Rodgers in Crittenden County while trying to talk to a group of sharecroppers. Rodgers was released with a warning to leave the area, but Smith was jailed and, by his own testimony, beaten up by deputies. Other union leaders, realizing that it was crucial to demonstrate that they could protect their organizers, conducted a desperate search for an attorney and finally retained C. T. Carpenter of Marked Tree, a well-respected lawyer who had come to Arkansas in 1903 to serve a term as president of Woodland Baptist College in Jonesboro. Carpenter's father had fought under General Robert E. Lee, a fact that enhanced his reputation in the area. His strategy for dealing with the Smith case was to have Mitchell and East pack the courtroom with menacing-looking white farm workers. This show of support had the desired effect, and Smith was released to a jubilant crowd of friends. It was a tiny victory, but it launched the union.[8]

By the mysterious grapevine that connects distant southern communities, the news of Smith's release spread from plantation to plantation across eastern Arkansas, and union groups sprang into existence more quickly than the few official organizers could attend to them. Once these gatherings were brought into the STFU structure, they were chartered as "Community Councils" under the leadership, often, of whichever member could read and write. It cost a dime to join and 10¢ a month for dues.[9]

The preamble of the union's constitution demanded the return of "land to the landless." This dream gave the STFU crusade the character of a holy movement for the people who joined. Their meetings were full of hymns and prayer and sermons about a richer life coming closer with each moment spent packed in the dimly lit fieldside churches. The successful organizers were all preachers, most notably a black man, the Reverend Edward Britt McKinney, who was later described by a friend as "a devoted Socialist and a spell-binding Baptist preacher who can shake a laugh out of a cold New England audience and bring tears to a sophisticated college audience at will." But in the early days of the STFU, McKinney was a tenant farmer widely known as a former labor recruiter for northern industry and as a circuit rider for several black congregations. He and many other unschooled white and black ministers were the backbone of the STFU. Upon this foundation in the local community church the radical gospel prophets—Ward Rodgers, Claude Williams, and Howard Kester—came to build.[10]

Kester arrived in Arkansas soon after concluding his investigation of the Claude Neal lynching. Mitchell had invited him with these words: "I know you have your hands full but I would like for you to come over here sometime and see what Ward Butler and I have got started, and attend one of our meetings with white and black share-croppers and hear their fundamentalis preachers preach revolution to them. . . . We have taken in about 2,000 members in the union in the past two weeks and I am damn near worked to death. . . . Lucien Koch attended one of our meetings and remarked that the Revolution started in Arkansas in the broken down church we met in."[11]

Mitchell also urged Kester to "bring your artillery," but, though Kester talked much about revolution, it was he who impressed the tactic of nonviolence upon the union militants as the STFU moved onto the national stage. Kester also gave the union a direct link to the Socialist party. While he was technically the agent of the independent Committee on Economic and Racial Justice, Kester traveled to Arkansas with funds raised by Norman Thomas, and he was accepted there as Thomas's semiofficial representative. He functioned less, however, as a socialist theoretician in union ranks than as the STFU's ambassador to what later came to be called the "eastern liberal establishment."[12]

The STFU's growth in stature, from a localized protest movement to a national farm workers' lobby, began in December 1934 when McKinney and another black minister, N. W. Webb, drove to Washington with Mitchell and a sharecropper named Alvin Nunnally and gained an interview with Secretary of Agriculture Henry Wallace. They explained to the secretary that sharecroppers were being evicted and tricked out of their crop support payments with the connivance of local AAA officials. Somewhat to their surprise, Wallace promised a thorough investigation.

On its way home in January, the delegation sent a telegram to Ward Rodgers instructing him to organize a rally in Marked Tree on the sixteenth to spread the news from Washington. A

crowd of about two thousand was milling around this Poinsett
County town when the four travelers arrived in Mitchell's
1926 Moon car. Rodgers was at that moment addressing the
rally, and he was heard to say, "If I wanted to do so, I could
lead a mob to lynch any planter in Poinsett County." The
crowd responded with cheers and hat throwing. When Rodgers was done, Mitchell took the platform to relay the promise
of the secretary of agriculture to investigate abuses in the
AAA program. [13]

The crowd dispersed peacefully later that afternoon, but as
Rodgers prepared to leave he was arrested and carried to jail
in Harrisburg, the county seat. Later he was taken to Jonesboro, in a neighboring county, for safekeeping. The charges
lodged against him were promoting anarchy and barratry.
When word of this arrest spread, Mitchell and Nunnally fled
to Memphis after pausing to notify Carpenter, the union's attorney, of the developments. The STFU "office" in Tyronza,
a back room in Mitchell's dry-cleaning shop, was raided by
the local sheriff, and many union records were confiscated.
Lyndell Mitchell followed her husband to Memphis, and a
new, two-room union headquarters was established at 2527
Broad Street. Desperate for help, the union wired the director of Commonwealth College, Lucien Koch, "Organizer
Ward jailed can you come?" Koch had led a similar mission to
Harlan County, Kentucky, in 1932, and he drove to the plantation country with several students. They were intercepted
by lawmen in Gilmore on February 1, pistol-whipped, and
run out of town. It was now evident that the public officials of
Arkansas meant to crush the sharecroppers' revolt by whatever means were handy. [14]

Mary Connor Myers, the Boston attorney dispatched to Arkansas by Secretary Wallace, attended the Rodgers trial. She
had spent the past two weeks collecting affidavits from tenant farmers in Marked Tree, a town which, a New York reporter wrote, "squats with sullen ugliness in the heart of the

troubled area." Rodgers now was charged with blasphemy, as well as anarchy and barratry, and the trial attracted considerable local and national publicity.[15] In fewer than fifteen minutes Rodgers was found guilty, fined $500, and sentenced to six months in prison. Myers was probably shocked by these proceedings, and her report to Washington evidently triggered a power struggle in the Agriculture Department between those who favored vigorous enforcement of the AAA protections for sharecroppers and those who did not.

The sharecroppers' allies were Jerome Frank, AAA general counsel, and his aides, Alger Hiss, Lee Pressman, and Francis B. Shea. Also on this side were Victor Christgau, deputy to the AAA administrator, Frederic C. Howe, head of the Consumer Protection Division, and his assistant, Gardner Jackson, who had been a leading crusader in the defense of Sacco and Vanzetti. Across the political fence stood Chester Davis, the Midwestern agribusinessman who headed the AAA, and Cully A. Cobb, a former farm journalist who directed the key Cotton Division. These men insisted that the AAA contract, by which planters promised not to grow cotton in return for a federal subsidy check, did not require that sharecroppers be kept on the land. They also denied that there had been any large-scale evictions of sharecroppers or that the AAA program had been anything less than "fair and just."[16]

The matter reached a head when Frank's legal department sought to intervene on behalf of the tenants who had been evicted from the Hiram Norcross plantation. Ample argument for joining this case, the attorneys evidently felt, could be found in the flagrant abuses chronicled by Myers's report. Cobb and Davis resisted any departmental action to aid the sharecroppers. When nine STFU pickets paraded in front of the AAA headquarters in May 1935, Cobb told the New York *Times* that the demonstrators "would not know a cotton stalk from a jimpson weed" and that "they seem to resent the im-

Constance West at the time of the Angelo Herndon trial,
Georgia, 1933 (*courtesy of Don and Constance West*)

proved economic conditions brought about by the cotton program because it makes it all the more difficult for them to
spread unrest upon which they feed." The dispute was laid
before the secretary of agriculture.[17]

Wallace made the political decision, and it was one in which
liberal New Dealers could take little pride. He ruled that the
AAA would not intervene in the Norcross case. During the
first week of February 1935 he fired Frank, Shea, Pressman,
and Jackson. Howe was demoted, and Hiss and Christgau
soon resigned. This elimination of the "liberal bloc" in the
Agriculture Department signified the power held within the
New Deal coalition by southern Democrats, particularly Joseph T. Robinson of Arkansas, majority leader in the United
States Senate. Lacking the support of the AAA, the suit
against Norcross was thrown out on the grounds, ironically,
that the evicted sharecroppers had no standing in court since
they were not parties to the contract between Norcross and
the government. During the shake-up Myers's report was so
completely suppressed that no copy found its way into the
public eye or even into the National Archives.[18]

The purge encouraged the plantation owners of Arkansas to
do as they pleased. Almost as quickly as Ward Rodgers was
bailed out of jail in Jonesboro to await the result of his appeal
he was arrested again, along with a sharecropper named Robert Baker and three of the people from Commonwealth College, for trying to speak on the streets of Lepanto. They spent
two nights in jail before being bailed out with funds sent by
Norman Thomas, and they kept the town awake during their
incarceration by singing revolutionary hymns. On the charge
of blocking traffic Rodgers and Lucien Koch were both fined
$100. The ACLU and Thomas organized an Auxiliary Com-
mittee for the Defense of Ward Rodgers to fight the convictions. The young minister planned to demand blacks on his
jury on the grounds that he was a "renegade white" and that

Negroes were his true peers, but both cases were dismissed on appeal.[19]

Alva Taylor read about Rodgers's repeated arrests, and the Social Gospel theologian who had planted the seeds now disavowed the harvest. The row in Arkansas, he told a friend, was "a forced socialist affair, made spectacular by two of my one time students [Ward Rodgers and Claude Williams] whose fine impulses lack adequate balance in discretion and good judgement." He guessed it was of small importance in the whole southern situation.[20]

There was a grain of truth in what Taylor said in that the sharecropper movement had Socialist support, and its organizers knew, or quickly learned, how to attract the attention of news media. It was through newspapers and radio that the STFU hoped to touch the conscience of the public, and until the union's first strike revealed its economic potential, public sympathy remained its only source of power. But the movement was not "forced"; it grew naturally from the inherently unstable agricultural system of the South and the drastic federal policies designed to regulate it. The union saw the flaws in the economy and exploited them because its goal was not a labor contract with the plantation owners but "land to the landless": the abolition of the plantation culture and the advent of socialized cooperative agriculture. The importance of the STFU movement can best be judged by the resistance with which it was met.

A sidelight of the STFU was that it revealed the different faces of the church. There would have been no union without the unprofessional fundamentalist country preachers, and the movement would have died young without the organizational skills of the radical gospel socialists. But its path would have been easier to travel had not other churchmen tried to block the way. One of these was the Reverend J. Abner Sage, the minister of the Southern Methodist church in Marked Tree. Sage had studied theology and taught hymnology at Emory

University, and he said that the school's first chancellor, Bishop Warren A. Candler, "is like a father to me." Yet he was incensed when an Emory undergraduate named Glenn Hutchinson wrote an "open letter" to the Methodist *Christian Advocate* criticizing the arrests and trials of Ward Rodgers. Sage replied, in a letter of his own, that

the facts are that Ward Rodgers and Howard Kesler [*sic*] joined in with a disreputable lot of Communists and for months sought to throw this country into a class and race war. In one of the letters taken from Rodgers when he was arrested, there was a letter to Communist headquarters (in Chicago, I believe) [Sage undoubtedly meant the Socialist party headquarters in Chicago] in which he expressed himself as in favor of the "united front" between all radical organizations. "What we want," he said, "is REVOLUTION under any name." – – – I cannot go into details, because it would require the writing of a small book. But these men, when things finally got so bad that they were run out of Arkansas, took up residence along with some renegade negroes at "2595 School Street," Memphis.[21]

Sage did not mention that he had organized a Marked Tree Cooperative Association to find jobs and new homes for any white sharecroppers who would renounce the STFU. The Negro sharecroppers, he thought, were shiftless and got their ideas from northern agitators. The cooperative association never posed a serious challenge to the STFU, but union organizers believed, though it was never proved, that Sage was behind more sinister activities. They were convinced, for example, that Sage had encouraged a mob to attack a peaceful union rally in Marked Tree early in 1935, and even that he had purchased machine guns to mow down the marchers. This story originated with the "conscience stricken" gun salesman who confessed the plot to the union, but he could not explain why the massacre, if indeed one was planned, had not taken place. Sage's own version of this event was that he had prevented a white man from shooting into the parade, but,

he added, "I don't know, though, but what it would have been
better to have a few no-account shiftless people like that
killed at the start than to have had all this fuss raised up."[22]

Getting Abner Sage became a personal vendetta for Howard Kester. He tried unsuccessfully to get his Scarritt College
friend, the Reverend Albert Barnett, to organize a Methodist
group to censure Sage. Kester had to content himself with
attacking Sage several times in his 1936 book about the union
movement, *Revolt among the Sharecroppers*. First he char-
acterized the "planters, riding bosses, deputies" who were in
Sage's church as being "more ruthless, vicious and callous
to human suffering than Chicago gangsters." Then he wrote
that "the kind of Christianity represented by the Rev. Mr.
Sage cannot pollute its pristine purity with poor whites and
colored people. To have a kind of brotherly feeling toward
poor whites and to respect the personality of Negroes by addressing them as mister is, according to this archbishop of the
plantation interests, to commit the crime of crimes."[23]

Kester also took a swipe in his book at the southern liberal
establishment. The unnamed target was Will W. Alexander,
who had moved from the Commission on Interracial Cooperation to the post of assistant director, and then director, of
the New Deal's Resettlement Administration. "Inter-racial-
ists of the Atlanta school," Kester wrote, " . . . take great de-
light in attempting to show that the rich man with his vast
benevolence and paternalism is the Negro's best friend, con-
veniently forgetting that if the poor white man is the Negro's
worst enemy it is the members of the so-called 'best families'
who force these equally exploited groups to struggle against
each other."[24]

Norman Thomas, accompanied by Jack Herling, the executive secretary of the Emergency Committee for Strikers Relief, made a second visit to Arkansas in March 1935. They
began their tour by meeting Governor J. Marion Futrell in
Little Rock and asking him to give police protection to union

gatherings. The governor said there was nothing he could do. Chauffeured by Mitchell and Kester, the party spent the next two days traveling through the Delta farm country and appearing before large and small gatherings of workers. In a memorable incident they came upon a white family camped with all their belongings by the roadside. The father explained to Thomas that the family had been evicted because he had tried to take legal action against a plantation riding boss who had raped his fourteen-year-old daughter. Thomas asked the union attorney to see what could be done to bring this "abomination to mankind" to justice, but nothing could be accomplished through the local courts. All that the union could offer the family was a few dollars for food. "It was," said Kester, "from beginning to end a heartbreaking and maddening experience for all concerned."[25]

On Friday, March 15, Thomas came to the hamlet of Birdsong in Mississippi County. It was here that Powers Hapgood, an itinerant union organizer and member of the national executive committee of the Socialist party, had been run out of town for trying to speak to an STFU assembly a few weeks earlier. About five hundred people came to see Thomas, most of them black. The Mississippi County sheriff told Thomas he expected trouble, and, in fact, the elder Socialist never even reached the podium. Kester climbed the steps of a church to introduce the distinguished visitor, but when he said, "Ladies and gentlemen . . ." an armed white man muscled his way forward to yell, "There ain't no ladies here, and there ain't no gentlemen on the platform." He and a swarm of others clambered up the church steps and pushed Kester and Thomas into the street.

Thomas waved a copy of the Bill of Rights over his head while he was manhandled through the crowd. Herling, standing beside the church, was struck from behind with a billy stick, then dragged, kicked, and shoved along with the rest of the party back to their car. They left quickly, with thugs beating the fenders, and drove to Memphis for a hasty press conference before boarding a train for the safety of home. Kester saw them off, and then returned to Nashville for the first time in a month to see his wife and family. There he received a letter from C. T. Carpenter imparting the rumor that the Ku Klux Klan was planning to deal with the STFU organizers. Travel only by daylight, Carpenter recommended. "Please remember me very kindly to Mrs. Kester and say to her that I do not wish her to be a widow."[26]

On the following Wednesday morning the home of an organizer, the Reverend Arthur B. Brookins, was fired upon. STFU president W. H. Stultz found a note on his front porch telling him to leave Marked Tree within twenty-four hours. He and another union man, Ed Pickering, were "arrested" and locked in a warehouse for three hours of questioning. That night an STFU meeting in Marked Tree was raided by Police Chief E. L. Shinabery, who declared that there would be no more union talk in his town.[27]

Lawyer Carpenter was told that a group of planters had put a $2,000 bounty on his life. After nightfall on March 26 Mrs. Carpenter peered through her bedroom window to see masked men surround the house. They called for her husband to come out, and when he refused they opened fire on the house and then departed. A little later the Carpenters' son was run off the highway by an unidentified vehicle.[28]

Mitchell and Kester sent a telegram to Norman Thomas summarizing the rush of events with the words: "ENTIRE POPULATION TERRORIZED." And the campaign of terror was not yet over. On March 30 night riders shot up a Negro church in Lepanto while the congregation huddled beneath the pews, and two days later, organizer Walter Moskop was chased from his home in Marked Tree by a mob. Trying to be helpful, Elisabeth Gilman suggested that the Committee on Economic and Racial Justice buy Kester a life insurance policy, and the New England Socialist Alfred Baker Lewis offered to buy the STFU an armored car with a loudspeaker attachment. This idea was rejected in Memphis on the grounds that sending a small tank into Arkansas would be an invitation to further violence.[29]

The STFU wanted allies, and it looked first to the labor movement. But J. R. Butler, newly elected president of the union, suffered a stinging rebuff in August 1935 when he was denied a seat at the Arkansas Federation of Labor convention because of his Socialist politics. Claude Williams was permitted to make a speech to the convention, but it degenerated into an insult match between him and David Fowler, the powerful UMW president in Arkansas, which prompted Williams to say that Fowler reminded him of a little boy's bulldog: 1 percent dog and 99 percent bull.

When the STFU sent notice to the high council of the AFL expressing its desire to affiliate, a letter came back from Frank Morrison, the staunchly conservative AFL secretary, demanding to know what dues the sharecroppers paid, what the officers earned, and whether or not the union could support itself. One of the underpaid STFU officers sent a copy of this letter to Clarence Senior, manager of the Socialist party headquarters in Chicago, who remarked, "That fellow [Morrison] is one of the most useless personalities in the American labor movement and that is taking in a lot of territory."[30]

If the American Federation of Labor was not interested in organizing sharecroppers, the Communist party was. After it decided in 1930 to support the immediate demands of blacks and downplay an all-black state as its primary goal, the American Communist party helped to create a Share Croppers Union in the cotton belt of central Alabama. Few, if any, white sharecroppers were a part of it, and the movement was mostly underground. Outsiders who were allowed to attend the secret meetings almost always commented on the double-barreled shotguns and pistols kept close at hand.

The SCU suffered a major setback before it really got off

the ground. On the night of July 17, 1931, a black sharecropper standing guard over a meeting near Camp Hill shot and wounded the Tallapoosa County sheriff. A posse led by the town police chief cornered a group of armed blacks in a tenant shack. In the ensuing exchange, a black man named Ralph Gray was killed, and three blacks and two whites were wounded. Thirty blacks were later arrested for their part in the uprising.

The militant Tallapoosa County sharecroppers clashed with the law again in December 1932 when the tried to defend an SCU member, Cliff James, against eviction. The sheriff and two of his deputies were wounded, and, again, a black man was killed. It set off a wave of mob violence lasting four days in which an unknown number of black farmers died. Yet the following spring the SCU claimed three thousand members.[31]

In 1934 the Communist organizer Clyde Johnson, who had been working with Don and Constance West in Atlanta, moved into the home of a black party member in Bessemer, Alabama. When the house was bombed by a terrorist, Johnson shifted his base to the Birmingham home of Nat and Johnnye Ross, and then to the cotton fields when he began organizing for the Share Croppers Union. He oversaw its 1935 strike, aimed primarily at the J. R. Bell plantation, and survived the counterattack which claimed the lives of three SCU members and left at least thirty others wounded or beaten. The union claimed victory on the fourth of July, though a bitter-tasting victory it must have been, and stated that wages had been boosted to a dollar a day.[32]

Johnson, who was then using the name "Tom Burke," began talking with the STFU leadership that summer about a possible merger. Along with Al Jackson, a former steelworker who was the other chief SCU organizer, Johnson went to Memphis in August in hopes of reaching an agreement with the STFU to combine the two unions. Mitchell was not enthusiastic about the proposition, although he expressed much

admiration for the Communist party's financial and propaganda strengths. He confided to Kester that "in Ala. they [the
Communists] are organizing separate locals for the races for
the first time. If they were not such damn fools and some
method could be worked out for their organization to take
over sponsorship of the STFU they could raise sufficient
money to put the thing over in a big way, but then dictation
from above would tear it up completely I fear. Where is there
a place for us who want to do something to turn. I came in
the Socialist Party simply because there was no other place to
go to, we, you and I would not last as long as a snowball in
hell with the CP, I know this very well."[33]

Kester was also disillusioned with the Communist party,
but for different reasons. He was now considering forming a
left-wing Christian organization. Late in 1934 he wrote to Mr.
and Mrs. John Bergthold, two close friends from his Student
Christian Movement days:

In my opinion we are headed for some terrible and disatrous
interracial disorders. Further, I see no solution until we have
come to a definite crisis and I doubt if we have sufficient
imagination and social intelligence to meet the coming crisis
short of violent social upheaval and bloodshed. . . . (While I
have been extremely sympathetic with the Communist position and have been very close to the organsiers in this area I
am becoming increasingly skeptical of the validity of their position and of their political tactics. . . .) While I despair of
present day religion as it is portrayed by our contemporaries
becoming an instrument of deliverance I think it is probably
not too late for a genuine prophetic religion to be of immense
significance in the coming struggle. That is my main concern
these days.[34]

Norman Thomas said of the proposed merger that he suspected the Communists wanted only a "Trial marriage" and
that they might "end the honeymoon with poison." Joining
with the Alabama union, he told the STFU leaders, "will raise
the cry of Communist against you in any strike you will un-

dertake without compensating advantages," and "it will enormously complicate your relations with the A. F. of L." These were arguments that the STFU officials found to be persuasive.[35]

Despite the terrorist campaign, the Southern Tenant Farmers' Union expanded rapidly in the summer of 1935. A part-Cherokee named Odis Sweeden organized thirty-seven locals in the dust bowl counties of Texas and Oklahoma, and a grant from the Garland Fund enabled the union to employ eight organizers in Arkansas. By midsummer the STFU claimed fifteen thousand members and felt strong enough to call its first wage strike. But the treasury was so low that Kester offered Mitchell one of his family's heirlooms, a gold watch, to pawn, and the STFU secretary would have quit for lack of funds had not Norman Thomas repeatedly written to praise him for the "magnificent work" he was doing. A trickle of funds from the Committee for Strikers' Relief solved the problem temporarily. On September 1, 1935, the union's executive council met to authorize a strike during the cotton harvest.[36]

Kester described the scene as E. B. McKinney rose to speak:

The men knew what this meant. They knew that before the strike was over some of them would be in jail, some would have been driven from their homes and some would be dead. . . . The gray-haired preacher and veteran organizer of the union lifted his head and prayed God's benediction on their work, he prayed for the men to be guided to the right cabins and along the unguarded roads, for all the organizers to escape from the hands of the law, to give all the people courage when they needed it and to seal their struggle with victory. When the meeting broke up I felt that the men and women who had heard the preacher's words and understood what he was saying would wade through hell and high water and not be afraid nor turn back. Some of them went through hell but they never turned back.[37]

Bundles of strike leaflets were printed and hidden until 11 o'clock on Sunday night, September 11, and then tacked up on trees and fence posts throughout eastern Arkansas. Carrie Dilworth, secretary of the Gould local, took part in this late-night sortie.

It was Sunday night. We got our papers together at eleven o'clock exactly. Everyone, all over Arkansas where there was an organization alive, had to be on the job at 11:00 passing out leaflets. We'd cover this street, then we'd go to another. We ain't supposed to go back there on the same route because if you do, somebody is gonna see one of them things. Oooh, I don't know how many we passed out. We spread them handbills saying, "Don't go to the fields and pick no cotton," over every street in this town.

I was riding in my car. Marie Pierce, a student from Memphis, was riding in the back seat with Mr. Bolden. Mrs. Burton and I sat in the front. I was laying down on my stomach holding the door cracked open, and I'd push the leaflets through the crack and spread them out in the street. You pick up speed and that'd just make them things go flying all over the yards.

By the time we got down to Mr. Dean's house, we had done the whole route. Then this car came swooping by us. I said, "Cut the lights off and let's go right into these woods." We got down in a little curl and cut the motor off. If they had caught us, I don't know what they would have done to us. But, they couldn't tell where we was. . . .

White folks thought a plane had flown over there and spread all them leaflets. They were all over the state.[38]

The strike call was generally heeded. It is likely that at least five thousand workers stayed off the job on the first day. There were no picket lines. It was simply a sit-down strike in which most of the participants sat down on their front porches and waited. In terms of the wide territory affected, the strike was unprecedented in the history of plantation labor relations.

But it was not a peaceful vacation for the idled cotton pickers. Scores of men and women were arrested for vagrancy if

NEGROES
BEWARE
DO NOT ATTEND
COMMUNIST
MEETINGS

Paid organizers for the communists are
only trying to get negroes in trouble.
Alabama is a good place for good negroes
to live in, but it is a bad place for negroes
who believe in SOCIAL EQUALITY.

The Ku Klux Klan
Is Watching You.
TAKE HEED

Tell the communist leaders to leave.
Report all communist meetings to the
Ku Klux Klan
Post Office Box 651, Birmingham, Alabama.

Warning to members of the Alabama Share Croppers Union,
1935 (LABOR DEFENDER 11 [June 1935]: 24)

they dared to show themselves in public, and many of these were then "released" into the custody of their landlords. In Cross County, Hes Redmond and George Fly were beaten with ax handles by overseers, and three people were jailed for a week in Blytheville for "agitating." An STFU meeting led by J. E. Cameroon was broken up in Parkin, and the white sharecropper described the confrontation this way:

In the middle of my speech up drove 3 men in cars. Came rite on in cussing and abbusing every body as they came till they got to me. . . . what in the hell are you doing here you son of a bitch shut up or I knock your brains out you damn bastard. . . . such as that went on till the most of the crowd had runn off The[y] loaded me up and said wel take you to Forest City you low down son of a bitch. so they took me and cussing and abbusing me every way they could think of they had a little Jack Leg Law so they said but had no warrant so when they got me their the Sheriff Refused to Lock me up so they took me where they got me and warned me never to be seen back there again.[39]

The plantation owners were caught off balance by the suddenness of the strike. The cotton crop stood a chance of being ruined in the fields by autumn rains and frosts. Going into the second week, the landlords began offering higher wages, and when the figure reached 75¢ per hundred, the pickers began returning to work. On October 4 the strike was declared a victory, and interracial solidarity was given the credit. H. L. Mitchell provided the best epilogue in a letter he wrote to the head of the Widener local: "It is very important that we organize the Whites as well as the Negroes. . . . For many years the Boss Class has succeeded in keeping the two races divided, and at the same time robbed both the Negroe and the White equally. . . . There are no 'niggers' and no 'poor white trash' in the Union. These two kinds of people are all lined up with the Planters. We have only Union men in our organization, and whether they are white or black makes no difference."[40]

The sweet smell of victory swept thousands of new members into the Southern Tenant Farmers' Union. In the two months after the strike was called, new locals were chartered at seventy-one plantations. On December 4 Kester sent word to Reinhold Niebuhr (to whom he usually did not exaggerate things) that the union now had twenty-five thousand members, including many Choctaws and Mexicans in Texas and Oklahoma. [41]

To hammer home the success Kester went to the Fifty-fifth Annual Convention of the American Federation of Labor, which opened in Atlantic City on October 5, 1935, to try again to get organized labor's recognition of the battle-tested farmers union. He met privately with AFL President William Green, numerous union leaders, and with the secretary-treasurer, Frank Morrison, whom he uncharitably described as "the biggest dumbell there by all odds." The insult was born of frustration since Kester failed to sell the argument that a union of America's poorest workers deserved the AFL's financial support for the vital role it might ultimately play in a general strike or the final struggle for control of the government. Kester succeeded, however, in persuading A. Philip Randolph, head of the nation's most powerful black union, the Sleeping Car Porters, to offer a resolution giving AFL "endorsement" to the STFU and calling upon union members to contribute money to the sharecroppers. [42]

Seventy-five poorly dressed but high-spirited delegates opened the second convention of the STFU (the first had been the informal meeting at which the union constitution was drafted) on January 3, 1936, with a rendition of the movement's official song, "We Shall Not Be Moved." President Butler announced a goal of one hundred thousand new members in the coming year and brought to the podium UMW District President David Fowler, whom he introduced as John L. Lewis's personal representative. Fowler explained that within the past two months Lewis and the presidents of

seven other AFL unions had taken the historic step of creating the Committee for Industrial Organization (CIO), and
they planned to launch a militant organizing drive in the basic
industries: steel, rubber, automobiles, and textiles. Naturally,
the STFU delegates hoped that agriculture would be one of
the CIO's targets, and Fowler suggested as much.

There was a women's caucus at this convention led by Evelyn Smith, a young Socialist from New Orleans who was employed as the office manager of the union in Memphis. A
great many of the STFU leaders at the local level were
women. Eight of the twenty-five Crittenden County locals,
for example, had female business secretaries, as did at least
ten of the thirty-one St. Francis County locals. Smith herself
had been made director of women's work by the STFU executive council in December. All of these officers politicked hard
at the convention and saw the union constitution amended to
suit them. Women were explicitly made eligible for the same
union offices and would pay the same dues that men did. It
was decided that women's locals would function separately
from men's wherever "it was so wished," and that women
would be admitted to men's organizations "whenever it was
thought advisable." The constitution did not say who would
do the "wishing" or the "advising," but places were made on
the executive council for two women: the first elected were
Marie Pierce, a black, and Myrtle Moskop, a white.

The delegates endorsed in principle a "New Homestead
Law" drafted by H. L. Mitchell and William Amberson. It
was the union's clearest proposal yet regarding the future
ownership and use of America's farmland. Under this scheme
a National Agricultural Land Authority (NALA) would be established to buy up and regulate all farmland in the United
States except tracts smaller than 160 acres, farms managed by
producers' co-ops, and farms operated by local governments
in accordance with NALA principles.

To purchase this boundless estate NALA would issue $10

110

billion in bonds and use them like money to compensate the former landowners. The bonds would be redeemed at low interest over twenty years, but to keep big landowners from profiting too much, $100,000 was set as the maximum payment. NALA would lease its holdings to bona fide farm families and cooperatives for ninety-nine years. Each tenant would be assigned the acreage NALA judged sufficient to support a family or a cooperative, and 25 percent of the crop would serve as rent. Ten directors would head NALA: three to be appointed by the president with Senate approval and seven to be elected by farm organizations in the seven geographically distinct farming regions of the United States. They would be responsible for designing a modern farming system for the nation, instructing farmers in the best crops to raise, and introducing laborsaving equipment.[43]

It was a novel blend of socialist theories—government expropriation and management of land—with American ideals—the direct election of governors and thriving rural communities inhabited by prosperous self-sufficient farmers. The plan exactly described the dream of most of the STFU's members, and it was clearly an alternative to the forced collectivization of agriculture envisioned and enacted by more rigorous socialists. The sharecroppers' socialism was the flexible sort, and not the least of the reasons was that, as Ward Rodgers recorded in 1938, he and five others were the only Socialist party members in the union. Kester provided a 1935 tally when he wrote that six of the fourteen members of the STFU executive council were preachers, and four of these were Socialists: "They believe in the tenets of Isaiah and of Jesus and of Marx and they are by their deeds social revolutionaries with a religious drive that keeps them in the midst of battle."[44]

V Gaining Ground

The new year of 1936 began tragically in Arkansas when an Earle planter named C. H. Dibble set off a new wave of evictions by ousting twenty-one of his tenant families. Before long 105 people, 28 of them children less than fifteen years of age, were stranded on the roadside begging food, clothing, and shelter. The union carried many of these families to a Negro Baptist church situated near Earle on U.S. Highway 64 where some were housed in the building and the overflow slept beneath crude shelters made of quilts in the churchyard. A union meeting was held that night at a Methodist church nearby, but it was broken up by deputies who shot two sharecroppers, Virgil Ligons and Ed Franklin, and arrested a third, Jim Ball. They put Ball, the father of five now-homeless children, on trial, and upon the shakiest of evidence saw him convicted of assault with intent to kill. He was sent to prison for more than a year.[1]

A meeting called to protest the shootings was held the next afternoon in a Baptist church near Parkin. Kester was the main speaker. He drove from Memphis with Evelyn Smith and Herman I. Goldberger, the attorney who was unsuccessfully fighting the evictions, and they found more than 450 white and black sharecroppers at the church. Kester had barely reached the pulpit when a squad of men armed with ax handles and guns broke into the building and began clubbing the people in the pews. They waded through the church, striking and cursing anybody they could reach. Some of the sharecroppers escaped through the church windows, taking glass and sash with them, but Kester continued with his speech. What kept him in the pulpit, he said, was the example of a group of black women seated directly in front of him who refused to acknowledge the mayhem to their rear. Soon, however, there was no one left but these few and the mob, whose leader strode up to Kester demanding, "Are you coming peaceably or will we have to take you?" Kester replied, "I am breaking no law, and if you want me you will have to take me." Whereupon they did, forcing the feisty preacher from the pulpit and out of the church. They sat him behind the wheel of his own '32 Chevrolet, put two gunmen on the running boards, and ordered him to follow their lead car out of town.

Kester was taken through the darkened streets of Earle. Once he had to slow abruptly to avoid hitting a small dog. The gunman beside him snarled, "You care more about dogs than you do about white people," but Kester reflected that he would have given pretext for an even angrier outburst had he hit the dog. Past Earle, they took a dirt road into the woods and halted. The captive was pulled from his car and a hangman's noose dangled before his eyes.

Kester summoned all his persuasive powers and began speaking loudly to one of the leaders of the gang, a man he recognized as an Earle cotton broker. He had harmed no one, Kester pointed out, and since he was not from Arkansas his murder would be investigated by federal authorities. The abductors could be identified by scores of people back at the church and were sure to be convicted. The kidnappers drew aside for a private discussion, but Kester overheard the words, "This man is telling the truth. We could get in a peck of trouble." The broker put an end to the talk by saying he had decided to escort Kester to the Mississippi River bridge into Tennessee, but that if he ever returned to Arkansas, "We'll shoot you on sight." Kester drove the twenty-five miles back to the river, and across it, in a cold sweat.

Meanwhile, union members had carried the word to Memphis that Kester had been captured and likely lynched. Mitchell called the Associated Press bureau chief, who relayed the news to New York City. It was soon told to Norman Thomas, who was addressing a meeting at the Hotel Roosevelt. Thomas sadly announced the fate of his friend, and shortly several listeners were sending telegrams of condolence to Alice in Nashville. It was not until several hours later, after her husband had collected his wits and found a telephone, that Alice learned he was still alive. Howard drove to Nashville that night, reaching home around 4 o'clock in the morning. He and his wife spent the remaining hours of darkness huddled together in front of the fireplace, Alice weeping.[2]

The indifference of the government to the eviction drama was recorded by William Amberson, who wrote late in January:

I fear that events in Crittenden are moving to a very bitter climax. Kelly Williams told me last night that the men at Earle had agreed to bring weapons to their next meeting, called for Friday night, and to defend themselves if again attacked by the planters. . . . Unless some agency of government steps in at *once* there is likely to be a most grievous situation. . . . The bitterness is being fanned by many evictions. One white woman and eight children were forced to live in the railroad depot at Earle for some days. She appealed to . . . the mayor and he spurned her. The Williams collected three dollars to send a wire to Futrell. Thereupon [the mayor] agreed to give her shelter and food. This was the only case which we could find in which any relief had been given, other than Union relief. There was absolutely no case of WPA action anywhere. Washington *must* move to do something about all this. . . . The men will delay further meetings if they think there is the slightest chance that some other way can be found. But . . . another whitewash of this stinking mess will be the last straw to break the patience of these people.

I must say that I have never been so nauseated by this

114

situation as on this trip. The utter brutality and callousness with which the planters are throwing off families is beyond belief. We visited among others the Hightower family, a widow and seven children, negro. She made ten bales of cotton, but has been ordered evicted without a cent of settlement, and her two mules and all her tools have been taken from her. They were to be moved today into a miserable wreck of a house, absolutely falling to pieces. We gave Marie Pierce $3.00 from the relief funds to feed these people. The Avery group of families also need relief, but the money is more than gone . . . the Parkin local promised to take a collection but the last meeting was called off because they feared an attack.[3]

Kester's narrow escape from the hangman's rope got the union some press attention, however; and Gardner Jackson arranged a dinner at Washington's exclusive Cosmos Club for several senators and congressmen who wished to learn more about civil liberties violations growing out of the union movement in Arkansas. Jackson, one of those purged from the Agriculture Department, now chaired the National Committee on Rural Social Planning and bore credentials making him the STFU's official spokesman in Washington. The dinner was held on February 21, 1936, and Kester was the featured speaker.

Jackson had persuaded Senators Edward P. Costigan of Colorado, Robert M. La Follette, Jr., of Wisconsin, Lewis B. Schwellenbach of Washington, and Burton K. Wheeler of Montana and Representatives Carolina O'Day of New York, Maury Maverick of Texas, and George P. Schneider of Wisconsin to sponsor the meeting. In all, about fifty politicians and church and labor leaders, including John L. Lewis, showed up. Kester spoke about the atrocities visited upon farm workers in Arkansas and read letters from Amberson testifying that conditions were becoming steadily worse. The only hopeful sign was the presence in Arkansas of Dorothy Day, who had founded, with Peter Maurin, the Catholic

Worker movement, and Sam Franklin, assistant to the international Christian crusader Sherwood Eddy, who were searching for a tract of land which might sustain the evicted tenants. They had located a tract in Poinsett County but needed $15,000 from the Resettlement Administration to buy it. The money was nowhere in sight.

A second report on the "Southern situation" was given by Clyde Johnson and Al Jackson from the Alabama Share Croppers Union. Jackson's head was wrapped in bandages, protecting, he said, wounds he had received in beatings by Alabama plantation owners. John L. Lewis, fresh from a CIO meeting which had rejected an AFL ultimatum to disband, followed this testimony with a demand that some federal protection be given to workers trying to organize unions. He expressed doubt, however, that Congress would do anything until blood flowed in the streets.

Senator La Follette concluded the meeting by promising definite action. True to his word he introduced, on March 23, a resolution in the Senate to create a subcommittee of the Committee on Education and Labor which would concern itself with violations of the rights of free speech and assembly and with interference with labor's right to organize. The La Follette Committee, as it became known, was created on June 6; besides the Wisconsin senator its members were Elbert D. Thomas of Utah and Louis Murphy of Iowa. It began hearings just as the CIO launched an organizing campaign in the steel industry, and it rendered great service to the labor movement by exposing the violence that big companies aimed at unions and the armies of gangsters, or detectives, that corporations marshaled to fight the union movement in the steel, coal, automobile, rubber, and electrical industries.[4] But the La Follette Committee never tackled agriculture, the industry where civil liberties abuses were so massive and obvious that the testimony of Kester, Johnson, and Jackson had been used as the springboard for the entire Senate investigat-

116 ing effort. Agriculture was always the "next" topic on the agenda—the one never reached because of the power in the Senate of southern Democrats. The day after the dinner at the Cosmos Club a parcel of dynamite was thrown into the sharecropper tent colony in Parkin. By some miracle it did not go off.

Even with the silence of the La Follette Committee it could not be said that the unpleasant news from Arkansas did not reach the president's ear. At a cabinet meting on March 6, Labor Secretary Frances Perkins suggested that a federal mediator be sent to the Delta. Vice-President Garner overruled the idea, fearing to cause embarrassment to Senator Robinson of Arkansas. Instead, Roosevelt had Rexford Tugwell contact Robinson and ask him to work through private channels to stop the bloodshed. The president also sent a telegram to Norman Thomas on March 13 saying that he had asked Governor Futrell to name an investigating committee. Thomas replied that Futrell had had ample opportunity to intervene in the crisis but had not done so. Mitchell sent a similar telegram to Roosevelt, but he did not enjoy the same direct access to the president that Thomas did. His telegram was answered by R. F. Croom of the AAA Compliance Division who said that conditions in Arkansas in regard to the cotton program had been investigated and found to be in good order. Mitchell sent a blistering response to this and received in return Croom's final words on the subject: "our own very extensive researches indicate that the program has . . . been administered . . . with helpful results to all people everywhere."[5]

The Southern Tenant Farmers' Union could not bear the burden of paying out roughly $100 weekly to the displaced families in the tent colonies. Late in February, Amberson wrote to Kester, who was trying to raise funds in Boston, that the last of their provisions had been handed out. "The money is gone, Amberson wrote, "it is either the WPA or starvation for these people from now on."[6]

Four semipermanent tent camps remained by the highway as the chill winds of early March gusted across the barren cotton fields. They were in plain sight of the motorists who passed by Earle or Parkin, but the sight of hoboes by the roadside was too common in 1936 to enable these castaways to make much of an impression upon the agencies that might have helped. The sharecroppers were huddled beneath the most makeshift of shelters to escape the rain and frost. Strewn about their camps were all of the household goods and farming implements that they had carried with them in their hurried exodus from the plantations. How they found the little food they shared was a mystery to all. H. L. Mitchell remarked bitterly that "I wish we had enough money to send them all to Washington and let them camp on Aubrey Williams and Rex Tugwells front door steps, and maybe they couldn't get around feeding them."[7]

Suddenly a partial, but most welcome, solution presented itself. The evangelist Sherwood Eddy and his assistant, Sam Franklin, located a plantation in Mississippi which could be used as a resettlement farm for the squatters, and Eddy decided to invest the initial cash needed to buy the place. He met with the STFU's officers to describe the venture. Afterwards Kester wrote, "I felt as though the Kingdom was really being born and that something of historical importance was about to make its appearance on earth." It would be a cooperative farm and would demonstrate, Kester said, that "the rural life of America may be lifted to a new high through our community ideal. . . . Don't think me either drunk or delirious. I was never more sane. This thing is of breath-taking importance and someday must be reckoned as one of the really important adventures in faith on the part of a disinherited group."[8]

Eddy had purchased a farm in Mississippi rather than Arkansas for reasons of safety, but Mitchell, with greater foresight, observed that "Eddy refused to invest money in Arkansas saying that he would not set a co-operative in the midst of a volcano, knowing the Delta as I do I greatly fear that they are jumping from the frying pan into the fire."[9]

The cooperative was soon christened Rochdale Farm in honor of the textile manufacturing town in England that had been the center of the British cooperative movement a century before. It consisted of 2,000 acres in Bolivar County, 800 of which were ready for cultivation. There were large stands of timber and eleven tenant houses and barns. Eddy bought the plantation with $1,000 in cash and a mortgage for $16,500, but it was eventually deeded to a board of trustees, the most active of whom were Reinhold Niebuhr, William Amberson, and John Rust. Rust and his brother Mack had perfected an invention that would dramatically change southern culture, the cotton-picking machine. The brothers, both Socialists, were unusual inventors in that they worried about the effect on the workers that their contrivance would have. They were quite slow to market the picker, but in anticipation of future profits they directed that most of the proceeds go into a foundation intended to support Rochdale Farm and other alternatives to plantation society. They knew that the economic system which sustained several million people was dying with nothing to catch the inevitable victims. Oddly, the Rust cotton picker was first produced by the government of the USSR and only later did it enter the United States as the basis for the Allis-Chalmers machine. In neither case did it reward the Rust family with great wealth.[10]

The first "social administrator" of Rochdale was Sam Franklin. Born on 1902 in Dandridge, Tennessee, Franklin had attended nearby Maryville College, McCormick Theological Seminary in Chicago, and the University of Edinburgh. He married Dorothy Winters of Maryville, and they had gone as

Presbyterian missionaries to Japan in 1929 to direct the Fellowship House in Kyoto. They lived there in a cooperative
household with Japanese and Formosans and worked among
factory workers until the rise of Japan's war-hungry right wing
forced their departure in 1934. Like his employer Eddy,
Franklin was a relentless social visionary, and he considered
himself a socialist during the Depression years. Upon hearing
of Franklin's appointment to Rochdale, another southern religious activist wrote happily to Kester, "You don't need to be
told that Sam Franklin is all wool and a yard wide."[11]

Soon after Rochdale was created, A. Eugene Cox was hired
to be its accountant. The son of a Texas sharecropper, Cox
had quit school in the seventh grade, been a bookkeeper for
Standard Oil, administered migrant relief, and pursued, for a
time, a ministerial career. After five years as a student at
Texas Christian University, he met Eddy at a revival and became interested in the Rochdale project. He joined the farm
staff in June 1936 and devoted the next twenty years of his
life to this unique experiment in cooperative community.[12]

Kester was also considered a staff member. He resigned
from the Presbyterian church in the summer of 1936 because
it was evident that it would not ordain him, and in October
he was officially accepted into the Congregational church
ministry. There were signs that other Congregational pastors
would resist Kester's ordination, but Fred Ensminger, a
church leader in Tennessee, saw that the ceremony was conducted without incident. Kester's formal assignment within
the church was to serve as the chaplain of Rochdale, but it
was mainly an honorary position since he never lived in Mississippi.

The first seven families arrived at Rochdale in March. All
had been evicted from the Dibble plantation, and all were
white, though soon the black families began to arrive. While
this group was in transit, another eight families were evicted
from the M. E. Holland plantation near Wynne, Arkansas.

"We have no relief money, and are at a loss as to what to do," wrote Mitchell. "I greatly fear that the co-operative may drain away from the Union resources which might be available for relief." And to Kester: "You fellows must realize that just by taking 25 or more families off to Mississippi doesn't solve the Relief problem . . . those people in these tent colonies look to me for every thing and believe me it is a one man job to tell them there is nothing for them. . . . If we can build the Union we will take over all the damn plantations and won't bother to pay for them again, as Dr. Eddy et al are doing with this one." Yet Mitchell defended the costly cooperative experiment to Clyde Johnson. "It is paternalistic an all of that," he wrote, "but what about your Soviet Collectives, weren't they too the same. The State took the place of the Philanthropist." He told the Alabama organizer that the sharecroppers had already paid for the land a "thousand times over" and would not buy it again, but if the Rochdale Farm was successful it would prove that the American farmer did not "have to be forced into collectivism."[13]

Despite the evictions the STFU membership voted overwhelmingly in the spring of 1936 to go on strike for a ten-hour day. The inflated voting tally (6,118 to 384 was the official ballot count) hid the disrupted condition of the union. Many locals did not bother to vote because their organization had been shattered by nightly terrorist raids. In one of these, near Earle, a group of masked men murdered Willie Hurst, the eyewitness to the scuffle between Jim Ball and the deputies that had resulted in Ball's prison sentence. Pressure from Washington forced Governor Futrell to make a cursory investigation of this vigilante war, but he told the press:

I am reminded of the play, "Much Ado About Nothing". With slight modification, this fits the situation in Eastern Arkansas with reference to the Tenant Farmers' Union. It is much ado about a very little. . . . Some of these negro tenant farmers wanted to join a union. They had the legal right to do so. The

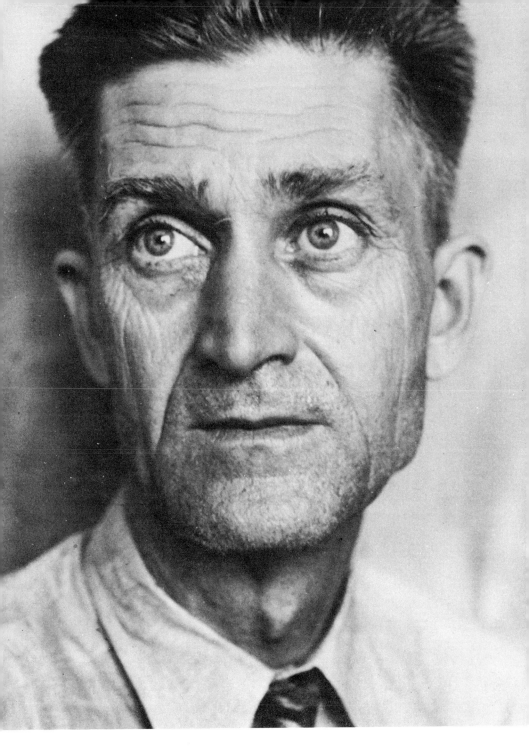

J. R. Butler, president of the Southern Tenant Farmers'
Union, June 1938 (*Dorothea Lange, Farm Security
Administration*)

land owners conceded this, but they are afraid. They know that
the negro is easily excited into the most unbridled violence. . . .
They remember vividly the Elaine affair, where the negroes,
under the guidance of white men, had planned to dispatch
several owners of land in that country. . . . You cannot get this
fear out of the land owners. They don't want trouble. They
don't want agitators around. . . . A good negro, in the eyes of a
white man, is one who attends to his business, works his crop,
stays sober and keeps out of mischief. . . . *There is no way to
make a man keep a negro on his place if he does not want to
keep him there. Most of these landlords will not keep a tenant
who is a member of the Union, and, knowing the situation as I
do, they are correct in this position.*[14]

As the strike date approached, an unwelcome announcement came from John Brophy, director of the CIO. Since the
CIO was directing its energies toward workers in mass industries, Brophy wrote, "it is inadvisable for the C.I.O. to deal
now with the subject of the building up of a union of workers on
the cotton plantations of the South. This is really out of our
field." The STFU would go into its 1936 strike without the
backing of the big powers in organized labor.[15]

The STFU could count 150 active locals in Arkansas, 60 in
Oklahoma (though some of these may have existed only on
paper since Odis Sweeden did not have the money to keep
himself in the field), and 15 or 20 others scattered about Tennessee, Missouri, and Mississippi. There were fifteen organizers on the job, and four or five more teaching or training at
Commonwealth College. Some of the best were absent. Kester
was in Nashville tending Alice, who was suffering from bursitis
that crippled her left arm. Walter Moskop and E. B. McKinney
were on an extended fund-raising venture to New York and
Boston. A feud had flared between the two men at the Little
Rock convention after Moskop, the white, had lost a close race
for the union vice-presidency to McKinney, who called himself
"black" even in those days when the term "colored" was more

common. They traveled together so that each could keep an eye on the small sums of money they collected. Yet the members wanted to strike because they were desperate. Lula Parchman, the secretary of Local no. 2 at the St. John Plantation, spoke for many when she described her own situation.

I am a widow woman and tries to lives peaceable. . . . I would given them a days work every year I been here and payed rent in 1934. . . . its (3) three empty houses here now but this man is too unjust to let people live in them unless he can use them as tools for a little or nothing. . . . oh he is unjust. it is same as a slave farm. he aint got enough mules. nor food stuff neather wagon and trying to run a big plantation. . . . They work from sun to sun at one dollar $1.00 per day. Conditions are pityfull with we poor peoples. the landlords and renters on some farms is unjust and unfair if they cant work we poor people for nothing scarcely. they will tell us to move and claim that we wont work. . . . I want only a chance to make my own liveing and not the others get the profit of my labor and I suffer. I am tired of being drove from place to place and being denied of the chance to live independent. I dont want what belongs to others. I only want the portion due me for comfort. [16]

Aiding in the strike was an organization of the unemployed in Memphis, the Workers' Alliance, which was supported by both Communists and Socialists. It was active in the Memphis slums among the people who waited in long lines each day to be bused to Arkansas to work for 75¢ per day. With the cooperation of Dave Benson, the alliance organizer, the STFU executive council voted to ask these day laborers to stay off the job. The officers left it up to each STFU local whether to call the more vulnerable Arkansas tenant farmers on strike as well. Work was to stop on May 18, coincident with the beginning of the Cotton Carnival in Memphis.

On that day, members of the Memphis Workers' Alliance picketed the Tennessee side of the Harahan Bridge and forcibly prevented the trucks of labor recruiters from entering

or leaving the city. Four of the picketers were arrested, and
Police Chief Will Lee testified at their trial that the defendants had turned back seven hundred workers and unloaded
forty trucks at the bridge. The word was out, and day laborers
stopped coming to the morning lineup. From Cross County,
Arkansas, W. L. Blackstone wrote, "I Believe the Strike Will
go over—Dont you—We gaining ground Every Day Every
thing looks good to me." Even AFL President Green seemed
impressed, and he asked his affiliated unions to send contributions to the striking agricultural workers.

The reaction of the plantation owners was immediate. On
the second day of the strike some thirty-five union members
were rounded up in Earle and thrown into jail. Their crime
was vagrancy; in other words, they were not in the fields
chopping cotton. Reports reached Memphis from all over the
Delta that men and women were being herded to the fields
at gunpoint. To verify one of them, Evelyn Smith and Maxine
East, Clay East's wife, sneaked onto the plantation of Earle
City Marshal Paul D. Peacher and discovered a rude stockade
in which thirteen black men were being held captive. The
spies were apprehended by the marshal's men, however, and
their camera was smashed. A second reconnaissance was
made by Sherwood Eddy and a sharecropper named Roy
Morlock. They got inside the stockade, took down the names
of the prisoners, and got out unscathed. Driving away, however, they were picked up by two deputies and taken to a
plantation commissary for questioning. But Eddy's talent was
talk, and he persuaded the lawmen to release him. Once back
to safety, he sent a telegram to United States Attorney General Homer Cummings which said: "I have today witnessed
most flagrant violations of the Federal Peonage act by the
killer P. D. Peacher in the lawless county of Crittenden, near
Earle, Arkansas. Our histories should be revised in mislead-
ing us that slavery was ever abolished in Arkansas."[17]

The union sent Newell Fowler, its attorney, and Aron Gil-

martin of the Workers' Defense League back to the Crittenden "concentration camp" to demand the release of the prisoners, but Fowler got into a fistfight with a deputy, and
Gilmartin was arrested for "disturbing labor." The young Socialist, who later became a Unitarian minister, had to post
$150 bond to get out of the Earle jail.

The STFU's charges of involuntary servitude reached the
desk of the United States attorney in Little Rock, a plantation
owner named Fred A. Isgrig, who responded by saying that
his office would need proof, such as signed statements from
the workers held prisoner, before it could proceed. He
added, "This is not intended to put the burden upon you to
investigate, but at the same time you may know if the Government was put to the expense of chasing men all over the
country simply on rumors we would not have any time left for
the actual and active enforcement of the law."[18]

Meanwhile the strike was failing. C. J. Spradling of Earle
wrote: "Our Beloved President of Local #102 . . . is in grave
Danger. . . . Yesterday the 23rd Day of May Preacher and
Dr. Watson was hunting for him with clubs and Boss Dulaney
and Arby Landcaster and R. E. moore has threating to hang
his hide on a pole. I will tell you things is get serious around
here." Before the strike was over this local president, Kelly
Williams, was forced to leave the state.

Hughel Haywood and Jim Brown, officers of the Cecella
Local in Whitmore, wrote that "the strike is on in our community an it has got some of our members in critical condition they are Day Hand have no crops they have not
nothing to eat an just about to get out of homes unless thay
continue to work like the land law say We who have crops
are Dividing our food with them the best we can the way
the thing is now we will soon Hafter quit . . . if we Dont thay
will quit furnish us so we want to here from you at once just
what to do about it Whether to tell them to go on to work
or to Continue to obey the Strike order."[19]

By the end of May the union was claiming only three thousand people on strike, down from five thousand at the beginning, and the local leaders met in Memphis to assess the situation. Rashly deciding to try to reverse their setbacks by counterattacking, they called for all of the tenants and sharecroppers who held allegiance to the STFU to join the day laborers on strike. They called it a "General Strike" and printed and shipped twenty-five thousand handbills to the locals. Certainly this was the most audacious and all-inclusive strike ever called among farm laborers in the South, and one of the least well supported.

Roving picket brigades, each numbering a hundred or more men and women, moved through the plantation backroads of Cross and St. Francis counties calling the stooped laborers to drop their hoes and join the strike. The tactic was quite successful. Governor Futrell called up the state militia; but when the troops arrived in one area, the picketers simply disbanded and regrouped in another. Dave Benson and a companion named Rose Mason joined the roving pickets, but since Benson was driving a car he was quickly located and arrested by the police. He was jailed in Forrest City on charges of rioting, interfering with labor, and having out-of-state license plates.

Clay East and a union attorney from Little Rock, M. D. Moody, came to Benson's trial on June 4. They got to see the organizer in jail and found him "scared to death," convinced that he was about to be lynched. He feared that any legal defense would only make matters worse. Obligingly, the attorney entered no plea, and Benson was fined $1,060, which he did not have, and was returned to jail. [20]

James Myers, the industrial secretary of the Federal Council of Churches, was on a four-day fact-finding trip through Arkansas, and he watched these proceedings. A white-suited planter sat next to the churchman and remarked that they should lynch Benson and be done with it. Myers said that he was "a little surprised" to hear that and was told, "You'll be surprised at a Hell of a lot more things if you stay around here long enough." He took this to be a threat and left town immediately after the guilty verdict came in.

Had Myers stayed a few minutes longer he would have seen what the man was talking about. Clay East was set upon by a crowd of whites when he left the courtroom, and he was on his back kicking wildly at his attackers when Sheriff J. C. Campbell rescued him. The sheriff locked East in Benson's cell and made preparations to defend the jail. The swelling crowd surrounding the courthouse turned on other strangers, jostling and interrogating a reporter for the St. Louis *Post Dispatch* and Joe Jones, a highly acclaimed painter of Depression scenes who had rendered a mural of coal miners and sharecroppers for the Commonwealth College dining hall.

A contingent of Arkansas state rangers arrived just in time. East was shoved into a patrol car and raced to the Mississippi River Bridge with the sirens wailing. Benson was forced to remain, but the rangers stood guard until the mob dispersed. Fearing that the planters might use Rose Mason to frame Benson on a "more serious charge," Mitchell sent her to the Highlander Folk School. When things calmed down later in the week, a judge lowered Benson's fine to $100, and he slipped out of town.[21]

The Memphis police joined in on June 8 when they raided the home of E. B. McKinney. He was not caught, but the officers arrested five sharecroppers who had taken refuge there. All were sentenced to the workhouse on the charge of vagrancy.[22]

From Earle, where City Marshal Peacher's stockade was located, union secretary Spradling wrote on June 8: "the planters are all mad   to day Dr. Watson and Boss Dulaney, and Buford Ray Did give one negro woman a whipping with sticks and strape of leather. And Ed Isom   white   was Following the gang   Dr. Watson Dulaney liked to Beat him to

Death. Be sure and send protection here and send me as much money a you can for Relief." On the same day the STFU members in Crittenden County planned a march through Earle. Two of their leaders, Frank Weems, a black, and Jim Reese, a white, scouted around town before the march began and concluded that there were too many armed white men on the streets for safety. As they left town to warn the marchers, Weems and Reese were overtaken by several carloads of planters, who surrounded the pair and beat them senseless. When Reese came to he could not find Weems, and he assumed, as did almost everyone else, that the black man had been killed and his body dropped in the river. [23]

The Weems murder received national publicity. Though there was no body, the Weems family and the union decided to hold a funeral service on Tuesday, June 16, at the Band Mill Church near Earle. Claude Williams, who was visiting in Memphis, volunteered to take over the pastoral duties. He set out on Monday morning for Crittenden County accompanied by Willie Sue Blagden. As they threaded through the backroads in search of the church, they were intercepted by a band of planters who hauled them into a soybean field and beat Williams bloody with a leather mule harness. The planters then turned their attention to Blagden. They were chivalrous enough to separate the barbed-wire strands so that she could climb into the field without scratching herself, but then they whipped her several times upon her thighs. Blagden was driven back to Earle and put on a train for Memphis. Williams, on the other hand, was driven around for hours while his captors talked about killing him. He was finally returned to his car and permitted to go. He arrived home in Little Rock in the early morning hours and collapsed in his wife's arms. [24]

Though her treatment was by far the less severe, it was the "flogging" of Willie Sue Blagden that outraged critics across the South and the nation. Whatever brutal acts the Arkansas planters had committed in the past had been excused by a great many people on the grounds that they were in defense of southern values and virtues. But the planters had violated the code by frightening and hurting Blagden because she was a white woman from one of the best families in Memphis. The STFU, exhausted in treasure and morale after months of violence and a failing strike, was brought back to life by an outpouring of public sympathy and cash contributions.

Norman Thomas sent a telegram to President Roosevelt about the beating asking that he act "in this monstrous perversion of everything decent in the American tradition." Jack Glenn of the "March of Time" film series arrived in Memphis a week later to begin shooting a half-hour movie entitled *Land of Cotton* that would be seen in theaters across America. In the film, marching sharecroppers sang, Governor Futrell declared that there was no peonage in Arkansas, and Blagden and Williams reenacted their abduction and whipping. Their scene was the climax of the film.[25]

The STFU executive council met in Muskogee on July 3 to declare the seven-week-old strike victorious. In fact, the 1936 strike had been a disastrous defeat. Wage increases were scarce, and the local organization was scattered. Had not the Blagden flogging and the resulting publicity occurred when they did, the union might have faded from history that summer.

Norman Thomas brought up Frank Weems's disappearance again in a speech he gave in September entitled "Arkansas' Shame." "In this region there is or there was a man whose name has become a symbol for our shame. It is the name of Frank Weems, colored farmer." Where is Frank Weems, Thomas demanded. Months later Weems turned up alive in Chicago where he had fled after his beating. The union made public the story of his harrowing ordeal after his escape, but Weems's reappearance did not attract the same attention as his "death."[26]

The only true victory to result from the 1936 cotton strike was the successful prosecution of Earle Marshal Peacher for holding workers in peonage. He was indicted on eight counts of violating the federal antislavery statutes. The STFU was jubilant, and the Workers' Defense League commemorated the event by distributing "Celebrate Arkansas Centenial, Abolish Peonage" stamps designed by Rockwell Kent. An assistant attorney general, Brien McMahon, was sent from Washington to present the case, and Peacher was found guilty on November 25 by an all-white jury and fined $3,500.

After local planters paid the fine, Peacher walked out of the courthouse a free man, but his conviction unhorsed one of the main adversaries of the sharecroppers' union. This case, the publicity generated by the STFU movement, and the dust storms that were burying Oklahoma made rural problems a key issue in the presidential campaign. A few days before the election, Roosevelt announced that he had ordered Henry Wallace to name a President's Committee on Farm Tenancy to recommend a new agricultural policy for the nation's poorest farmers. This committee would pave the way for the creation of the Farm Security Administration.[27]

The simmering hostility between Socialists and Communists in the farm worker movement was intensified by the national spotlight. In October the STFU executive council ruled that it opposed sending union students to either Commonwealth College or the Highlander Folk School because neither school would allow whites and blacks to be in residence or in class at the same time due to state segregation laws. Actually, race had nothing to do with the decision but was used as an excuse to sever ties with Commonwealth. The officers believed the school had come under increasing Communist influence since the departure of its Socialist director, Richard Whitten. Furthermore, Walter Moskop, while in residence at Commonwealth, had staged a lunatic assassination attempt against H. L. Mitchell, and, though there was no

evidence that Moskop's malice had any basis in political ri-
valry, Mitchell admitted that "this was the beginning of my
anti-communist paranoia." The mention of Highlander in the
ruling served mainly to obscure the issue since very few Arkansas sharecroppers had ever attended the school. It was
also well known to the STFU officers that Highlander quietly
but openly flouted Tennessee's race laws. To Myles Horton,
Mitchell wrote: "Due to Commonwealth's interference into
our affairs I am afraid that we can not send students even to
Highlander for this year."[28]

On a motion by Kester, the executive council also withdrew
its endorsement of Donald Henderson's *Rural Worker* because Henderson had written an editorial espousing the
Communist party line that sharecroppers and farm owners
should be organized into one union and wageworkers into another. This was precisely the course followed by the Share
Croppers Union in Alabama. It turned its farm-operating
members over to the National Farmers Union and created an
Alabama Agricultural Workers Union, which was chartered
by the AFL in 1937, to house its wageworkers. The STFU
had already refused to dismember itself along these lines,
preferring instead a loose structure that enabled neighbors on
the same plantation to be members of the same organization.[29]

In taking a stand on Communism the STFU was entering a
quagmire that confounded almost all of the radical movements of the 1930s. It was difficult to remain silent on the
issue because Communist party members and sympathizers
were a potent force in the labor and liberal community and
because there was constant public pressure upon all human
rights organizations to define their political alignment clearly.
The Highlander Folk School tried to find neutral ground by
stating that it would work with and support all democratic
groups, but, while this sounded fine to some liberal ears, it
was unsatisfactory to many of those on the firing lines of po-

litical activism. The result, in Highlander's case, was that both Communists and Socialists tried at various times to sabotage the school's programs. The possibility of peaceful coexistence between those who saw Communism as the wave of the future and those who viewed it as a monstrous totalitarian scheme vanished rapidly as the decade progressed and as more was learned about Stalin's purge of his enemies and the USSR's dealings with Nazi Germany.

For a labor organization like the STFU to welcome the support of the Communist party would have been to commit organizational suicide considering the political climate of the South; yet to denounce Communism would leave the organization open to accusations of "red baiting" and destroy much of its prestige on the left. The union viewed its quiet salvos against Commonwealth College and Donald Henderson as a discreet declaration of independence from Communist influence, and at first they had the desired result. Henderson quickly apologized for his editorial, saying it was meant only to apply to the Share Croppers Union and that he had no intention of forcing the Communist line "down the throats" of the STFU, but the reconciliation did not take.[30]

In particular, Henderson had not wanted to upset the delicate relationship between the STFU, the Share Croppers Union, his own periodical, and a farm workers local he was backing in New Jersey. All of these received equal shares of the money raised by an agency which Gardner Jackson had created, the Committee to Aid Agricultural Workers. This arrangement, however, was very uncomfortable for some STFU supporters, like Norman Thomas, who complained that the good name of the STFU, earned through great hardship, was being used to raise money for the coffers of Communist unions. Walter White likewise objected that he had heard Clyde Johnson speak at a New York fund raiser, and it seemed to him that Johnson had tried to claim some credit for the peonage conviction of Marshal Peacher in Arkansas.[31]

Gardner Jackson was under the impression that John L. Lewis, whose UMW was then financing a massive organizing drive in the steel industry, was about to announce a campaign to organize farm workers and hire Jackson to run it. This was an additional reason for the agricultural unions to appear to be friends. Jackson, therefore, had Mitchell, Kester, and Henderson accompany him to the AFL convention in Tampa, Florida, in November 1936 to lobby the CIO leaders, but their mission was lost sight of during the tumultuous meeting. After a prelude of mutual bombast and insult, the AFL formally expelled all ten CIO unions from the "House of Labor" and thereby divided skilled craftsmen and assembly-line workers into warring camps. In the months ahead the contest turned bloody as the competing labor giants tried to lasso each other's members. Mitchell met Donald Henderson for the first time in Tampa and formed an immediate dislike for the man. His impression was that "Henderson is a well intentioned, zealous person, very hard to understand, but thoroughly devoted to his party and policies which it puts forward. Two or three centuries ago, such people as Henderson were out hunting witches, and it is to be regretted that they are now engaged in attempting to organize farm laborers."[32]

When Reinhold Niebuhr asked Kester to explain exactly what were the differences between the STFU and the Share Croppers Union, he was told that the STFU was interracial while the SCU was entirely black, that the STFU was larger, claiming about fifty thousand members, and that the STFU was "non-political" while the SCU was "communistic." Although it was true that the Socialist party did not govern the Southern Tenant Farmers' Union, it was certainly inaccurate to say that the union was nonpolitical. The STFU president, J. R. Butler, ran for governor of Arkansas in 1936 on the Socialist party ticket, and Claude Williams shared the bill as the party's candidate for the United States Senate. The socialist views of Kester, Mitchell, and E. B. McKinney were also

Jim Ball, secretary of St. Peter's local, STFU, near Earle, Arkansas, in 1936. He served one year in prison for disarming a sheriff's deputy at a union meeting. (*Southern Tenant Farmers' Union Papers, Southern Historical Collection, UNC, Chapel Hill*)

quite pronounced. Mitchell and William Amberson joined
Myles Horton, Elizabeth Hawes, and a handful of other party
members in January 1937 at the Socialist Southern Conference in Norris, Tennessee. They heard Frank N. Trager, the
party's labor secretary, call for "a real revolutionary organization for the overthrow of capitalism and the establishment of
socialism."

But the only "mass organizations" that the party was working with in the South, Trager admitted, were the Southern
Tenant Farmers' Union and the Workers' Alliance, and he
stressed repeatedly that these must be kept out of the hands
of the Communists. Pressures such as these upon the southern movement, originating with party tacticians in New York
and Chicago, generated a feeling of hostility among activists
who otherwise worked well together. The overall result was
the fracturing of the radical movement throughout the region.[33]

VI Southern Radicals and National Unions

Trager's directive to fight Communists was probably taken least seriously by Myles Horton and James Dombrowski, who, notwithstanding the isolation of their educational community atop the Cumberland Plateau, were committed to the philosophy that the Highlander Folk School should nurture all "democratic" movements. The school's main source of operating funds was a diverse group of "drawing room radicals" whom both men diligently cultivated, and their program involved a wide range of grass-roots organizations. Highlander, therefore, never forged bonds to the Socialist party equal to those accepted gratefully by the Southern Tenant Farmers' Union. Consequently, Horton and Dombrowski were both criticized by Kester, as he moved deeper into the orbit of the Socialist party, for standing too far to the left. It was an irony that Kester alone among this group of Christian radicals rated mention in Elizabeth Dilling's 1934 anti-Communist handbook, *The Red Network*, and he and Alice suffered the late-night phone calls and other harassments because of it.

Some leftists, on the other hand, accused Highlander of being overly academic. This was a charge easily countered, however, for the school was very active in the trade union movement. It sponsored Elizabeth Hawes's organizing for the Amalgamated Clothing Workers in eastern Tennessee, and she and Dombrowski were behind-the-scenes advisers to striking textile workers in Harriman in 1934 and Soddy and Daisy in 1935. The school's librarian, Hilda L. Hulbert from Wellesley College, was wounded by police gunfire while leading a parade through Daisy.[1]

The Soddy and Daisy strikes were also supported by the Fellowship of Southern Churchmen, successor to the Conference of Younger Churchmen. The Reverend A. J. DeJarnette, Soddy's Congregational missionary and an ardent FSC member, offered his home as a strike headquarters, and he and the Reverend "Scotty" Cowan of Norris attended cockfights together to talk up labor unions among the workers. One of the Highlander students who lived in the DeJarnette home while working on a strike newsletter was Zilphia Mae Johnson, a concert pianist and a graduate of the College of the Ozarks, who had been one of those young people "awakened" by Claude and Joyce Williams. Her father was the coal mine owner in Paris, and her allegiance to the Williams family had divided her own. With Kester acting as a go-between, Zilphia went to Highlander in January 1935, and, at the conclusion of the Daisy and Soddy strikes five months later, she was married to Myles Horton by the Reverend Mr. DeJarnette. She became proficient with many musical instruments and contributed to the labor movement as a drama teacher and a collector of songs. At least ten books of protest songs were produced at Highlander under her direction, and in 1939 the Textile Workers' Union published a volume she had compiled.[2]

The Highlander staff had a vision of a radical southern labor movement allied with the AFL, and in May 1935 Horton and Dombrowski convened the All-Southern Conference for Civil and Trade Union Rights in Chattanooga. A Communist delegation composed of several Alabama trade unionists was brought by the party organizer in Birmingham, Nat Ross, who was then using the name "J. Harris." The aura of a "united front" was created by the addition of Kester's and Mitchell's names to the program. Kester's had been used without his consent, however, and he did not attend the conference because it conflicted with a meeting of his Committee on Economic and Racial Justice in New York City. Mitchell, then busy picketing the Agriculture Department in Washington, D.C., also could not come. Among those who did attend were John Mooney, whose brother Tom had been in San Quentin Prison since being convicted of throwing a bomb amidst the 1916 San Francisco Preparedness Day Parade, and a delegation from Commonwealth College led by a promising young student named Orval Faubus.[3]

The meeting at the Negro Pythian Temple had barely begun when a band of policemen and American Legionnaires surrounded the hall, forcing the conferees to flee quickly to their cars and regroup forty miles away at Highlander. Here they were not molested, but the significance of the meeting was questionable. The mainstream trade unionists whom Horton and Dombrowski had hoped to draw into an alliance with the radicals had not made an appearance. The Reverend Eugene Sutherland, a Unitarian pastor from Louisville, was there, and he commented on this problem: "it remains a question," he wrote, "whether we can work successfully with the A.F. of L. Unions while co-operating with the Communists." As events repeatedly proved, the answer was no.[4]

The reluctance of the AFL to deal with "reds" was demonstrated clearly by the experience of Don West, who had been more deeply involved in Communist causes than any of the others who had been in his class at Vanderbilt seminary. After being hounded from Atlanta for his work on behalf of Angelo Herndon, he moved to Burlington, North Carolina, to take on another case embraced by the International Labor Defense. The principal facts were these.

At 3 o'clock on the morning of September 15, 1934, a dynamite bomb exploded in the yard of the E. M. Holt Plaid Mill near downtown Burlington. It cracked a cement walkway and broke some windows but did no further damage. Since there was a strike on at Holt and every other mill in town—part of a brash national walkout—management immediately accused the millworkers of the bombing. The Alamance

County sheriff, H. J. Stockard, found a second unexploded bomb the next morning at the Stevens Cotton Plant, but his conduct of the investigation was too slow to suit the millowners; they imported four "detectives" from Pennsylvania to solve the case. All four had extensive experience as company policemen and strikebreakers in the employ of the A. C. Fricke Coal Company of Uniontown, Pennsylvania. They drifted into Burlington posing as American Legionnaires "loafing along" toward Miami, rented a room at the Correct Time Inn, and proceeded to construct a case of conspiracy against the local union leaders.

The strike had already begun to crumble by that time. One after another, the South's governors called out the National Guard, and millowners unleashed their company gunmen and strikebreakers. North Carolina's Governor John C. B. Ehringhaus sent the militia to Burlington to break up picket lines with bayonets, tear gas, and fire hoses, and, to display their mastery of the situation, the Guards paraded captured strikers through town on the hoods of army vehicles. The national leadership of the United Textile Workers caved in and surrendered, while pathetically claiming victory, on September 22.

In hopes of eradicating the union in Alamance County, Burlington's millowners filed charges against ten textile workers over the bombing incident. The case soon achieved notoriety as the Burlington Dynamite Plot. A defense organizer, who called himself Jim A. Weaver, then appeared on the scene. This man with so appropriate a name was actually Don West. He was still a fugitive from an Atlanta warrant charging him with inciting insurrection, thus the alias. When the trial began on November 28, 1934, West organized a Burlington Ten Defense Committee with himself as its chairman.

The union claimed, of course, that the bombing incident had been staged by the millowners to put the strike leaders behind bars, but the five-day trial was a disaster for the de-

140

fense from start to finish. Three of the defendants, after being sequestered for several days in the Alamance Hotel with the Pennsylvania "detectives," decided to testify against the other suspects. Then a fourth confessed that he had been driving the car from which the bombs were thrown. He later repudiated this statement, saying he was drunk when he signed it, but the judge allowed it into evidence.

The alleged ringleader of the plot, John Anderson, whom the prosecutor called the "Al Capone of Alamance County," was sentenced to eight to ten years; his six codefendants received terms ranging from two to six years. Of the three who turned state's evidence, one served eight months in jail and the others were set free; all three returned to their jobs in the Burlington mills.[5]

West interested the International Labor Defense in becoming co-counsels for the appeals of the convicted, and with Walt Pickard, a local union organizer, he wrote a pamphlet called the *Burlington Dynamite Plot* which the ILD sold on street corners for 2¢. At the time the Wests were surviving on about $8 per week donated by sympathetic townspeople.[6]

The defense team succeeded in bringing several members of the University of North Carolina faculty into the case. English professors J. H. Wisherd, J. O. Bailey, and E. E. Erickson all presided at meetings held on the Chapel Hill campus to protest the trials. The student paper, the *Daily Tarheel*, criticized one such gathering as "an impudent move" which threatens "to jeopardize the interests of both strikers and University"; it disliked the "feeble, misdirected and ostentatious efforts that characterize such strivings toward social justice as this." A young history instructor, C. Vann Woodward, objected to this editorial in a letter to the paper in which he argued that the interests of the strikers were already in jeopardy whether or not a campus meeting was held, and that the interest of the university in preserving freedom of speech was jeopardized more by the editors' attitude than by the meeting itself.[7] W. T. Couch, head of the university press, wrote a series of magazine articles pointing out inconsistencies in the state's case, and the playwright Paul Green, a Pulitzer Prize winner for *In Abraham's Bosom*, contributed several hundred dollars to the defense fund. Communist activists in the state also lent their support.[8] One of these was Paul Crouch, a party district organizer who later changed sides to become a featured government witness at numerous federal hearings on un-American activities.

In his address to the North Carolina Supreme Court in Raleigh, ILD attorney David Levinson offered a most cogent question concerning the case. "Suppose," he said, "instead of this slight injury to the mill the dynamite had been thrown against the union headquarters, would the authorities have prosecuted anyone? Would they have imported four 'detectives' from Pennsylvania to 'investigate?' Would a $1000 reward have been offered to catch the offenders? Would anyone have been sentenced to ten years, as the defendant, Anderson, has been sentenced in this case?" Unmoved, the court upheld all of the convictions but one, and six men went to prison.[9]

While leftists rallied to support the Burlington defendants, the AFL United Textile Workers tried to distance itself as far as possible from the case. The bombs had hardly gone off when the Burlington UTW president threatened to call off the strike. When his membership voted to support the accused men, he closed the union hall and declared the local defunct. The state president of the UTW brought in a New England Socialist, Leonard J. Green, to conduct a "confidential investigation" which convinced the AFL leader that the men were probably under the influence of left-wing agitators and guilty as charged. Green, whom West bitterly described as an "insane, raving person," then wrote a letter to a Burlington newspaper shortly before the case reached the state supreme court in which he exposed "Jim Weaver" as Don West, Communist organizer.[10]

Fingering an activist to the law was an act that not even Green's fellow Socialists could tolerate. Howard Kester and others called on Norman Thomas to censure Green, which he did. Thomas printed a statement in the *Socialist Call* saying that the alleged Socialists who were disrupting the defense efforts were "inspired I suspect by some Chamber of Commerce stool pigeon" and that "emphatically I support the Burlington Defense." West, concerned lest he be hauled to jail and extradited by Georgia, went underground once more and left the state.[11]

He and Constance settled on Greasy Creek in Bell County, Kentucky, where there were still some remnants of the unsuccessful Communist push to organize a militant National Miners' Union. Don took a job at the Kayjay Coal Mine, but he was quickly tagged a Communist agitator. Deputies raided the Wests' home in the spring of 1936 and arrested them both. Their two-year-old daughter, Ann, was bundled off to her grandmother's home in Corbin.

They were charged with "banding and confederating" to foster insurrection, and though Constance was released after an overnight stay in the Pineville jail, Don was kept six weeks awaiting trial. It was not easy to endure. "Bed bugs and crabs never tired," he wrote. "Their wiry legs made ceaseless motion. Their everlasting vigil kept us on keen edge. Sleep would have been difficult without the vermon. The filthy blankets, the ragged mattresses smeared with dirt, bloodstains and excrement, would alone have made sleep a fitful dream."

He and a handful of codefendants were prosecuted by Commonwealth Attorney Walter B. Smith, who called them the "Red Vultures," but the courtroom was packed with miners who supported them. "Workers are not afraid," West wrote. "These miners who face worse than death every day, how foolish of Walter B. to think he can make them afraid to be Communists." The state really had no case, and the court released each of the men under a $5,000 "peace bond."[12]

143

West left the area for Louisville, where he became general organizer for the Kentucky Workers' Alliance. After 1936 the alliance was a "united front" group with a Socialist president and a Communist organizational secretary. This uneasy partnership had been created by the merger of several organizations seeking to represent public works employees and the jobless. Calling himself "George Brown," West organized the Kentucky chapter with Allen McElfresh as its secretary and Giles Cooper, a carpenter and head of Wage Earners, Inc., as its president. They demanded jobs for all, a wage of $40 per month for everyone employed by the Works Progress Administration, and an end to discrimination against Negroes; and they led marches to the courthouses in Lexington, Paintsville, and Louisville. West was jailed briefly in Paintsville, but he was released upon the demand of insistent coal miners.[13]

A high point of the alliance came at the close of its state convention in Frankfort in October 1936 when a delegation went to keep an appointment with Governor A. B. "Happy" Chandler. The governor tried to duck the meeting and sent an aide to tell the protesters that he was out of state. Doubting this, the delegates marched on the Governor's Mansion, where both Chandler and his wife appeared on the steps to hear their grievances. Two of the demonstrators, Thelma Stone and Avenell Sexton, wrote a song about this confrontation:

> *When I went to Frankfort Town*
> *Many workers did I pass,*
> *'Twas there I saw the Governor,*
> *And I kicked him on the—Hocus, Pocus*

Sonny Bocus
And you may think I lie
But if you'd been down in Frankfort Town
You'd done the same as I. . . .

The goat that wears these shiny clothes
Is surely not so rich
The bosses call him loving son
While workers call him son of a . . . Hocus,
*   Pocus, Sonny Bocus*
And you may think I lie
But if the rich were poor like us
They'd call him the same as I. . . .[14]

The alliance also staged a hunger march in the nation's capital in 1936. West led three hundred WPA workers to this demonstration. They camped in Potomac Park, and some met with Aubrey Williams, deputy director of the WPA, to complain that the agency's "southern differential" meant that public works jobs north of the Ohio River paid $60 per month against $22 in Kentucky. Williams was sympathetic but said he could only administer the laws as Congress wrote them.

Had his cover not been stripped away in Burlington, West might have taken part in the textile union's second major drive of the decade to weld southern and northern millworkers into a powerful national union. The CIO directed this campaign under the banner of the Textile Workers Organizing Committee (TWOC) and placed a man who had never suffered a serious defeat in any labor contest, Sidney Hillman, at the helm. Between March 1937, when the campaign began, and March 1939, when it ended, almost $2 million was spent to bring textile workers into the union. Most of this was contributed by Hillman's Amalgamated Clothing Workers, the United Mine Workers, and the International Ladies Garment Workers. This was the first time that American labor had brought such a war chest to the South.[15]

Yet never had the House of Labor been more bitterly divided. The southern director of the AFL, George Googe, charged publicly that the CIO textile drive was controlled by Moscow, whereas his own organization represented "100% Americanism." Representative Eugene Cox from Georgia called John L. Lewis a Communist on the House floor and charged that the "flower of Southern Manhood" would resist the "Carpet Bag Invasion." More ominously, the Imperial Wizard of the Ku Klux Klan, Hiram W. Evans, warned that "the Klan will not sit idly by and allow the C.I.O. to destroy our social order."[16]

In the early months of the movement TWOC had 650 people on its staff, most of whom were native to the region. Hillman wished to blunt the charge that his people were "outside agitators." Abused by speedups and stretch-outs, thousands of southern millworkers signed TWOC cards. It was the union's policy not to charge them any dues, or even to charter locals, until it won a formal agreement with management.[17]

Highlander Folk School had for five years been training many of the leaders of the southern textile union movement, and thirty to forty of its former students were hired as organizers by the TWOC. Most of the school's faculty also joined the campaign. Elizabeth Hawes took charge of the TWOC headquarters in Greenville, South Carolina, aided by Highlander's Becky Barton. Dombrowski went to Atlanta to edit the union's newspaper. Zilphia Horton moved to La Follette, Tennessee, where a former Highlander student, Charles Handy, was leading a hosiery workers' strike; when these workers won on Labor Day, their victory celebration became the climax of a movie made by Frontier Films called *People of the Cumberland* which was shown for years thereafter to labor audiences across the South.[18]

Myles Horton went to Bennettsville and McColl, South

Carolina, to organize the Marlboro cotton mills owned by D. K. McColl. Blacks made up a large portion of the work force, but the towns were for whites only. Each evening at 6 o'clock the Bennettsville fire whistle signaled Negroes to leave the city limits.[19] A strike was already in progress at the Bennettsville plant, and the McColl workers came out soon afterwards. Since the governor refused to summon the National Guard, the strikers were free to hold picnics on the railroad tracks leading into the mills to block shipments of fabric. In less than a month the Marlboro management granted the union demands for reduced hours and the minimum wage. These were the first contracts to be won in the TWOC southern campaign. The victory was only temporary, however; McColl shut the mills down a year later to avoid operating under a union contract.

Horton went on to Lumberton, North Carolina, to organize the H. B. Jennings cotton mill. On his first night in town he received a delegation of workers in his hotel room. Later that night the windows in these workers' homes were broken by rocks and bullets. The union organization grew quickly, however, under Horton's leadership. Described by a visiting reporter as a man "whose dark skin is almost smooth and whose glasses and keen eyes given him a more or less academic appearance, despite his plain dress, with collar open and up-rolled sleeves," he built strong workers' committees to handle union business. Within a month they had brought 90 percent of the employees at the Jennings mill and 65 percent of those at the companion Mansfield mill into the TWOC.[20]

On the day before the National Labor Relations Board was scheduled to hear the case, June 7, 1937, the Jennings workers struck to protest a production stretch-out, and the Mansfield workers soon came out in sympathy. This strike was the first to confront the NLRB in the South since, on April 12, the Supreme Court had upheld the board's right to exist un-

der the Wagner Labor Act, and it therefore became a test of
the NLRB's ability to settle a major industrial dispute.

As the preliminaries for an NLRB election were slowly
hashed out, H. B. Jennings cut off the strikers' credit at his
company store. The union responded by sending teams into
the countryside to beg food from farmers and by leading two
thousand marchers to the courthouse to demand surplus government commodities. The company brought in strikebreakers under the protection of a National Guard unit housed in
the same hotel where Horton was staying, and this sparked
the one major clash of the strike.

A large body of strikers went to the mill gates to ask for
their jobs back. Once inside the gates they raced through the
factory ejecting strikebreakers through the windows and
doorways. When the state militia rushed in to retake the
plant, the strikers followed union orders and departed peacefully—except one, a Lumbee Indian, who knocked a trooper
down a flight of steps. He was arrested and tried for assault,
but when the trooper took the stand to testify he claimed that
he could not identify the man who had hit him. After the
hearing Horton took the guardsman aside to thank him for his
lapse of memory, and the trooper replied, according to Horton, "I couldn't squeal on a guy who could pack a wallop like
that."

Sixty-five union people were arrested during the course of
the strike, but none served time in jail. Horton was arrested
with nineteen others for blocking a road leading into the
plant, and he was detained a second time, on charges of inciting a riot, when a union meeting turned violent. A heckler
started a fistfight by calling one of the union men a "bean
eater," and, though Horton was not involved, he was sentenced to six months on the chain gang. He appealed, and the
state dropped the matter after the strike was settled.

The NLRB election took place in September, and the union

Sharecroppers evicted from the Dibble plantation camp in a churchyard near Earle, Arkansas, January 1936 (*Howard A. Kester Papers, Southern Historical Collection, UNC, Chapel Hill*)

150   won by a vote of 321 to 179. All of the striking workers were
reinstated, and contracts were signed at both the Mansfield
and Jennings mills the following January. A union member
was elected county sheriff after the strike, and the contracts
at the plants endured. The Jennings plant closed down in
1944, but the union local at Mansfield existed into the 1950s.

Horton was promoted to TWOC organizing director for
North Carolina, but he was ill-suited to office work and asked
to be returned to the field. Oddly, his request was refused.
He guessed that the TWOC high command disapproved of
his "democratic organizing," particularly his practice of passing out his salary and expense money to volunteer local organizers who signed up a great many members but did not
always take orders from above. He returned to Highlander in
November 1937. Later he reflected on his experience as a
union organizer:

I was convinced, even before I started organizing . . . that
the difference between an educator and an organizer is pretty
fundamental. . . . You have got to be the charismatic personality that stands up and fights the state, fights the courts,
fights the sheriff and fights the bosses and defies the
press. . . . They've got to do that, and that's the role that I
found rather heady but not satisfying. . . . The truth about
the matter is that I enjoyed tremendously being able to slap
these people around, because I had the backing of the working people. . . . But I think that if you did that for two or
three years, you would lose your perspective and begin to
think that it was you instead of the workers.[21]

Elsewhere in the South the TWOC racked up steady gains.
The main strike in the region took place at the Dallas Manufacturing Company and other mills in Huntsville, Alabama
(where once Victoria Price and Ruby Bates, the women involved in the Scottsboro case, had been paid $3.60 weekly
and had been forced to turn to nocturnal activities to support
their families). It was eventually won because the union per-
severed in the face of hostile police and because Governor

Bibb Graves refused to send in troops to break up the picket lines. This opened the door to the rest of the South, and by 1939 the union claimed contracts with twenty-seven manufacturers employing 27,000 people, election victories at sixty more plants employing 40,000 workers, and another 85,000 members spread across the region.

Elizabeth Hawes left the Highlander staff at the end of 1937 to work full time for the Amalgamated Clothing Workers. Franz Daniel, her husband, made a rousing speech at the 1939 convention that closed out the TWOC and launched the Textile Workers Union of America (CIO). Southern millworkers, he said, "are no longer content to go on day after day, month after month, bringing their children into the . . . mills to be used to make another fortune for the same bosses." These people, he said, "are beginning to think of themselves as children of God the same as anybody else." Bowing to the enthusiasm of all of its southern delegates, the new union pledged to make organizing the South its "Number One task." But neither it nor any future AFL or CIO union was ever able to gather the energy or the resources to mount the major organizing campaign necessary to consolidate the gains made by the TWOC. The victories of 1937, scant though they were in comparison to the vast field to be conquered, would remain the high point of textile unionism in the South for decades to come.[22]

Like most domestic concerns, the union movement was sidetracked by the coming war. The conflict in Spain came home to Americans when young men and women began volunteering to go abroad and join the Republican armies. Two Kentucky Workers' Alliance leaders, Fernando Burch and Roy Swanson, went overseas to fight and lived through the campaigns. Jack Adams, the brother of Constance West, was one of the many who died on a Spanish battlefield.

The Southern Tenant Farmers' Union and kindred organizations suffered financially as their contributors began donat-

152 ing instead to the forces resisting Francisco Franco. The union tried to reverse the trend by holding a National Share-croppers Week, an idea first conceived by Kester. He envisioned selling bolls of cotton with pamphlets attached, for "there are hundreds of thousands of people who have never seen cotton in the raw and to have a piece . . . to hang on the wall or put in a vase would take with many who wouldn't give a whoop about the Union."[23] When the event took form under the direction of Sidney Hertzberg in 1937, the cotton-selling plan was dropped. Benefits for the STFU, sponsored by the Workers' Defense League, were held in a number of cities during March, and the Sharecroppers Week was repeated each year until the war came. Though the funds raised never made the union rich, they were a dependable source of income, and, later on, the annual affair became a permanent organization called the National Sharecroppers Fund.

More debilitating to the STFU than financial hardship was a schism that developed between Claude Williams and other union leaders during the STFU's 1937 convention in Muskogee. The meeting started off on the wrong foot when a delegation from Commonwealth College arrived early and made statements to the press that were misquoted to depict the convention as a communistic forum for free love and racial equality. The UMW's David Fowler, scheduled to give the keynote address, then denounced the STFU in the name of "God and Country" and withdrew from the meeting.[24]

The planners of the event, Mitchell, Kester, and Gardner Jackson, were dismayed. Fowler's presence was intended to seal a bond between the union and the CIO. The three spent hours trying to reach Fowler's boss, John L. Lewis, but the crusty labor leader was tied up in negotiations with General Motors. Claude Williams, an old enemy of Fowler's, allied himself with the Commonwealth crowd and insisted that the STFU have no more to do with the UMW or the CIO. Fowler's action particularly irritated Williams since the minister

had bowed to the wishes of his friends in the STFU leadership and dropped out of the race for a seat on the STFU executive council. It was a job that Williams badly wanted, but
other officers believed that John L. Lewis still bore such a
grudge against Williams for encouraging the miners' autonomy movement in Arkansas that his election to a prominent
position in the STFU might prevent an alliance with the
CIO.[25]

When it became obvious that Lewis could not be reached,
Jackson, Mitchell, and Fowler met privately and produced a
document stating that "it was agreed by the Southern Tenant
Farmers' Union that they were unintentionally put on the
spot by people attending this convention . . . and that they
would divorce themselves from this element and would cooperate with the United Mine Workers of America and all
other legitimate labor organizations in furthering a campaign
to the best interest of the workers, whether he be on farm,
mine or mill."[26]

Now Fowler felt that he could speak at the convention.
Williams, however, was furious. He construed the hazy accord as a repudiation of Commonwealth College and himself,
coming at a time when the Arkansas state legislature was de-
bating a measure aimed at closing both Commonwealth and
his own New Era School for offering courses on Marxism. He
believed that the officers, Mitchell in particular, had "sold the
union down the river" when they should have been defending
the free speech of Commonwealth students. Defending this
principle was particularly important to Williams because he
had just been elected a national vice-president of the American Federation of Teachers.[27]

Most of the 150 delegates, "their clothes or overalls . . .
mere crazy-quilts of patches," were hardly aware of these behind-the-scenes clashes. They wanted to talk about building
the STFU, which, by its own count, now numbered 30,827
members spread over seven states. They had so little interest

in the arguments preoccupying their leaders that they voted not to be affiliated with any political party or labor school. Their motivation and vision were expressed in the resolution demanding that all "actual tillers of the soil be guaranteed possession of the land, either as working farm families or co-operative associations of such farm families, so long as they occupy and use the land."[28]

The delegates ratified a slightly revised union constitution. Its preamble read in part:

We maintain that the earth is the common heritage of all, and that the use and occupancy of land shall constitute the sole title thereto. This organization is dedicated to the complete abolition of tenantry and wage slavery in all its forms, and to the establishment of a new order of society wherein all who are willing to work shall be given the full products of their toil. We seek to establish a co-operative order of society by legal and peaceable methods. . . .

We stand ready, at all times, to affiliate with other agricultural workers' organizations, whose principles are in accord with our own, and to build one big union of all agricultural workers.[29]

The goal of building "one big union" seemed nearer when the chairman read a telegram from the AFL's William Green. "Labor is deeply interested in economic improvement of agricultural workers and of those classified as sharecroppers," Green wrote. "I urge that you unite and fight to improve and maintain decent economic standards." This was met with thunderous applause, and the delegates hoped to hear next from John L. Lewis.[30]

The climax of the convention was the performance of the *Ceremony of the Land*, a ritual conceived by Kester and Evelyn Smith. A responsive reading, its central passage, delivered by Kester, was: "We came of all races and nationalities to this land to make a home and a better life for our children. We live in a land of plenty, and yet the products of our labor will not support our families and educate our children. We work all the days of our life and are yet cast aside in our old age. There are those who would deny us the God-given right to act together for self-improvement." To which the audience responded: "To the disinherited belongs the future." The delegates then marched forward one by one to receive a handful of the native soil of their own state, and they mixed their bit in a common pile, mingling together the many soils of the South and Southwest.[31]

It was a considerable disappointment that the much-awaited telegram from John L. Lewis did not arrive until after the convention ended. And while the message was warm and sympathetic, it did not promise that the CIO would support the farm workers in any future campaigns. The union paid much for this faint praise. Williams left the convention angry at Mitchell, whom he accused of trying to "crush Commonwealth College and stamp out the 'reds.'" He denounced Fowler as "racketeering, red-baiting and dictatorial," and he condemned Jackson for coauthoring the nebulous agreement with the UMW leader. Williams took his complaints to the Arkansas Socialist party and persuaded its executives to censure Mitchell for his actions at Muskogee. Mitchell appealed to the national executive committee of the party, which restored him to good graces, but he wrote angrily that "as long as I have anything to do with the work of the STFU, Claude will not be used without my consent for anything."[32]

Then, on June 7, 1937, a surprising letter from Fowler came to STFU headquarters inviting J. R. Butler to Muskogee to talk over the possibility of affiliating the STFU with the CIO. Butler made the trip without delay. The CIO's sudden interest in agriculture was due to the fact that John L. Lewis had made a pact with Harry Bridges, the radical leader of California's longshoremen, who wanted to expand his domain to include warehousemen and farm workers. Bridges wanted, in fact, to be placed in charge of all CIO organizing in the Pacific region. Lewis was interested because Bridges was aggressive, popular, and a veteran opponent of the American Federation of Labor. Lewis was especially taken with the theory that the CIO, under Bridges, could capture the AFL's cannery unions, thereby depriving the AFL of roughly $3,600 in monthly dues and channeling this money instead into the CIO. Lewis's sights were set higher than California, and he now saw possibilities in the idea of a national agricultural workers union. He authorized Donald Henderson, a Communist and a man acceptable to Bridges, to convene an agricultural workers' convention in Denver for the purpose of creating a new union.

Gardner Jackson was the first one in the STFU network to learn of Lewis's plan. He urged the sharecroppers to heal their factional differences in anticipation of an invitation to Denver. But he advised that the STFU could expect support from big labor "only in accordance with the systematic effort that is put in to make your membership truly union-conscious by regular payment of dues, regular meetings, etc." The STFU leaders should have paid more attention to this warning.[33]

The STFU officers gathered at the Rochdale Cooperative Farm to discuss the proposition. Mitchell argued that affiliation with the CIO be considered only on the conditions that the STFU retain its name, "which has more prestige than any other union in the field," and that it remain "autonomous" within the international. He warned that these stipulations might be opposed by the Communist delegates in Denver. The council accepted Mitchell's plan and furthermore insisted that the STFU must be given jurisdiction over all cotton and tobacco workers in the South and Southwest. To return Claude Williams to the fold, Kester and E. B. McKinney moved that he now be elected to the union's executive council. Over Mitchell's objection the motion passed. But the healing did not go deep.[34]

The First National Convention of Agricultural, Cannery,

and Fruit and Vegetable Packing House Unions got underway at the Fraternal Hall in Denver on July 9, 1937. Fifty-four unions, all but ten of them formerly connected to the AFL, endorsed the meeting, and the CIO paid the bills, even the travel costs of nine STFU delegates. Though the sharecroppers came prepared for a "big fight" with the Communists, things went smoothly. On the fourth day a constitution was ratified which created the United Cannery, Agricultural, Packing, and Allied Workers of America (UCAPAWA). It divided the country into seven districts; the STFU, along with smaller organizations in Texas and Alabama, fell into District IV. It was understood that the STFU could remain self-governing and elect its own officers, but the exact measure of autonomy granted beyond that was unclear. The minimum dues for sharecroppers and the unemployed were 25¢ per month.[35]

Since Henderson carried the blessing of John L. Lewis he was overwhelmingly elected president. To satisfy the Socialists and the STFU, which, according to its membership claims, was the largest union there, J. R. Butler was elected vice-president. The new executive board met immediately and petitioned the CIO for a loan of $20,000 and eighty-seven organizers, but they learned the limits of Lewis's commitment to agriculture a week later when the CIO informed UCAPAWA that it would receive just $2,000 and twenty-four organizers, eleven of whom were already on the CIO payroll in California. The STFU got a salary for only one person, Butler.[36]

A special STFU convention was called to consider the merger, but the delegates found their leaders divided on the question. Williams, Butler, and most of the field organizers favored the merger. Mitchell was for it if the STFU's autonomy could be preserved, but Kester was flatly opposed because he feared the affiliation would put the STFU under the domination of the Communist party.[37]

Kester still played an important role in developing the South's image in the eyes of the rest of the nation. While deeply involved in union activity, he wrote a report on the lynching of two black men, Roosevelt Townes and "Bootjack" McDaniels in Duck Hill, Mississippi, which was published and widely distributed by the NAACP. Charged with murdering a white storekeeper, the pair were being led from the courthouse in Winona, Mississippi, on April 13, 1937, when twelve armed whites quietly and calmly kidnapped them. They were driven to a field near Windham's grocery in the community of Duck Hill, chained to two lonely pine trees, and then burned up with blowtorches. Their bodies were left hanging from the chains until a local white minister finally prevailed upon a Winona undertaker to cut them down and conduct a funeral service in the back room of his mortuary. The corpses were buried in a single pine box.

Piecing the scene together two weeks later, Kester found that "of the scores of people with whom I talked not a single one greatly deplored the lynching. The citizens of Duck Hill seemed rather well pleased with themselves." Kester's testimony before Congress about this lynching provoked the House of Representatives to pass a federal antilynching bill by a vote of 277 to 120. In January 1938 it reached the Senate, where it finally went down to defeat after one of the longest filibusters in history.[38]

Kester played a role, too, in transmitting to southern dissenters the disputes of the national radical parties. The intense quarreling among intellectuals on the left had hardly mattered in the South, where the problems of survival were terribly real, but as the southern movement integrated with national causes through its growing partnership with the CIO, leftist parties, and the New Deal, it, too, became split along ideological lines. Kester was a catalyst in the process.

He had risen to the top of the Socialist party due to his friendship with Norman Thomas and the fact that the party was down to a few thousand scattered members, almost none of whom "represented" the South. At one point Kester was considered as a possible running mate for Thomas. He was elected to the party's national executive committee in March 1937, and, along with Mitchell and Myles Horton, he was put on its Negro Work Committee in May. In August he was elected to the party's National Agricultural Labor Committee with Mitchell, Butler, and Ward Rodgers. Kester's participation in all of these committees was largely limited to naming alternates to their New York City meetings, but, in 1937, when a crunch developed in the party's dealing with the Trotskyites, Kester was summoned north. The affair left him forever antagonistic toward disciplined, secretive political groups on the left.[39]

Norman Thomas had made a mistake in 1936 when, vainly trying to infuse new blood into his shrinking party, he had welcomed the Trotskyites as members. They were followers of Leon Trotsky, who found his final refuge in Mexico after being exiled by Stalin in 1928. Their leader in the United States was James P. Cannon, and the faction achieved its greatest influence in the citywide Teamsters strike in Minneapolis in 1934. In that year the Trotskyites merged with a more numerous body, the American Workers party, whose secretary, A. J. Muste, was a longtime pacifist who had come to believe in the class struggle. The Trotskyites then became attracted to the radical youthful wing of the Socialist party to which Kester, Dombrowski, Rodgers, Hawes, and many others belonged. In the elaborate theoretical construction of the Trotskyites it was essential to capture this Socialist left wing to keep it out of the hands of their archenemies, the Stalinists.

Cannon's group began to infiltrate the Socialist party, and in 1936 Thomas invited the Trotskyites to dissolve the American Workers party and join his own. "We went into the Socialist Party confidently because we knew that we had a disciplined group and a program that was bound in the end to prevail. When, a little later, the leaders of the Socialist Party began to repent of the whole business; wishing they had never heard the name of Trotskyism, wishing to reconsider their decision to admit us, it was already too late," said Cannon six years later.[40]

The Trotskyites established a power base within the party and took over locals wherever they could. They gained editorial control of an official party paper, the *Socialist Appeal*, and pushed their view that the Socialist party should become a smaller, more disciplined group in the vanguard of the workers' struggle. The Socialist leadership allied with Thomas, on the other hand, wished their party to have a wide appeal to the American public.

When the traditional Socialists finally awoke to this internal threat, they banned the *Socialist Appeal* and began purging "disrupters." At the request of Ward Rodgers the party suspended its entire California wing because it was dominated by Trotskyites, and in August 1937 the New York party expelled fifty-four of Cannon's followers. The Trotskyites fought back, and the issue reached a head at a special meeting of the party's national executive committee held in September 1937. Cannon's followers were represented on the committee, and Thomas needed all of his supporters present to uphold the ouster of the Trotskyites. He begged Kester to attend and invited the southerner to lodge with him and his wife, Violet, at their New York City brownstone.

Kester accepted, and at the noisy committee sessions he voted with Thomas on every question. The Trotskyites were expelled, the California party was suspended, and Kester cast the deciding vote in favor of a measure to permit the New York party to cooperate with the union-affiliated American Labor party. This cleared the way for Thomas to withdraw from the New York mayoral race in favor of a man he highly esteemed, Fiorello La Guardia.[41]

Thomas termed Kester's presence at the New York meeting "invaluable. . . . Without him and his vote the result would have been for a Party for which I for one would have had little hope or little use." Yet the party that emerged from the "ravages of the NEC meeting" was little more than a shell. Though the Trotskyites had entered the Socialist party only a few hundred strong, they carried with them more than a thousand members in California, New York, Minnesota, and Ohio when they left. Cannon labeled the sidelining of the Socialist party "a great achievement" of his group. They went on to form the Socialist Workers party, which proved to be so deeply infiltrated by the FBI that it is possible that at least some of the "Trotskyites" responsible for the disruption of the Socialist party were government agents.[42]

The voice of Socialism was not silenced. Thomas ran for the presidency three more times, but his party was finished as an effective political instrument. Kester, for one, emerged from the fracas bitter and vigilant against the subversive tactics of communist parties. He was now especially wary of cooperating with communists in the southern farm workers' movement.

STFU convention in Cotton Plant, Arkansas, 1938, where
Claude Williams was expelled. Left to right: Evelyn Smith,
E. B. McKinney, Douglas Cobbs (Twist plantation local),
Leon Turner (Jefferson County local), Claude Williams,

W. B. Moore (Blytheville local), W. C. Banks (Widener
local), John Alford Gammil (Roundpond local). (*Southern
Tenant Farmers' Union Papers, Southern Historical
Collection, UNC, Chapel Hill*)

VII
Wild Enthusiasm, Disruption, Confusion

Despite Kester's warning that the union faced Communist domination, the sharecroppers who came to the STFU convention in Memphis on September 24, 1937, voted with "wild enthusiasm" to join UCAPAWA and the CIO. "The people look upon the CIO as a sort of Santa Claus who will give them everything and crown all their efforts with victory," was Kester's sour explanation. He wrote to Norman Thomas that it was now necessary to "make a go of our affiliation." We can always get out later, he added.[1]

Delegates from the other unions scattered about District IV arrived the next day to ratify the new constitution and hear a speech by Aubrey Williams, director of the National Youth Administration. Most of the newcomers were from Hispanic locals in the Rio Grande Valley, organized by James Sager of the CIO, and the Alabama remnants of the Share Croppers Union, now headed by Walker Martin. Clyde Johnson had left the South for Washington, D.C., to be research director for UCAPAWA.

The document they ratified preserved the "identity and administrative self-government" of the STFU, subject to the rules of the international union, and it listed certain goals, none of which have yet been attained by most agricultural workers. Among these were the establishment of collective bargaining, old-age pensions, workmen's compensation, unemployment insurance, the abolition of child labor, the creation of adequate educational facilities and opportunities for the children of farm workers, and the securing of equal pay for equal service regardless of sex, race, or nationality.[2]

Butler was easily elected president of the district; he was also president of the STFU and vice-president of the international. Mitchell, however, fought a much harder battle to retain his job as STFU secretary-treasurer. Since the Muskogee convention, Claude Williams had been made director of Commonwealth College, an appointment which led Reinhold Niebuhr to comment: "Is that school going to the dogs completely. He certainly lacks the balance to run a school." Williams, "in a carefully prepared oration," nominated a young black leader from Jefferson County, Arkansas, Leon Turner, to fill Mitchell's position. This was a strong challenge because the membership of the union, if the delegate tally can be used as a rule, was now about 70 percent black. Kester preached long in defense of Mitchell, urging the delegates to consider experience, not race, and he helped to sway the crowd. Mitchell beat Turner 83 to 32, and the black was then elected to the new post of assistant secretary. It seemed a peaceful solution, but it turned out to be the beginning of a struggle for black control of the union, spearheaded by Williams, a white, and E. B. McKinney.[3]

Mitchell wrote that Williams's actions "have aroused a feeling of prejudice among our people that had not existed in our organization before." He was now convinced, moreover, that Williams was secretly a member of the Communist party. Mitchell claimed that Williams had shown him his party membership card, made out in the name of "John Galey," at the Denver convention. He now wrote to Donald Henderson, whom Mitchell viewed as a member of the Communist hierarchy, telling him to see that Williams "attends to his own affairs over at Commonwealth" or else Mitchell would expose Williams.[4]

Norman Thomas suggested that Mitchell formally charge Williams with holding dual party membership in front of the Arkansas Socialist party. He also proposed that Mitchell "make some of our colored friends understand that Williams himself is now the head of an institution which does not admit colored people." Kester was less severe in his estimate of Williams. When Roger Baldwin, director of the American Civil Liberties Union, asked him to appraise Commonwealth College, Kester wrote, "if the policy and program related to me by Williams is . . . followed . . . Commonwealth may make the contribution to southern labor so earnestly desired by all."[5]

The dispute continued to grow, and it tainted the relationship between the STFU and UCAPAWA. Mitchell began to complain regularly to Henderson about the bureaucratic pressure the international was applying to the STFU. UCAPAWA, for example, required extensive monthly reports, but Mitchell argued that "there are not 10 local Secretaries who could make out an understandable report on the complicated blanks that you have. . . . Please realize Don that we are here dealing with a group of people whose educational standards, are lower than any other group in all America."[6]

Worse than this was the matter of UCAPAWA dues, which were a minimum of 25¢ per month, more than twice what the STFU members had been asked to pay before. As a white organizer from Colt, Arkansas, Myrtle Lawrence, expressed it: "us poor people that haven't got jobs can't pay such dues. There is 6 in my family which would be $1.50 per month. Ben only makes $21.00 per month. It may be a good thing but I can't see it that way."[7]

When Thomas wrote to Mitchell in October to declare that Williams should be kicked out of the Socialist party, he went on to ask the really important question: "Is the new union making definite and concrete demands? What active work is it going to do in the cotton fields just now?" What was being done to enforce the UCAPAWA demand that cotton pickers must be paid $1 a hundredweight? The reality was that the STFU was so enmeshed in rearranging its records and hand-

ing out new UCAPAWA charters that it had almost no energy
left over for confronting the plantation owners.[8]

Only one brief strike occurred in the STFU territory in the
fall of 1937. It took place on the Belsha plantation in St. Francis County, but it fizzled after its leaders were jailed for "in-
terferring with labor." The union's attorney, C. A. Stanfield,
went to their trial, but he was ordered out of the courtroom
by the county health officer and roughed up before making it
back to his car. The three defendants were also beaten in the
jail. All that the STFU could do about these matters was to
report them to the La Follette Committee, which it still
hoped, groundlessly it turned out, would give national publicity to troubles in the cotton country.[9]

The coming of winter intensified the sharecroppers' difficulties. A survey commissioned by the STFU quickly pin-
pointed 3,931 Arkansas families in need of immediate relief.
One survey form came back with this note attached: "This is
to inform you That all of These Names I have ritten here They
are in Real need of food and clothes. Their land lords has
taken Every Thing they made an left Them Nothing to live
on   naked + Bare footed + The[y] needs help right away
So pleas do Some Thing for us at once."[10]

Besides presenting these grim statistics to congressional
committees, there was little the union could do to get at the
cause of the problem: the growing preference of plantation
owners for day laborers at the expense of tenants and sharecroppers. The STFU was also deteriorating internally. At its
fourth annual convention in Little Rock in February 1938,
E. B. McKinney made a determined effort to elect an all-
black slate of union officers. But two other black leaders,
Leon Turner and J. E. Clayton, turned against him, with the
result that blacks won only two of the ten posts on the executive council. McKinney almost lost his vice-presidency to
Owen H. Whitfield, a black organizer from Missouri; the out-

168

come was so close that a post of second vice-president was created for Whitfield. Kester was reelected to the council with the votes of all but two of the eighty-three delegates, after which he gave a long speech appealing for race brotherhood.[11]

National Sharecroppers Week was also afflicted. When its director, Harriet Young, discovered that Claude Williams was raising money in Cleveland just days before Kester's fundraising engagement there for NSW, she construed it as "definite and willful C.P. sabotage." Walter White complained angrily that Communist toughs in Newark had attempted to prevent the NAACP from staging NSW activities on the grounds that its sponsoring agency, the Workers' Defense League, was not a legitimate representative of the sharecroppers. And Communists in New York returned en masse the tickets they had purchased to an NSW benefit concert at Carnegie Hall. Only a $5,000 personal gift to the STFU by Harriet Young helped repair the damage.[12]

The accord between the STFU and UCAPAWA began to break up at the same time. Donald Henderson refused to concede that the STFU's cherished "autonomy" meant that sharecropper locals could send their dues to Memphis or that the STFU had the right to organize in Texas where UCAPAWA had an active pecan-shellers union. The Oklahoma section of the STFU, which had eyes on Texas, was so infuriated that it officially and publicly resolved "to war on communism and other political opportunists within the movement."[13]

A meeting of the UCAPAWA executive board was held to iron out these differences in Washington on April 28, 1938. John Brophy, the director of the CIO, attended and threw his considerable weight behind Henderson. The STFU must abide by the rules of the international, he insisted; anything else smacked of "dual unionism." Both Kester and Evelyn Smith made vain efforts to speak at this meeting, but they were kicked out on the grounds that neither was a member of the executive board. Kester stormed away saying, "This isn't the first time a member of the Southern Tenant Farmers' Union has been evicted."[14]

This meeting was final proof for Kester that "the CP controlled UCAPAWA is out to liquidate the STFU" and that his union must fight back or be "smashed like a potato bug." Mitchell feared the reaction of the labor movement if the STFU seceded from the CIO, but he advised his locals to cease doing business with UCAPAWA and "sit tight, keep up your Union work and wait for developments." Privately, he asked Gardner Jackson to find out if John L. Lewis wanted to use the scrap between the unions as an opening wedge to expose the Communists in the CIO and get rid of them. Might not Lewis want to "clean house all down the line," Mitchell wondered? It is not certain that this inquiry ever reached Lewis, but the CIO obviously did not want to force the issue then because many of its best organizers were Communist party members. Not until 1949 were the Communist-dominated unions expelled from the CIO.[15]

Other inquisitors were thinking the same thing. In June 1938 the House Committee for the Investigation of Un-American Activities was formed under the chairmanship of Martin Dies of Texas. The first notable witness was John P. Frey, head of the Metal Trades Division of the American Federation of Labor. The gist of his testimony was that his rival, the CIO, was saturated with Communists. Harry Bridges and Donald Henderson got special attention, and the STFU was among the 280 unions Frey named as having links to the Communist party. Norman Thomas urged Mitchell to refute this charge vigorously, adding a caution which reflected the paranoia of the times: "I suggest that you be careful about letters though since letters have a way of being taken and read by the wrong people. . . . Moreover, you can't always tell whose the wrong person these days."[16]

170

Another star witness appeared in August. He was J. B. Matthews, the former Scarritt College professor whom Kester had eleven years before recommended for the secretaryship of the Fellowship of Reconciliation. The two had been kicked out of the FOR together for seeming too willing to use violence on behalf of the class struggle. Matthews had gone on to become a leading participant in "united front" organizations. He and Francis Henson from Virginia had been the Socialist contingent in the headquarters of the American League Against War and Fascism—counterbalanced by Donald Henderson and Ida Dailes—and his close association with many leading Communists made him an ideal government witness when he repented his leftward drift.

Matthews named scores of people as Communists or "fellow travelers," and he made a famous gaffe when he mentioned that certain film stars, Clark Gable, James Cagney, and Shirley Temple among them, had sent anniversary greetings to a French Communist paper. The press had a field day with the idea that Shirley Temple was a servant of the international Communist conspiracy, but Matthews survived the incident to become the chief paid investigator for the Dies Committee.

Perhaps the sensational crusade to root out and humiliate Communists affected J. R. Butler, for when he found an incriminating document in Claude Williams's coat he went straight to the newspapers with it. The document was a proposal, addressed to the central committee of the Communist party, requesting funds for Commonwealth College. It came to light when Williams forgot his coat at Butler's home. Butler's nephew wore the coat, but first he removed several papers from the pockets and laid them on a bookshelf where the STFU president stumbled across them.[17]

Like all proposals, this one perhaps stretched the truth. It boasted that twenty of the twenty-five people on the Commonwealth staff, including Williams, were Communist party members. It enumerated several contributions the college was making to the grand Communist design, then went on to say: "A situation has now arisen which offers us an extraordinary opportunity to move into the most important organization in the agricultural South: the STFU."

The rare "opportunity" was that Mitchell had left Memphis to take a temporary job evaluating National Youth Administration projects for Aubrey Williams. In his absence, Butler had invited Commonwealth students and faculty to organize STFU meetings in Arkansas and Missouri. With the proper financial backing, the peculiar document continued, Commonwealth could exploit this invitation, organize sympathetic locals, "capture the union for our line at the next convention," and establish "a real party base in the STFU." The author requested a grant of $500.[18]

Butler had previously refused to believe that Commonwealth or Williams, his old friend and Socialist running-mate, had subversive intentions. Now he was convinced of it, and he called a press conference to denounce Williams as a "red." He wrote to demand Williams's resignation from the union and ordered him and his associates to cease presenting themselves as STFU organizers. (One of these "associates" was Lee Hays, a young man haunted by "the debts which long generations of slave owners and exploiters in my family have incurred," who had come under the sway of Williams while a student at the College of the Ozarks. He later provided the resonant bass voice for the folksinging quartet the Weavers.) Butler enclosed his resignation from the board of Commonwealth College, and he signed himself, "Your one time friend."[19]

Mitchell was in North Carolina when he read about this controversy in a newspaper. He condemned Butler for going to the press in such haste; Mitchell would have preferred to use the document in some more effective and private manner. When Williams saw the story, he rushed to Memphis to insist

172

that he was not the author of the proposal and that, in any event, it was "largely fictional in nature." Butler was persuaded, and, "in a moment of weakness," he withdrew his demand that Williams resign from the STFU. Then he repented and wrote to Kester to ask if he would want to accuse Williams formally before the union executive council.[20]

The request hit Kester while his disenchantment with the left was at its apex and mattered more than a decade of friendship with Williams, whose "prophetic witness" against capitalism he had defended on numerous occasions. With a second from Dave Griffin, a white organizer in Arkansas, Kester sent notice to Williams to appear before the union council to face charges of using "disruptive tactics against and planning harm to the Southern Tenant Farmers' Union."

This was a major blow to Williams's effectiveness as director of Commonwealth College. His union office had provided the school with its main connection to the national labor movement and to the race relations struggle. If it lost this, the college would have little reason to exist, and if the charge that Williams was a Communist could be sustained, the school might be snuffed out entirely by witch-hunters in Arkansas.

A second difficult issue confronted the STFU executive council. Several members had charged Vice-President McKinney with trying to organize a separate black union. Their evidence included letters McKinney had written to Wiley Harris, a black union member in Parkin, Arkansas, in which McKinney described the STFU headquarters as "an office full of poor white people, who had nothing before this organization was set up, but now in a time when a man can hardly live they are buying big fine car, sending their children to school, and Women . . . while your old servant must walk and work to build up the union." These whites, some of whom he noted even ate with blacks, pretended to be great friends of the Negro, but "they aim to move in on us and be our next masters."

"These facts Brother Wiley, do not come from any prejudice that may be thought that I have towards the white people . . . but I must admit that I am very suspicious of them." It had been the blacks, McKinney maintained, who had lost their homes, their livelihoods, and their lives for the union, but the whites were getting the glory. "At the rate we are now thinking," McKinney complained, "we are just manufacturing some new masters who have always wanted to get the opportunity to handle the Negro."[21]

The case of McKinney was disposed of quickly because he did not show up for the council meeting. After his letters were read, he was expelled from the union. His place on the council was taken by F. R. Betton, an organizer from Woodruff County, Arkansas. Betton had a college degree, was a high school teacher, and had held, in Prairie County, the distinction of being the only black justice of the peace in the South. The officers then began the "trial" of Claude Williams, who was there to defend himself. With him was almost the entire faculty of Commonwealth College.

The "awful document," Williams said, had been written as a class exercise by Ralph Fields, a student just back after eighteen months of fighting in Spain. Combat had left Fields a "nervous wreck," Williams said, and nothing he wrote could be taken seriously. According to the minutes taken by Evelyn Smith, Williams admitted that he had shown his "red card" to Mitchell in Denver, but he insisted that he had quit the party upon being appointed director of Commonwealth. He had run the school on a nonsectarian basis, and, though Communists like Alfred Wagenknecht had been permitted to hold meetings on campus, the students were forbidden to join political parties.

Fields was brought in to substantiate what Williams had said, and he stated further that, although he was a Communist, there were so few comrades at Commonwealth that he felt lonesome. Williams admitted that he had once advised

Butler to push the STFU "closer to the Communist Party" and that, in preparation for a fund-raising trip to the West Coast, he had asked Communist theoretician V. J. Jerome for an introduction to the party's "Hollywood group," but he denied that either incident was linked to the case at hand.

Butler doubted the Fields story because he thought the document revealed so much inside information about the union that only Williams could have written it. It took a vote of the council to get Williams to leave the room. When he was outside, Mitchell warned his fellow officers that one of the most important union presidents in the country, David Dubinsky of the ILGWU, had advised the STFU to "clear itself of communist implications." The men and women at the table then stripped Williams of his union membership. He left the meeting "grieving," as he put it, and returned to Mena a bitter man. He planned to appeal the entire matter to the next union convention.[22]

This larger meeting took place four days after Christmas at the Arkadelphia Presbyterian Academy in Cotton Plant, Arkansas. Williams had drafted a "10 Point Action Plan," signed also by McKinney, which they thought would restore the lost sense of militancy to the STFU. It called for separate state organizations allied with the CIO and an end to "Negro Baiting, Red Baiting and Jew Baiting."[23]

McKinney withdrew his name from this plan at the very last minute, thus paving the way for his reinstatement in the union. He pledged allegiance to the STFU and said, "It was always my desire to see the two races organized together, being convinced by 30 years of organizing that it was the only way that they could correct a situation which was mutual to both." Recalling the early days of the STFU, McKinney said, "It seems like just tonight when H. L. Mitchell proposed we have a five-mile march with the Negro marching behind the white man. I said I would not stand for it. I said I would stand for a double row, with a row of Negroes marching beside a

row of white men. . . . I was feared of trouble and I didn't
want the white man—who was in front—to die for me. I was
willing to die with him. I said to Mitchell, I wouldn't follow
him anywhere, but I would go with him anywhere."[24]

The case of Claude Williams, however, was not so easily
dispatched. It came up late at night, and Williams tried to
have the hearing delayed until the following morning when
he expected an ally, Owen Whitfield, to arrive. Whitfield
had recently been named to the international board of
UCAPAWA, and he was a strong CIO supporter. Chairman
Butler was determined to end the issue, however. After cor-
ralling the janitor to stoke up the furnace against the winter-
time chill, he read the charges and invited Williams to answer
them. The defense was a lengthy one, but it did no good. The
delegates upheld Williams's ouster from the union by a vote
of 58 to 7.[25]

The STFU might have survived this public trial of a here-
tic, and the alienation of his supporters, were it not also being
torn apart by its dispute with UCAPAWA. After the banish-
ment of Williams, Donald Henderson lectured the convention about the benefits they would derive from better cooperation with the CIO. Butler rose from the floor to rebuke
him and make a final plea to the international to grant the
STFU autonomous status and some relief from the oppressive
dues, which had just been raised to 60¢ per month for sharecroppers. Mitchell recited the indignities he had suffered at
the second UCAPAWA convention in San Francisco where
the STFU delegates representing 146 locals had only been
given nine votes. There was no room for compromise, and all
mention of UCAPAWA was stripped from the STFU constitution; it was ordered that sharecroppers' dues henceforth be
sent to Memphis, and that locals ignore any future correspondence from UCAPAWA headquarters.[26]

The acrimony between the various factions in the leadership of the sharecropper movement prevented all of them

James Dombrowski at Highlander Folk School, c. 1936
(*Highlander Research and Education Center*)

from responding well to its most critical test: the massive eviction of union sharecroppers that began on January 1,   177 1939, in the bootheel of Missouri. Several hundred families were put out of their homes on that date in what seemed to be a well-coordinated offensive by the plantation owners designed to restructure the area work force on the basis of day labor.

The STFU was represented in this fertile territory by Owen Whitfield, a black minister who, along with his predecessor, John Handcox, had brought about two thousand plantation workers into the union. A conflict arose because Whitfield was also an international vice-president of UCAPAWA and a close friend of Claude Williams. He credited Williams with turning his eyes from the "blue prints of Heaven" to the oppressiveness of the world. A recurrent story in Whitfield's sermons was that in a moment of desperation he had said to God, "You promised that if I preached your word, my children would not go hungry. Well, they are hungry. They would beg, but there is no one to beg from." And God had replied that He had kept His promise by giving Whitfield sun, rain, blue sky, and land, but that He had never promised to keep other men from stealing it.[27]

The mass eviction was anticipated well in advance, and the STFU locals in the area instructed about nine hundred affected families to "pile their household goods on [the] sides of the highway and see what happens." Whitfield went to St. Louis to organize a support committee made up of the CIO unions, the Urban League, the Federal Council of Churches, and several Communist activists. He introduced to the Missouri sharecroppers a Communist organizer, Al Murphy, who began planning resistance, both peaceful and armed, with some union members. Murphy had earlier been the chief black organizer for the Alabama Share Croppers Union under the name of "Jackson."[28]

Whitfield was present in the bootheel when the dreary

procession to the roadside began on New Year's Day, but he then retreated to St. Louis for safety. Neither he nor his St. Louis committee gave any further practical aid to the sharecroppers during the first critical days of the encampment. They publicized the situation, but the skeptical press continually referred to the event as the "Missouri Highway Demonstration," as if the people by the road had some other place to go.

Whitfield ceased to correspond with the STFU office in Memphis, and he even sent a telegram ordering Mitchell to "Keep out." It was not until January 9, when Butler read in the *Post Dispatch* that seventeen hundred people were camped out, that the union president realized the extent of the crisis. With organizers W. M. Tanner, F. R. Betton, and W. B. Moore, he drove to Missouri and located the squatters' settlements along U.S. Highways 60 and 61, which were being cordoned off by state police. The four spent only a minute with the sharecroppers before they were arrested and taken back to the state line under escort.[29]

The people in the camps were on their own from then on, isolated by the police and lacking any effective leadership from either the CIO or the STFU. Militants in some of the groups began drilling with weapons and planning for the defense of their camps. Into this breach stepped the Fellowship of Southern Churchmen, the only organization sufficiently "nonaligned" to coordinate a relief effort. Since Kester was the FSC's secretary, Communists could not support its activities with much enthusiasm, but it was the choice of northern donors who refused to send supplies directly to either the STFU or UCAPAWA until the feud between them was resolved.[30]

When Howard and Alice Kester reached Missouri, at least thirteen hundred people were bivouacked in churches, by roads, and in barns aroud the towns of Sikeston, Charleston, Hayti, and Caruthersville. One small party had taken refuge in Baby Red's Dance Hall in Charleston. It was snowing, and those living outside were sheltered by rag tents pitched amidst household goods, furniture, and farm animals.

The Kesters believed it was too dangerous to set up their relief office in the bootheel, so they established the FSC headquarters across the line in Blytheville, Arkansas. Supplies began arriving from the Federal Council of Churches, the Washington Committee to Aid Agricultural Workers, and STFU locals, and the Kesters passed them out by the carload to sharecroppers who managed to run the police blockade. To make contact with one group of 146 people abiding under police "protection" at the Sweet Home Baptist Church near Charleston, Betton took a 50¢ a day job on an adjacent farm. Dave Griffin successfully slipped a load of provisions to another camp only because his car bore New York plates and he convinced the deputies that he was a federal agent. More than five tons of food reached Missouri in this way, but the few miles that separated Blytheville from the scene of this conflict prevented many of the homeless from receiving any supplies at all.[31]

Mitchell went to Washington and, with the aid of Aubrey Williams and Will Alexander, got an appointment with Eleanor Roosevelt at the White House. In their short talk he begged the First Lady to use her influence to get army field kitchens and tents sent to Missouri. She expressed her concern and soon inserted an appeal for food and clothing in her regular newspaper column. In time, the field kitchens also arrived, but not before police had broken up most of the encampments.[32]

Led by an army veteran, the sharecroppers living between New Madrid and Lilbourn had planned to resist any police assault, but they were tricked into laying down their weapons and peacefully boarding trucks on the pretext that they were being taken to a Farm Security Administration resettlement community. Instead they were carried to a remote marshland known as the New Madrid Spillway and unceremoniously dumped without shelter or any sort of provisions. The other settlements were scattered simultaneously by the state troopers, and the "demonstration" was suddenly at an end.[33]

Whitfield's St. Louis allies, an ad hoc CIO agency called the Missouri Agricultural Workers' Council and the St. Louis Committee for the Rehabilitation of the Sharecropper, helped to rescue the spillway refugees. They purchased ninety acres of land just south of Poplar Bluff and offered this as a haven. A visitor to this farm in July 1939 found forty Negro families living there in eighteen tents while four white families camped in a separate area. They got minimal help from welfare authorities until finally they were rehabilitated by the Farm Security Administration, which used this group as the nucleus of its Delmo Homes resettlement project. When in 1945 the Delmo Homes were auctioned off during the nationwide liquidation of FSA property, the Congregational church's "farm worker minister," the Reverend David Burgess (a Fellowship of Southern Churchmen officer), persuaded Congress to give the 549 resident families the right to buy the property at a preferred rate of $800 per dwelling.[34]

The Missouri fiasco irrevocably divided the STFU and UCAPAWA factions. All that remained were the formalities of separation. Late in January, Henderson officially demanded that STFU members send their dues to Washington, and Butler officially refused. The membership hardly knew what to make of it since a constant barrage of mail from both sides overflowed their rural mailboxes. The beleaguered organization simply began to dissolve. Martha Williams wrote from Wilson, Arkansas, that her local was "scaterd." The secretary of the local in Charleston, Missouri, reported that only half of the members had attended the regular meeting. From the union's birthplace in Tyronza, where McKinney was busily agitating on the side of UCAPAWA, the news was that "our local has split up. We are not sending money no where."[35]

The final break came when Whitfield issued a call for a Missouri sharecroppers convention at which the STFU locals would be reformed under the CIO. Mitchell sent cables to John L. Lewis and John Brophy demanding that they put a stop to this splinter movement, but they would not. On the day that Whitfield's convention took place in St. Louis, March 12, 1939, the STFU executive council issued a press statement announcing the union's withdrawal from UCAPAWA. One of the reasons it cited was its desire to remove the STFU from "control by Communists."[36]

The public cry of "Communist" brought an immediate request from Representative Dies that Butler appear before his committee. Butler stalled for a time, during which he received a stern warning from Norman Thomas cautioning him not to appear before the Dies Committee unless subpoenaed. No subpoena was issued, and Butler did not testify.[37]

Thirty-two delegates, all but two of them blacks, attended Whitfield's meeting. The STFU countered with a convention of its own. While Butler was in the field recruiting delegates, Mitchell guarded the union headquarters against a raid by the enemy. The STFU pulled 116 sharecroppers to its convention, and they endorsed the withdrawal from UCAPAWA, put dues back to a quarter a month, and boasted that they would organize farm workers from North Carolina to Texas.[38]

Henderson called this meeting "illegal" and invited the locals in Arkansas to send delegates to Memphis for a UCAPAWA convention in April. Rather than ignore this meeting, the STFU arrived in strength. Each loyalist received instructions that read, "Members of the STFU have always been told to show courtesy to friends and strangers. This time you are dealing with enemies. Give no quarter . . . nor should you expect any." Henderson opened the meeting by reciting the charges against the STFU officers. When Mitchell demanded the floor to reply, the chairman, McKinney, declared him out of order. Defiant, the eight

STFU delegates marched out of the hall. The fifty people who remained chartered the Arkansas District of UCAPAWA and elected McKinney its president and Leon Turner its vice-president.[39]

Neither union emerged from this collision a victor. The Southern Tenant Farmers' Union lost most of its members in Missouri, and it paid a staggering toll in organizers. Whitfield, McKinney, and Turner joined Claude Williams in the column of those departed. Odis Sweeden, the STFU's volatile western leader, was gone, too. He had carried his wife to Arizona the previous autumn to cure her respiratory ailment, but, when he asked Memphis for $25 to pay his way back home, all he got was pleas of poverty. Butler delayed sending the check until February, and by then Sweeden was furious. He rushed into the UCAPAWA camp as soon as he was back in Oklahoma and called a sharecroppers convention in Durant in March. Those who came affiliated with UCAPAWA. By these acts, the sharecroppers' union movement was shattered beyond recognition.[40]

In Arkansas, where most of the members had always been, both unions claimed the loyalty of the workers. But, in reality, the members had retired in frustration. In a private assessment of the situation to Norman Thomas, Mitchell wrote, "There is no denying that the split with the C.I.O. has done tremendous damage, not only with our friends on the outside, but in the field as well." He estimated that of the 200 active locals the STFU had had before the battle, UCAPAWA had gotten 12, the STFU was left with 40, and the rest were moribund. "The situation has become so confusing to the people that they have just shut down and quit for the time being, many of them disgusted with all unions."[41]

Many of the STFU's "friends on the outside" left it now. John L. Lewis, John Brophy, and all the CIO would no longer have anything to do with the renegade southern union. Just as damaging was the desertion of one of the STFU's firmest

allies, Gardner Jackson. He had told Mitchell in February
that, in his opinion, the STFU did not have a leg to stand on
in its dispute with UCAPAWA. He withdrew his support entirely when he learned that the STFU had seceded. No easy
course was open to Jackson since he now worked for Labor's
Non-Partisan League, the political action arm of the CIO. Finally, his Washington Committee to Aid Agricultural Workers
dealt the STFU a serious financial blow by voting to withhold
further contributions.[42]

UCAPAWA had won some of the STFU's best workers, but,
for all the seriousness with which it had fought, it had neither
the finances nor the inclination to conduct a major organizing
drive in the cotton belt. Though it remained active for a spell
in Missouri, claiming four thousand members in the summer
of 1939, UCAPAWA ceased trying to overrun the STFU in
Arkansas on orders from the CIO. Its representative in Arkansas, John Day, abandoned the union field altogether in
1940 to run for governor of Missouri on the Communist party
ticket. UCAPAWA also lost its base in Oklahoma when Odis
Sweeden quit almost as quickly as he had joined. Before a
year was out nearly all the fires UCAPAWA had lit in the
Mississippi River Valley were permitted to die out. The international itself was soon dismembered, and Henderson was
put in charge of a new Food and Tobacco and Allied Workers'
Union. The only former STFU officer to make the change
with him was Owen Whitfield, who saw service in a strike of
tobacco warehousemen in Winston-Salem in 1946.[43]

By a consent decree with UCAPAWA, the organization represented by Butler and Mitchell retained the name Southern
Tenant Farmers' Union. The STFU also protected its financial
lifeline, the National Sharecroppers Week, by incorporating
it in Woodruff County, Arkansas. An epitaph for the Southern
Tenant Farmers' Union as an active force in national and
southern politics was contained in a report from Mid Hayes,
who had tried without success to bring the union back to life

in Crittenden County: "i have talk With lots of the members about it and thay said thay Wouldent try it anymore Because the union Were Not Doing anything it said it Would Doe. . . . they Will not come together again. said Just Paying Money for Nothing it is Nothing i can Doe With them."[44]

The STFU was the most potent creation of the southern radical movement of the 1930s. The anguish of landless farmers inevitably had to find some political outlet, and through the interracial composition and peaceful tactics of the STFU it expressed itself in a way that was particularly Christian and socialist. Though the union failed to break the back of the plantation system, it added the word *sharecropper* to the language of Europe and America, however little it may have rewarded the members in terms of food on the table. These servants of the plantations became the symbols of the starving South and were unavoidable examples of America's failure to provide a livelihood to all its people and the New Deal's inability to cope with their tragic world of constant need. By their rebellion the sharecroppers proved to many who watched from the sidelines that human endurance had its limits and that cowed spirits could rise.

The American public did not long cry for the poor and homeless in the plantation South, but the knowledge of their distress did have tangible results. One was the creation of the Farm Security Administration in 1937 along lines recommended by the President's Committee on Farm Tenancy. It was the federal government's first "war on poverty," and during its brief existence, cut short by World War II, it provided cheap medical insurance, emergency loans, and the funds to buy land to thousands of sharecroppers and small farmers. In the West it created ninety-five migrant camps with bed space for seventy-five thousand people. Though the FSA never made a lasting impact upon the national economy, and was so mindful of racial mores that it never appointed a single black

senior county agent, it did offer immeasurable relief to many
of the rural families hit hardest by the Depression.[45]

The collapse of the sharecroppers' movement was due to
forces far removed from the muddy backroads, country
towns, and drafty shacks of Arkansas. More than anything
else its defeat was caused by the inability of its radical leaders
to work together. The ideals of a cleansing revolution and a
truly egalitarian society had bound Christians and socialists
together at the start of the decade, but the looming threat of
world war took utopia out of reach. Linked as they were to
the survival of nations, the debates of radicals assumed a
dreadful seriousness which could not endure compromise.

The South had also changed. Millions of rural workers were
moving northward and westward in search of urban jobs.
Soon, booming war industries and the needs of the armed
services would take millions more away from the plantations
and dusty towns. The moment in history when the crusade of
the Southern Tenant Farmers' Union had been needed, and
could flourish, had vanished.

Howard Kester, Black Mountain, North Carolina, c. 1945
(*Howard A. Kester Papers, Southern Historical Collection,
UNC, Chapel Hill*)

VIII
Progressivism
Besieged

One thing that most southern radicals had in common was their wish to summon the power of the federal government, national organizations, and northern indignation to rectify southern injustices. The CIO unions, the national press corps, church organizations, the Socialist party, and the Communist media were all used to give southern progressivism greater clout than it could develop on native soil. The last major initiative of southern dissenters in the decade was the Southern Conference for Human Welfare. Through it they hoped to put the moral and political weight of the New Deal behind a program for change which was relatively moderate yet assured of stiff resistance. In the case of the Southern Conference, however, it was unclear whose ends were being served—those of national politicians or those of southern radicals.

The exact genesis of the Southern Conference later became a matter of considerable debate, but there is little doubt that the event was inspired by Joseph Gelders, the southern representative of the National Committee for the Defense of Political Prisoners. He envisioned a gathering which would publicize civil liberties abuses, particularly the intimidation of Communist and union organizers in Alabama. Gelders enlisted the aid of Lucy Randolph Mason of Virginia, the most distinguished southerner in the employ of the CIO. Her forebears had been prominent in both the American Revolution and the Confederacy; her background was in YWCA work, and she had proved herself to be an ideal person to reassure small-town mayors that a union campaign did not portend armed insurrection. Mason was also a good friend of Eleanor Roosevelt, and Gelder's ideas were relayed through her to the president.

Franklin Roosevelt in 1938 was seeking ways to rid Congress of certain conservative members who were thwarting his program. His "southern strategy" began with the commissioning of a sweeping report on the economic conditions of the South, to be drafted by a diverse panel, which included H. L. Mitchell, under the guidance of the National Emergency Council. The completed document painted a dreary picture of life in the "Old Confederacy," and it concluded that the South was the "Nation's Number One economic problem."

Roosevelt's next step was to give his administration's blessings to a convocation of influential southerners who would decide what to do about this problem. The president met with Gelders in June 1938 and evidently encouraged him to convene such a meeting to address the problems that would be documented in the National Emergency Council report. Its special purpose would be to hammer away at state poll taxes, which constricted democracy and New Deal ambitions in the South.[1]

Roosevelt's direct assaults upon the South's reactionary politicians by and large failed miserably. Although the president was so blunt as to call for the defeat of Georgia's Senator Walter F. George while the grim senator sat behind him at a rally in Barnsville, Georgia, George was reelected—as were most of Roosevelt's opponents.

The conference of progressives, however, was more easily arranged. Gelders was assisted in the planning of it by the staff at Highlander Folk School, where he had had an eye-opening experience as a delegate to the aborted All-Southern Trade Union and Civil Rights Conference in 1935. Myles Horton and the other teachers contacted labor organizations and several congressmen and helped with promotional literature. Equally important, Gelders got the support of the Southern Policy Committee, a liberal forum organized in 1935 by Francis Pickens Miller. Its chairman, H. Clarence Nixon, and the members of its Alabama branch made most of the arrangements for the conference. One of these members, Birmingham's Judge Louise O. Charlton, agreed to serve as chairwoman of the first Southern Conference for Human Welfare.[2]

The four-day meeting was extremely successful. It began on Sunday, November 20, 1938, with a motorcade tour of Birmingham conducted by the Women's Civic Club. More than twelve hundred delegates, who qualified for a vote if they lived in the South, turned out; most of the whites stayed at the spacious Tutwiler Hotel, headquarters of the conference, while blacks were assigned to boarding houses around the city. Representatives of labor organizations were numerous; Dave Griffin and J. R. Butler of the Southern Tenant Farmers' Union were among the many who attended. The meeting was marred only by an order from City Commissioner T. E. "Bull" Connor that whites and blacks must sit on opposite sides of the municipal auditorium.

Eleanor Roosevelt was the major attraction. Rising from the chair she had conspicuously placed in the aisle between the white and black seats, she spoke about the power of democracy, its basis in universal education, and the need to be proud of the contribution of every citizen regardless of nationality or race. In case her participation was not enough to establish the New Deal's support of the meeting, the president had also sent a message:

The long struggle by liberal leaders of the South for human welfare . . . has been implemented on an unprecedented scale these past five and one-half years by Federal help. Yet we have recognized publicly this year that what has been done is only a beginning, and that the South's unbalance is a major concern not merely of the South, but of the whole na-

tion. It is heartening, therefore, to face these human problems, not locally or individually, but in a united front from
Fort Raleigh to the Alamo.

You know, from years of trying, the difficulties of your task.
I believe you will find it impossible in many instances to separate human from economic problems. But if you steer a true
course and keep everlastingly at it, the South will long be
thankful for this day.[3]

Delegates attended workshops on such diverse subjects as
prison reform, farm tenancy, and women in the work force
and then applauded an address given by Frank P. Graham,
the president of the University of North Carolina. A Thomas
Jefferson Award, dedicated to "the Southerner who has done
most to promote human and social welfare," was given to the
Alabaman whom Roosevelt had appointed to the Supreme
Court, Hugo Black.

Resolutions were adopted calling for more playground facilities for Negroes and a women's bureau in each state labor
department to oppose sex discrimination, but those that received the most attention dealt with race discrimination and
the abolition of the poll tax. Repeal of poll tax laws was an
object that Roosevelt shared with southern progressives,
since these statutes effectively disenfranchised the poor, and
the major activity of the Southern Conference during its
eight-year life span was lobbying for the free ballot.

The convention also resolved henceforth to meet only in
cities where the races would not be segregated. This was mis-
represented by the southern press as a call for an end to all
segregation. In fact, no such radical demand could have issued from the overwhelmingly moderate majority at the Birmingham convention. The delegates did, however, condemn
the Dies Committee, but not for its war on domestic Communism. Rather they faulted HUAC for its "obvious use of
Congressional investigatory power to discredit the present
administration."

Frank Graham left before the convention ended, but he was elected chairman of the ongoing organization in spite of the fact that he sent a telegram asking not to be considered. The meeting had hardly adjourned when Representative Dies charged that the conference had been covertly organized and entirely dominated by Communists. Indeed, 6 of the 1,200 delegates had registered as representatives of the Communist party, but Dies insisted that many more had been active behind the scenes. What this implied about the motives or intelligence of Judge Charlton, who had overseen the planning of the convention, was enough to bring out a stubborn streak in Graham. In order to show that he would not be badgered by "powerful and privileged groups," he refused to resign his unwanted post as conference chairman.[4]

Many other political figures, however, were quick to back away from the organization. Alabama Senators Lister Hill and John Bankhead, Congressman Luther Patrick and Birmingham Postmaster Cooper Green disavowed any further role in the SCHW, mainly, they said, because it had taken a public stand against segregation. Brooks Hays, a Democratic national committeeman from Arkansas, quietly withdrew, and Virginia's Francis Pickens Miller declined late in December to serve as a vice-president after reflecting that John P. Davis, another vice-president who worked also as the executive secretary of the National Negro Congress, was an "associate" of Communists and that Donald Burke, head of the Virginia Communist party, had been in attendance at Birmingham.[5]

Before Miller resigned he wrote to Howard Kester to ask who else, in Kester's opinion, was operating behind the scenes to subvert the Southern Conference. On this point, Kester had definite ideas. His connection with the Southern Conference was an odd one. When Gelders was first trying to raise money to finance the Birmingham convention, he secured a $1,000 contribution from a donor he did not want to identify. According to Kester, Gelders called him on the telephone to explain that the condition attached to this grant by the anonymous donor was that Kester agree to play an active role in planning the Birmingham meeting. Kester agreed, but, he later asserted angrily, he was never invited to any of the plenary sessions as promised. Since he was at this time closely identified in southern activist circles with the fight to get Claude Williams out of the STFU and the STFU out of UCAPAWA, Kester concluded that the real planners of the convention resented his anti-Communist views. His first impression of the Southern Conference, therefore, was that it was Communist dominated. This opinion was reinforced because Kester believed that Gelders was a Communist.[6]

Gelders did have close ties to the Communist party though he would later specifically deny that he had ever been a member. He was a native of Birmingham, and Kester had first met him when Gelders was a professor at the University of Alabama. The occasion of Kester's visit to the area was an investigation, partially sponsored by the National Committee for the Defense of Political Prisoners, of the lynching of three blacks in Tuscaloosa in 1933. Gelders was associated with this committee, and in 1935 he moved to New York City to be its secretary.

Numerous prominent Americans were also members of the National Committee for the Defense of Political Prisoners. Among these were Theodore Dreiser, Sherwood Anderson, John Dos Passos, Lincoln Steffens, Upton Sinclair, and Edna St. Vincent Millay. It worked closely with the Communist party and investigated mainly those cases in which the International Labor Defense was involved. The committee's headquarters was in a building in New York City which also housed the ILD, the Friends of the Soviet Union, the Communist Unemployed Councils, and several other groups that had party affiliation. Gelders returned to Birmingham in 1936 to serve as this committee's southern representative.

He soon received a bitter taste of the limits on civil liberties when he was kidnapped and flogged mercilessly by three assailants while seeking information about the arrest and conviction of Jack Barton, the Communist party secretary in Birmingham. This experience and the general "state of siege" then prevailing in Alabama against political agitators of all sorts gave birth to the idea of a Southern Conference for Human Welfare.[7]

Certain that Communists were lurking behind the scenes of the Southern Conference, Kester went to the Birmingham bearing credentials from Roger Baldwin making him an "observer and consultant" for the ACLU. He departed "convinced beyond a shadow of a doubt that the Birmingham conference was conceived and in the main executed by persons who were either members of the Communist Party and known as such, and well known and not so well known fellow-travelers."[8]

In answering Miller, Kester cited his evidence. The official speaker on farm tenancy had been Gordon McIntire, an organizer for the Louisiana Farmers' Union, rather than a representative of the Southern Tenant Farmers' Union. McIntire was a "very fine boy," Kester said, but a Communist nonetheless. Howard Lee, a "leading member" of the American Student Union, Kester said, had dominated the student workshops. Lee had joined the church of Claude and Joyce Williams while a high school student in Paris, Arkansas, and he traced his acceptance of Christianity as a means to end war, racial injustice, and economic exploitation to the Williamses' inspiration. And then there was Joseph Gelders, who had helped to plan the entire event.

"While I have no objection to Communists or any one else holding a conference designed to . . . promote the common welfare," Kester wrote, "I am wholly against any group using unsuspecting and sincere people to advance causes with which it is well known that they are not in sympathy. . . .

While the goal of Communism is one to which I subscribe I cannot accept nor sanction the methods which they espouse and employ in achieving their goal. The doctrine that the end justifies the means is, in my judgment, one of the most damnable and one of the most insane ideas that ever possessed the human brain." The party, he said, has "an enormous lust for power and in its efforts to achieve power it will stop at nothing."[9]

This letter was evidently circulated by Miller to Frank Graham, Brooks Hays, and Will W. Alexander, as well as to Barry Bingham and Mark Ethridge, publisher and editor, respectively, of the Louisville *Courier* and *Times*. Graham thought highly enough of Kester to send him a complete list of the past and present officers, committee members, and state leaders of the Southern Conference with the request that Kester identify those he knew to be, or suspected of being, Communists. The educator, describing himself as "a Democrat who as a boy shouted by William Jennings Bryan, who later followed Woodrow Wilson, and now as a citizen supports most of the policies of Franklin D. Roosevelt as a chief hope of the real American way of human liberty," included his own views:

I do not object to members of any political party Democrats, Republicans, Socialists, Communists, or what-not coming into an open democratic meeting so long as it is open and above board. Nor do I think that we should run when we find out that a handful of Communists joined the Conference or would like to manipulate it or claim it as their own.

I am in favor of the majority, who have a decent sense of fair play and a Christian sense of ethics . . . holding their ground and maintaining their control of the Conference against the devious methods of both Communists and Fascists.[10]

This statement relieved Kester of many misgivings concerning the conference leadership, but he did respond to Graham's request and identified the individuals whom he be-

194

lieved, on the basis of long association, to be Communists or
fellow travelers. There were no surprises: he named Gelders,
McIntire, John P. Davis, and Gilbert Parks from South Carolina—though Howard Lee came in for special mention as a
"not-so-well-known Communist." Lee was now in a position
of influence as the corresponding secretary of the Tennessee
chapter of the Southern Conference. Kester identified two
"fellow travelers": one was Edward Strong of Virginia; the
other was Myles Horton who, with Lee, was active in the
youth section of the conference and was one of nine Tennessee representatives on the conference's governing board. To
Elisabeth Gilman, Kester wrote, "While I have no positive
proof I am inclined to believe from all I hear that Highlander
is strongly CP."[11]

This statement marked the dissolution of the circle of
Christian activists who had just six years earlier proclaimed
with one voice a radical gospel, the collapse of capitalism, and
the coming of the Kingdom of God on earth. The final bonds
fell away when the Fellowship of Southern Churchmen, the
one regional ministerial fraternity that had clearly stated the
radical social implications of Christianity, denied membership
to Claude Williams and Don West.

This tiny organization, born as the Conference of Younger
Churchmen of the South, had become a loose association of
roughly 275 ministers and lay people tied together by a newsletter, an annual meeting, and a sense of sharing the work of
their secretary, Howard Kester. It did little, but it was the
"personal church" of a great many clergy who wanted more
from their religion than "a mere thing of wind and tongue." It
stood for the unification of the redeeming word with the redeeming deed, and its members professed to accept responsibility for "the present wide-spread poverty, class conflict,
racial bitterness, general unemployment, and the overt and
covert warfare, together with the consequent spiritual disin-
tegration, moral confusion and overwhelming sense of futility

and despair throughout the world today." The FSC called for
a deeper commitment to God, "a greater measure of justice
for the disinherited and oppressed," the abolition of "all arti-
ficial and accidental divisions of persons on the basis of race,
nationality, class, or creed," and the holding in common of all
natural resources and scientific processes. Yet it too splin-
tered on the issue of Communism. [12]

Hitler's annexation of Austria sparked heated debate at an
FSC meeting in Raleigh in 1938. The pacifists who had come
to the Reverend Hermann Voss's United Church were unable
to pass a resolution renouncing war in all its forms. A substantial number of the members, led by James Dombrowski, felt
it imperative to identify fascism as the malignant force loose
in the world and to take the position that "as Christians, we
cannot stand idly by while our fellowmen in other lands are
murdered, their homes and civilizations destroyed." Kester
and the FSC president, the Reverend "Scotty" Cowan,
thought that this view sprang more from sympathy with the
perilous situation of the Soviet Union, then facing Hitler's armies, than from Christianity; they feared that "those who follow the CP line" wanted to infiltrate their organization. [13]

Stalin's nonaggression pact with Germany in 1939, the German and Russian conquest of Poland, and the entry of Britain
and France into the war completed the division between
Communist and Western sympathizers. Claude Williams now
sought to renew his membership in the Fellowship of Southern Churchmen. Though he was willing to sign the FSC's
"Statement of Principles," hitherto the only criterion for admission, his application was regarded with intense suspicion.
The executive committee rejected it in secret session because
they doubted Williams's "readiness to give . . . undivided
loyalty to the cause of Prophetic Religion." Herbert King, a
black Congregationalist, led the opposition to Williams. Kester said he refrained from this debate, but sixteen years later
when he was himself pressed to prove that he had never been

a Communist, he illustrated his anti-Communism by citing his vote against Williams even though he had been "deeply devoted" to the man and "knew I would destroy a friendship of many years standing."[14]

Don West's attempts to join the FSC were rebuffed by the gentler tactic of not answering his letters. West had returned to his Georgia farm after severing connections with the Kentucky Workers' Alliance and some other leftist political associations. He sent feelers to the FSC seeking, he said, information and religious comradeship. Through oversight or intention his mail went unanswered. In March 1939 he moved to Bethel, Ohio, to pastor a Christian Fellowship Parish made up of three Congregational churches, and he again tried to engage Kester in correspondence. He criticized Kester for ignoring him when he was isolated in Georgia and unable to find a "crevice open wide enough for one of my color to scrounge through." He asked to be thought of as a friend; "that is," he wrote, "if you think your 'suspicion' can be put aside, and accept me even with the inferior background of having had a few tastes of hell in the scarlet stream of the labor movement."

Offended, Kester replied that he guessed West was still enrolled in the "Communist kindergarten," but that if he ever again wanted to join the FSC his application would be considered. Kester added, however, that "you will find a good many people in the Fellowship who have had 'a few tastes of hell in the scarlet stream of the labor movement' as you so dramatically put it, but who, unlike you, think nothing of it except that it is but part of the task of trying to bring some decency and justice into a world full of agony and despair. We haven't very many martyr's that I know of and as yet we haven't created a "hero's corner' but I suppose we might do it for those who consider themselves so almighty different from other 'Christians.'"

Strangely, these emotional outpourings seemed to relieve

198 both men, and in the future they communicated with something of their old friendliness. Though West did not again apply for membership in the FSC, he did thank Kester for the "currying down," even if he thought it unfair. When West returned to Georgia a year later, he sent the Kesters a copy of his new periodical, *The Country Parson*. Kester said he admired the paper, and he sent West some FSC pamphlets to read. Yet their days of working together in harness were finished, and gone with them was the dream, born in the seminaries, that their dedicated band of Christian visionaries would provide leadership of a revolution of poor and working people in the South.[15]

The
IX   War Years

Japan's sudden aerial bombardment of Pearl Harbor made the prospect of a second American Revolution all the more remote. Most foreign policy differences between left and right were erased by the Nazi invasion of Russia and the entry of the United States into the conflict, and the critical issue became winning the war, not reconstructing America. The organizations founded by southern radicals floundered for the most part; some passed out of existence entirely; others assumed a character less regional or apocalyptic. The passionate Christian activists who had been in the forefront of protest went separate ways. None totally abandoned politics; rather they continued with their work as ministers, educators, or self-styled prophets. Their messages differed in detail but were alike in linking the achievement of basic human rights with the attainment of socialistic economic goals.

Radicals, however, did not emerge as leaders in human rights causes after the war. The heady expectation of imminent revolution perished at Pearl Harbor, if not sooner, and so did much of the appeal of radical politics and religion. Liberalism, moderation, and gradualism were the catchwords of white southern progressives by war's end, and the dominant human rights organization to emerge under their leadership made no difficult economic demands. It did not, in fact, even denounce segregation in its statements of principles.

The New Deal died suddenly, replaced by the slogan "Win the War." The National Youth Administration, the Civilian Conservation Corps, and the Works Progress Administration were immediate casualties, and the most adventurous liberal experiment, the Farm Security Administration, was put on the auction block. In 1942 the Joint Committee on Reduction of Nonessential Federal Expenses, under the direction of Senator Harry F. Byrd of Virginia, condemned the FSA for soliciting clients, exaggerating the need for its programs, encouraging "socialist and impractical farming projects," and paying farmers' poll taxes. The FSA's argument that the small farmer, properly supported, could contribute more than his share toward the war effort was not persuasive to the senators. Congress stripped the FSA of its migrant programs, and in 1944 the agency began to liquidate its 152 resettlement farms and other holdings. Two years later this one and only New Deal program to benefit small farmers and tenants was abolished by Congress. At a time when millions were dying on the battlefields, curing rural poverty had become an extravagance.

The South underwent its own dramatic changes. War meant that jobs were available for nearly everyone able to work or to fight. Black and white laborers left the countryside by the thousands, most of them never to return except as visitors to the "homeplace." The mass exodus affected even the Rochdale Cooperative Farm in Mississippi and caused it to abandon most of its "socialist" principles. The cooperative had resettled in Holmes County in 1938 and taken the name Providence Farm. But after the calamity of Pearl Harbor, its manager, Sam Franklin, enlisted as a navy chaplain, and most of the farmers were drafted or moved north. The new manager, A. Eugene Cox, found that the cooperative simply could not compete with neighboring mechanized plantations, and he leased much of the acreage to private farmers. The only "socialist" programs to remain were a cooperative grocery and a credit union.[1]

Critical shortages of farm and cannery workers developed in the Southwest and along the Atlantic coast, and the Southern Tenant Farmers' Union arose from its slumber to meet a portion of this need. In 1940 the chief assets of the STFU had been forty-five dues-paying locals and an energetic young black woman, Pauli Murray, in charge of National Sharecroppers Week. But in 1942 the War Manpower Commission authorized the Farm Security Administration to transport two thousand STFU workers to Arizona, New Mexico, and Texas to pick the pima long-staple cotton needed to make parachutes.[2]

The approach of war had boosted the STFU in another way when its Alabama organizer, Holiness preacher W. M. Tanner, struck a deal with Roy E. Raley of the Laborers' Union to give STFU members hiring priority in Alabama's expanding defense industries. Many new members joined as a result, and Raley replaced J. R. Butler as president of the STFU in 1942.[3]

The arrangement by which STFU workers were sent to the Southwest ended in 1943 when Congress took the migrant programs away from the Farm Security Administration and gave them to the Extension Service of the Agriculture Department. Under the new rules a farm worker could not leave his home county unless the local extension agent certified that a labor surplus existed. Plantation owners in the cotton South considered plentiful labor too much of a blessing to let the government carry off their field hands, and, as a consequence, the United States was forced to begin importing Mexican braceros. Nothing could illustrate more clearly how bowing to one region's political establishment adversely affected the nation as a whole, for the bracero program fixed the reliance of western farmers on Mexican labor and helped to create an immense problem of illegal immigration. Allowing southern cotton field workers to remain under the thumb of their plantation bosses also added enormously to the welfare burdens of several states when machines began to replace plantation labor wholesale.

The STFU, still administered by H. L. Mitchell, put its

Cotton mill workers on strike in Lumberton, North Carolina, 1937; Myles Horton, center (*Highlander Research and Education Center*)

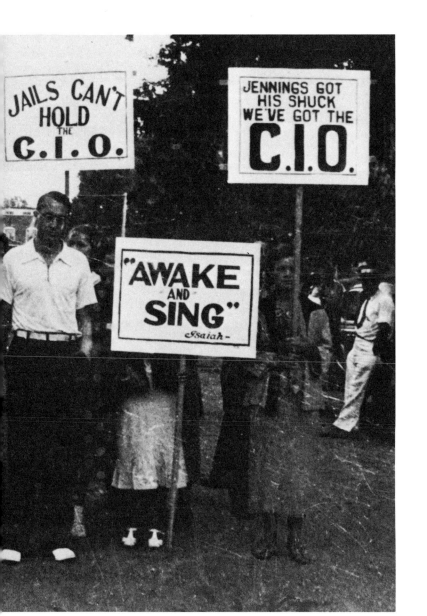

first 150 workers on trains for Swedesboro, New Jersey, in December 1943 to work in vegetable canneries under contracts arranged by the Amalgamated Meat Cutters. This was the first organized migration plan ever put together by an employer and a union without the assistance of government, and during the war it carried 12,000 seasonal laborers to Delaware, California, New Jersey, New York, and Michigan to work for Campbell Soup, H. J. Heinz, and other large employers. Union organizers followed these workers and handled their grievances. In 1946 the STFU was awarded a charter by the American Federation of Labor and changed its name to the National Farm Labor Union (NFLU). Mitchell moved to Washington, D.C., to represent the new union, and its organizers shifted to California in 1948 to conduct a strike of the 1,200 fruit pickers at the mammoth DiGiorgio Farms in Bakersfield.[4]

The radical gospel found new application in the wartime ministry of Claude Williams. He had left Commonwealth College after his expulsion from the STFU (and shortly before the school's charter was revoked in 1940) to create a new organization called the People's Institute of Applied Religion. Its purpose was to train grass-roots preachers from the "mass ecstatic religious sects of the South" in a Marxist analysis of the Bible. Williams had meticulously developed this analysis and illustrated its major points upon complex charts that served as visual aids during his sermons. It held that Jesus, the "Son of Man," had been the leader of an underground guerilla movement known as "The Way of Righteousness" which, when victorious, would usher in an age of brotherhood and plenty. Old enemies were the pharaohs; new ones were Nazis, fascists, and Klansmen. He counted Owen Whitfield, E. B. McKinney, and Leon Turner among the ministers of the People's Institute, and he laid grandiose plans for sweeping the South with its message. With the support of the National Religion and Labor Foundation, Claude and Joyce

Williams and a Methodist activist named Winifred L. Chappell held "Institutes" throughout Missouri, Arkansas, and Tennessee.[5]

Alva Taylor attended one such institute in Evansville, Indiana. The aging professor had finally been ousted from Vanderbilt by Chancellor Kirkland in 1936 largely because Taylor had supported a union drive at the woolens factory of John Edgerton, a university trustee. "I am no longer at Vanderbilt," he wrote. "The old Chancellor . . . a Bourbon as ancient as an Egyptian mummy and a certain rich man maddened by the New Deal and the TVA and possessed with a holy enthusiasm to protect the interests of their kind . . . contrived to abolish my chair." After a short stint as manager of the Cumberland Homesteads, Taylor became a federal labor mediator.[6] His report on the Evansville Institute showed that he still found merit in his former student's work: each word spoken there, he said, "rang with religious devotion. The simplicity of language, the picturesqueness of illustration, the sound Americanism of all references to our present situation, the broad plea for toleration and the exaltation of the Kingdom of God . . . marked the whole day's work as something to long remember."[7]

In 1942 Williams received a rare opportunity to redeem himself in the eyes of the Presbyterian church. The Detroit Presbytery asked him to be its industrial chaplain and work to reconcile the blacks and whites who had flocked from the South to labor in the vital war plants. Hatemongers were active in the working-class neighborhoods, Gerald L. K. Smith and the angry priest of the Little Flower, Father Coughlin, among them. In the powerful unions there was friction between the new arrivals and workers with seniority.

Williams held institutes for white and black union leaders, and when the city was engulfed in a bloody race riot in June 1943, he was a leader in the group that persuaded the mayor to call out the state militia. His following was greatest at Detroit's Packard plant where Virgil Vandenburg, a black auto worker and storefront preacher, organized a Gospel Preachers' Council of Applied Religion. For revival activities they got together a Brotherhood Squadron consisting of black and white orators and an integrated choir. The People's Institute demonstrated some influence in the labor community in July 1944 when it sponsored a Congress of Applied Religion, well attended by union members, at St. Paul's Cathedral. Never before had Williams's Christianity seemed so bellicose. He stated unequivocally that he loathed pacifism because it shielded "fifth columnists," gave support to the cause of Hitler, and was unscriptural. Denying the obvious interpretation of Jesus's admonition to "turn the other cheek," Williams declared that "the Son of Man did not fight back here because He was outnumbered. . . . That statement was given in a specific instance where to have resisted would have meant the annihilation of the entire group. But escapists and idealists have extended it and attempted to apply it to every situation, even to the beast of Nazism."

To claim legitimacy as a true church and challenge mainstream Christianity on its own terrain, the People's Institute began ordaining ministers and chartering local congregations on May Day in 1944. Williams planned not to establish a small sect on the fringes of the Christian church but to convert millions of people. By his claims, the People's Institute had field representatives in Connecticut, Florida, Illinois, Michigan, New York, North Carolina, Tennessee, Louisiana, Arkansas, and Georgia when the war came to an end.

Victory in Europe gave the Detroit Presbytery an excuse to abolish William's position, but this was only a small setback to the Marxist preacher. He moved with his family to Fungo Hollow, near Alabaster, Alabama, on a farm purchased with the help of northern friends. Here would be the Williamses' camp, their base, their conference center, and their contact with the labor movement in the nearby steel mills and coal mines of north Alabama.[8]

Howard Kester spent the war years as a teacher. His Committee on Economic and Racial Justice dissolved in 1941, partly because of political differences between Reinhold Niebuhr, who staunchly supported aid to Britain, and several pacifists who did not, and partly because Kester's increasing devotion to religious causes was not shared by all of his board members. The collapse of the old Southern Tenant Farmers' Union disenchanted Kester with unions, and he no longer relished a job requiring him to "barely escape a few lynchings now and then and spend the rest of the time lecturing for the Socialist Party." Saying that "my life and my work is today more firmly rooted in our Christian faith than ever before," he became the full-time secretary of the Fellowship of Southern Churchmen, and Alice became its office manager. Niebuhr welcomed this "change of strategy" and did his best to raise money for the Kesters' work, but the outbreak of war made the task virtually impossible.[9]

At the age of thirty-eight, Kester registered for the draft as a conscientious objector. Under his direction, however, the FSC called on the army to create an interracial volunteer combat division. It also published *That America Be Not Blamed*, a powerful statement against race bigotry signed by 100 well-known southerners. Five hundred people came to the FSC's 1943 meeting in Raleigh where they heard Lillian Smith denounce the fiction that blacks were lynched for the protection of white women and call for the right of the races to intermarry. Such boldness from a southern white woman brought the crowd to its feet cheering.[10]

The FSC also sponsored a tiny organization called Friends of the Soil which was created in 1940 to be "a distinctly religious movement founded upon the Lordship of God over man, the earth and its resources." Its guiding dictum was that "those who despoil the earth stand under the judgment of God, no less than those who oppress His people." Friends of the Soil never claimed more than 231 members, and like many FSC projects its significance lay less in the sphere of national politics than in the good works of those who believed in its blending of environmentalism, socialism, and Christianity. The guiding figures were Kester, an Englishman named Francis Drake, and the Reverend Eugene Smathers. Smathers was a Kentuckian who had come with his wife, Lucille, to the mountains of Tennessee in 1932 to pastor a small Presbyterian mission in the hard-hit community of Big Lick. He believed firmly that "souls cannot be saved in abstraction: soil, society and souls are bound together. . . . If Christianity is the truth about God, it is also the truth about the whole of life."

In line with their socialist ideas, the Smatherses taught advanced farming techniques and created a Calvary Church cooperative land-buying and home-building project to keep parishioners in the county. Their dream was to build a House of Recreation and a House of Health adjoining their church, and through their efforts a clinic was established that eventually was transformed into the county's major hospital.[11]

Many churches across the United States subscribed to Friends of the Soil publications, but this association was no better able than the FSC to pay its bills. Late in 1942 Ethel Moors, a faithful contributor to FSC projects, nominated Kester for the post of director of Penn School, a Christian institution on St. Helena Island near Beaufort, South Carolina. The first organized school for blacks in the South, Penn had been established at the very outset of the Civil War by abolitionists, most of them Quakers, as soon as the Yankee gunboats forced the whites to the mainland and claimed the plantations for the slaves. Two Philadelphia Friends, Laura Towne and Ellen Murray, started the school, and for the next forty years they were its faculty. With their passing, Rossa B.

Cooley and Grace B. House were recruited from Hampton Institute to continue the work of educating a people who spoke no language recognizable on the mainland, and, like their predecessors, these women each gave forty years.

Many of Penn's trustees had likewise served on the board for decades, and, according to a critical observer, the school suffered from "82 years of inertia and a charitable paternalism with all of its opiatic effects." After carefully scrutinizing the Kesters' credentials, the trustees, overwhelmed by glowing recommendations from black leaders like Walter White and Benjamin Mays, hired Howard as Penn's principal and Alice as head teacher. She wrote home to her sisters that "it seems especially fitting to go to such a job now when Christianity and Democracy are being challenged around the world. It is really a part of what we are fighting for. It won't be easy—but Guadalcanal wasn't easy—nor was Henry's job easy." This last reference was to her brother, Henry Harris, who was killed in the Pacific theater in 1942.[12]

Penn had 274 students and a faculty of 25 when the Kesters were inaugurated on January 9, 1944. The school's buildings, forests, and farm had been neglected, and the new principal enthusiastically embraced the opportunity to implement numerous theories on scientific farming which he had assiduously studied as a hobby. He went to work to improve the livestock herd, and he boasted that by May of his first year the students had spread 54 tons of fertilizer on the farm. He got the school to buy a new tractor, replacing its spiked-wheel antique, and boosted corn production from 16 bushels per acre to 64. To assure ample food for the coming winter the students canned nearly 3,000 quarts of fruit and vegetables. "Never in my life," Kester wrote, "has a job excited me more."[13]

Lectures against fascism became a part of the school curriculum. While some of Penn's best students were drafted to fight or to perform graveyard duty in the Negro regiments, the younger ones learned to recognize enemy aircraft and submarines in case the Nazis should try to sneak ashore through the marshes where the shrimp boats docked. But the school remained academically weak because the salaries it could pay its teachers were even lower than what the state doled out to black instructors.[14]

The Kesters were not universally liked by the islanders. Their attempts to impose traditional educational discipline upon the old institution were rebuffed by faculty and students alike, and the couple frequently took refuge from the hostility down by the riverbank where they could "cuss and discuss half the night." In 1946 Kester proposed an ambitious plan to reorient the school's program in light of the fact that Penn's financial mainstay, John D. Rockefeller's General Education Board, was withdrawing its support. He recommended shutting down the elementary grades entirely and turning these pupils over to state schools. He wanted to retain the high school since the state appropriation to Negro secondary schools was abysmally low, but only if sufficient money could be raised to hire qualified teachers. Kester also proposed to fulfill a personal dream by creating a "Seminary in the Corn Field" to train a new generation of rural ministers, and he wanted to begin a comprehensive program of community development through improved techniques of fishing, shrimping, and forestry.[15]

The trustees approved the plan, but though Kester was quickly able to organize a Sea Island Better Life Council he could not raise the funds needed for the cornfield seminary or for the improvement of the high school. Finally he was forced to recommend that Penn drop all of its formal child education programs in favor of community work, small farm and business demonstration projects, and selected ventures in adult education.[16]

Though the trustees ultimately endorsed this course of action, many of the islanders were angry. One wrote to Kester that "you and your dirty Georgia cracker wife is having Penn School going to hell. . . . You aint doing nothing but pulling confusion among many good people." Their position became untenable, and the Kesters resigned in June 1948. Before departing for a hilltop cottage they had built in Black Mountain, North Carolina, they oversaw the transfer of the school buildings to the state and the farm to Clemson College. Penn retained its meeting halls and, most importantly, its community programs. Though the Kesters' four and one-half years at Penn were not remembered with pleasure, either by them or by many of the islanders, they had affected the transition that would keep Penn relevant to the changing South. Their successors, Elizabeth and Courtney Siceloff, inherited a financial base sufficient to initiate a day-care center, a nurse-staffed clinic, a midwife program, and community recreational activity. The new directors also brought to life neighborhood political action groups to improve conditions for blacks on St. Helena, and by the 1960s Penn had become a training center for civil rights organizers.[17]

Don West was another who made a mark as an educator during the war years. He resigned his pastorate in Bethel, Ohio, in 1940 to work for a while as a deckhand on a Mississippi River barge between New Orleans and Pittsburgh, then received a call to minister to four small Congregational churches clustered around Meansville, Georgia. Here he established the Country Parson Press, and, in the days before the Soviet Union was attacked by Germany, he editorialized against intervention by the United States. One publication entitled *"Blessed Are the Peace Makers"* argued that Hitler's war machine had been built by American and British capitalists and that the war fever in the United States was being promoted by capitalists "just to make money."[18]

West explained to Alva Taylor, who raised the question, that he was not a Communist, but that neither was he an anti-Communist. "Somehow," he said, "I can't help but preach the only Jesus I know, and he is a very bothersome fellow, and he gets me in dutch time after time. Sometimes my wife may wish that I'd met that other Jesus, the one most of the churches have up in the stained glass. But I just missed him, somehow, and got all tangled up with the one that stirred up the people. He's a powerful interesting guy, but bad medicine for a pastor in modern churches, or ancient ones either I reckon."[19]

In 1942 West, whose academic credentials were impressive, was made superintendent of the small public school system in nearby Lula, Georgia. Now that both America and the Soviet Union were in the war, West had his office stationery imprinted with the slogan: "Education for Victory over Fascism Both Foreign and Domestic." The system as he ran it was as innovative as any in the country. Democratically elected student and faculty committees were put in charge of each school. The student government put on plays (one, called *Old Elrod's Defeat*, depicted the ouster of a school board member who had tried to fire West) and was given a weekly radio program where students could air their views on issues both immediate and international. Through this medium they conducted scrap drives for the military, and each student was on the program at least once. The young people also financed and published their own newspaper which they entitled, appropriately, *The Scrapper*.[20]

The Wests' living quarters were in an old school building that also housed a machine shop open to local farmers and a community cannery powered by a wood-burning steam engine. They had organized both of these enterprises, and Don West also established a National Farmers' Union chapter in the area.

He ran the Lula schools for four years and could have stayed longer, but in 1945 he accepted a fellowship from the Rosenwald Foundation for graduate study at the University of Chicago, Columbia University, and the University of Geor-

gia. He returned to Georgia at the end of the year to write
and to preach at churches around Lula. Constance West, now   213
the mother of daughters aged six and eleven, had found a
secure position as a school supervisor in Catoosa County. The
first year of peacetime was one of relative achievement and
fulfillment for the family. Don was invited by the owner of a
shirt factory in Martin, Tennessee, to conduct classes on the
benefits of unionism to his workers, and he spoke at strike
rallies in Andalusia, Alabama. In these sermons he called
Moses the first labor leader and the exodus from Egypt the
first strike. In May his most popular book of verse, *Clods of
Southern Earth*, was published, and the Southern Conference for Human Welfare gave the volume away free to new
subscribers to its newspaper. He finished his doctoral thesis
that summer and in the fall was hired to teach English and
sacred literature at Oglethorpe University in Atlanta. Speaking particularly of the healthy sales of his new book, but no
doubt reflecting as well on his victory over the poverty of his
youth in the north Georgia hills, West wrote to Myles Horton
that it "is a pleasing experience after so damn many years of
scraping bottom."[21]

Highlander Folk School's program during the 1940s was
inextricably linked with that of the Southern Conference for
Human Welfare. One unfortunate result of this was that textile organizer Franz Daniel, long considered a friend by both
Horton and James Dombrowski, announced at the Tennessee
CIO convention in 1941 that he and his wife, Elizabeth
Hawes, were severing their ties to Highlander because the
school's staff were "Communist stooges." The heat being applied to the Southern Conference also brought Highlander
unwelcome visitors from the Dies Committee and the FBI,
none of whom found anything of a seditious nature worthy of
public disclosure.[2p11,52]

Horton was active in both the youth section of the Southern
Conference, called the League of Young Southerners, and its

Eleanor Roosevelt, beside Myles Horton, speaking at
Highlander Folk School, 1955 (*Highlander Research and
Education Center*)

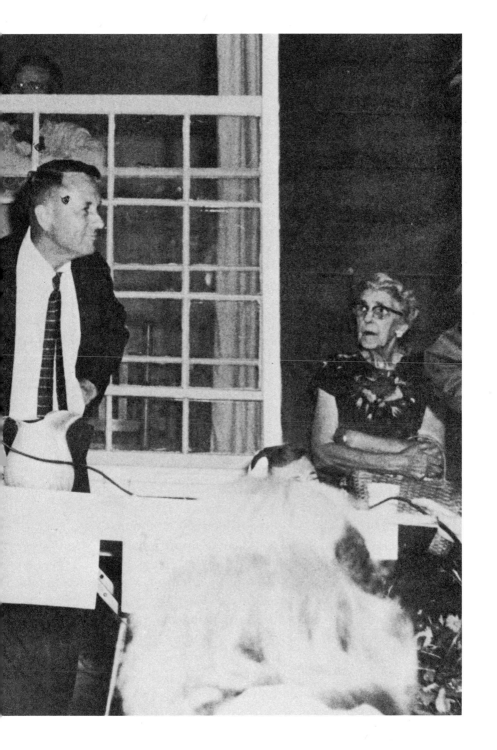

state organization in Tennessee. Under the direction of its new executive secretary, Howard Lee, the Southern Conference convened its second regional meeting in an unsegregated hall in Chattanooga in April 1940. Elected chairman to replace Frank Graham was the Reverend John B. Thompson, pastor of the First Presbyterian Church in Norman, Oklahoma, and professor of theology at the University of Oklahoma. A native of Tennessee, Thompson had earned his divinity degree under Reinhold Niebuhr, and he had been one of the original teachers at Highlander in 1933. Five months after becoming chariman of the Southern Conference, however, Thompson came under fire for accepting the presidency of the American Peace Mobilization, an organization which seemed to reflect the gyrations of Soviet foreign policy. It lobbied, for example, to keep America out of the war until Russia was attacked and then became fervently interventionist.

Frank Graham, in charge of the Chattanooga conference, took great pains to draw Howard Kester into the planning of it. Kester sent an endorsement of the meeting to Graham, "out of sympathy for what you are trying to accomplish," but he continued his private efforts to obtain evidence that certain members of the organization were secretly Communists. He was particularly interested in Howard Lee, and he wrote to the Socialist party labor secretary, Arthur McDowell, asking for proof that Lee had made pro-Communist statements. McDowell, however, could come up with nothing.[23]

The Chattanooga meeting was attended by more than a thousand delegates, the largest group of whom were mine workers sent by John L. Lewis. Eleanor Roosevelt spoke, as she had two years before in Birmingham, and again the conference passed its strongest resolution against the poll tax. What "Communist watchers" noticed, however, was that this convention, which took place while Hitler and Stalin were carving up Europe under the protection of their nonaggression treaty, took a stand in opposition to any United States

defense spending at the expense of domestic programs. This
was a position then being pushed by the Communist party,
and it was a reversal of a resolution favoring aid to European
democracies which had passed at the Birmingham meeting
two years earlier. All that was remarkable in this, however,
was that American Communists were latecomers to isolation-
ism; the major backers of the 1940 resolution against military
spending were members of the UMW caucus led by Katherine Lewis, who represented her isolationist father. Strenuous
campaigning by W. T. Couch and Graham compelled the conference to couple this resolution with another that condemned those Nazi, Communist, fascist, and imperialist re-
gimes that suppressed democratic liberties. While there
could be no concealing the fact that Communists participated
in the Southern Conference, its dominant liberal and labor
membership wished it understood that they, not the far left,
ran the show.[24]

But the cry of "communist" hurt and ultimately defeated
the Southern Conference. The participation of Thompson and
Lee in the American Peace Mobilization caused so much of
the labor and liberal membership to pull out that not even
the resignations of Lee and Joseph Gelders could improve
things. Lee went on to organize for the militant and leftist
International Union of Mine, Mill, and Smelter Workers. He
was first replaced as conference secretary by Alton Lawrence,
southern representative of Labor's Non-Partisan League
(CIO), who was loaned to the SCHW by John L. Lewis. Lawrence, who was a Communist, stayed only a short time with
the Southern Conference. He was withdrawn for other CIO
duties late in 1942, and soon he too signed on as an organizer
for the Mine, Mill, and Smelter Workers.[25]

Desperate for an administration unhampered by political
affiliation and supported by black leaders, the conference
turned to Dombrowski. His selection as secretary breathed
new life, temporarily, into the organization and enabled it to

finance a third convention in Nashville in 1942. Convening as it did just four months after the Japanese bombed Pearl Harbor, this conference adopted the theme: "The South's Part in Winning the War for Democracy." Eleanor Roosevelt was there, the president sent a greeting, and a host of dignitaries including Senator Claude Pepper, Mary McLeod Bethune, David Lilienthal, Charles S. Johnson, Rufus Clement, and Lillian Smith gave talks. But a decline to five hundred in the number of delegates showed that interest in the organization, and perhaps in the South as a topic, was on the wane. Thompson retired as chairman, and this might have mollified the liberals had not Paul Robeson, during a singing performance at the convention, made an embarrassing public appeal for the release of Communist party chief Earl Browder, then serving time for passport violations.[26]

Homer Price Rainey, president of the University of Texas, was elected to replace Thompson, but he declined the position after the conference adjourned. Finally, in June 1942, Clark Foreman took the post. Foreman was a Georgian who had served as Interior Secretary Harold Ickes's adviser on the economic status of Negroes. It was he who had originally suggested to Roosevelt the study of southern economic problems that led to the creation of the Southern Conference.

The SCHW was successful in drawing three thousand people to a "Win the War" rally in Raleigh in July, but this was the last major public event sponsored by the organization. Financial survival was its main concern for the remainder of the war, and its ability to issue statements condemning the poll tax and lynchings was made possible only by Dombrowski's skill at squeezing funds from reluctant foundations and the CIO. It saved its final breath to protest another travesty of justice that occurred in Columbia, Tennessee, in 1946. In February of that year a black veteran was charged with attempted murder for hitting a Columbia storeowner who would not permit the soldier's mother to try on a hat. The mayor thought a riot was imminent and called out five hundred National Guardsmen. The troops surrounded the black section of town, charged through it firing their weapons, and looted and destroyed several businesses. Dozens of blacks were arrested in the sweep, and many were bludgeoned insensible. Two captives were shot to death, and twenty-five blacks were subsequently tried for rioting.

The headquarters of the Southern Conference was thirty miles away in Nashville, and Dombrowski hurried to Columbia to investigate. The Southern Conference published his findings and was instrumental in drumming up twenty thousand letters of protest to Tennessee's Governor James Nance McCord. When, in the end, only one of the twenty-five defendants was sentenced to prison, the organization celebrated it as a victory.[27]

For all practical purposes the Southern Conference was out of business within the year, done in finally by a depleted treasury, internal feuding, lack of any support from the new Truman administration, and a congressional assault upon its politics and motives. Eleanor Roosevelt continued her support until the end. Though she did not attend the Southern Conference meeting in New Orleans in 1946, she sent her greetings.

The other southern organization she faithfully endorsed was the Highlander Folk School. In large measure this was due to the affection she felt for two of the school's closest friends, Lucy Randolph Mason and Virginia Durr of Alabama, the wife of a Federal Communications commissioner, Clifford Durr, and the sister-in-law of Supreme Court Justice Hugo Black. Mrs. Durr, often exhausted by her job as a politician's wife and center of enlightened southern society in Washington, wrote: "I often realize how rich my life is and how fortunate but occasionally it gets a little too rich—sort of like too much plum pudding—and then I lay awake thinking how much I would like to be at Highlander. . . . it is the only place I know of where I feel I am only myself and not Mother Daughter Wife Sister or So. Conference."[28]

Mrs. Roosevelt created a scholarship fund at Highlander that permitted union members like Nashville clothing worker Edward Blair to attend the school. She also allowed her name to be used at some of the school's fund-raising benefits and joined Highlander's national sponsoring committee in 1942. But she, or the White House, was concerned enough by rumors that the school was Communist-dominated to inquire whether Horton or Dombrowski had ever been connected with Commonwealth College. Her fears were allayed on this point by Virginia Durr, and she sent an endorsement to Highlander that read: "I have had the school checked by people in whom I have absolute confidence and am convinced that the newspaper attack and the groups which have been opposed to you are not opposed to you because of any communist activities, but because they are opposed to labor organizations and, therefore, labor education. I am continuing my support." With her permission, Highlander published the statement.[29]

During the war period, in fact, Highlander attempted the difficult task of steering a neutral course between the various political ideologies competing among the labor unions and civil rights groups with which it worked. Besides its involvement with the Southern Conference, Highlander had regular summer sessions for union members sent by their locals, ran a children's camp, held an integrated workshop for the United Automobile Workers in 1944, and even offered itself as a "defense training school" for union leaders. It accomplished these things while its staff and its supporters advocated different political ideas. Dombrowski could boast correctly to Eleanor Roosevelt that "what gives Highlander a unique significance is the confidence which it enjoys among many of the rival groups within the labor family." On the other side of the coin, where leftist politics were reflected, Dombrowski was being candid when he confessed to Virginia Durr that "from the beginning Highlander has worked on the basis of cooperating with all groups with a progressive point of view. This has meant that none of the radical groups have completely trusted us."[30]

Whether they fully trusted each other or not, the war had made radicals and conservatives work together for victory, but the alliance vanished in peacetime. The chill of the Cold War muted all dissent, and southern radicals, like men and women everywhere who had been touched by socialism in the thirties, found themselves exiled to points so far removed from mainstream political life that their continued activity, and their defiance of McCarthyism, went almost unnoticed. The vacuum created by their departure was filled by the resurgence of liberalism, led in the region by the Southern Regional Council. It was a progressivism shorn of any economic critique and absolutely unmarked by the radical protest of the past decade.

The council grew, in 1943, from the roots of the Commission on Interracial Cooperation. Its impetus came from Jessie Daniel Ames, head of the commission's Association of Southern Women for the Prevention of Lynching; its first president was also the final president of the commission, the sociologist Howard Odum, whose interests lay in scientific regional planning rather than political or religious crusading. The resolution that launched the council made no mention of redistributing the wealth or of segregation, though it did state that "the Negro in the United States and in every region is entitled to and should have every guarantee of equal opportunity that every other citizen of the United States has." Lillian Smith, and a few others who were invited, refused to join for this reason, and remained apart even after the council pledged itself in 1951 to work toward a day when "segregation will be recognized as a cruel and needless penalty on the human spirit."[31]

Nevertheless the council, standing though it did for gradual

Rosa Parks (left), her mother (right), and Septima Clark
(center) at Highlander Folk School, Christmas 1956
(*Highlander Research and Education Center*)

change, set the tone well into the 1950s for the progressive white southerner's position on race. It was a tone determined by the organization's desire to be practical and effective in a region overcome by a new wave of resistance to change of any sort. The experience of southern radicals who had immediate encounters with that fearsome resistance suggests that the path of the council may have been the only course on which survival was possible.

X Revolution Denied

In June 1938 Congress established the Special House Committee for the Investigation of Un-American Activities. Its chairman was Martin Dies of Texas, and its other original members were Arthur D. Healey of Massachusetts, John J. Dempsey of New Mexico, Joe Starnes of Alabama, Harold G. Mosier of Ohio, Noah M. Mason of Illinois, and J. Parnell Thomas of New Jersey. Its purpose was to investigate the clandestine or subversive activities of Communists and Nazis in the United States.

The first witness before this committee was John C. Metcalfe, who had information to give concerning the existence of a pro-Nazi underground. His appearance marked virtually the last time the committee heard evidence about the activities of fascist organizations. What fascinated it the most, and what it would dwell upon for the next thirty years, was naming Communists and people who sympathized with Communists and exposing activities having any possible link to the Communist party in the United States or anywhere in the world. The principal method of HUAC was to grant immunity to men and women who had had some connection to the Communist party in exchange for their testimony about their past associations.

The second witness to appear, John P. Frey of the American Federation of Labor, set the pace for those who followed by citing nearly every leader and union in the Congress for Industrial Organization as Communist. Two of the thousands of organizations and individuals he listed were the National Religion and Labor Foundation, headed by Willard Uphaus, and

226

Don West. He said that the latter was "formerly in charge of Atlanta, Ga., for Communist Party. . . . He sneaked out of Atlanta on a truck, under a load of gunnysacks, when Assistant Solicitor General Huston swore out warrants for his arrest. After a short period of time in New York City, he was sent to Kentucky and there made organizer." Frey missed the fact that West had worked in Burlington, North Carolina, as Jim Weaver.[1]

J. B. Matthews was the most credible witness to appear during this first round of hearings because he had been involved in many pacifist and leftist organizations and had been a leader of several "united fronts." He was so impressive on the stand, and so free with criticism of Communists he had known, that Dies hired him to be HUAC's chief investigator, a position he held until 1944 when he departed to amass a private set of files on suspected Communists and become a lecturer and consultant on the subject to business and government.

Though Dies made spectacular headlines with these early hearings, the sense of national unity invoked by the war forced HUAC into the background. After the Axis defeat, however, the United States resumed its tense confrontation with the Soviet Union, and in this climate of anxiety and suspicion HUAC flourished.

The Southern Conference for Human Welfare was the first organization in the South to come in for any serious attention by the Dies Committee. In June 1947 HUAC reported that the Southern Conference existed not to promote human welfare but solely to further the aims of the Communist party. This attack was a mortal blow to the Southern Conference. Alva Taylor, who described himself as "an ardent New Dealer," had served as treasurer of the Southern Conference since 1941, and he protested defiantly to the editor of the Nashville *Tennessean* that "we have never paid any attention to those who mouth the red-phobia, moronic yawp of 'Communist'; their Peglerian poison is falsehood beneath the contempt of progressives." But he was forced to confess to his friend Albert Barnett a year later that the "Communist front" label had cost the Southern Conference half of its membership and put the organization into debt. In November 1948 the remaining executives, Clark Foreman, Dombrowski, Horton, and Virginia Durr, quietly dissolved the Southern Conference for Human Welfare in a little ceremony in Virginia near Thomas Jefferson's home, Monticello.[2]

Dombrowski continued to direct the former conference's tax-exempt arm, the Southern Conference Educational Fund (SCEF). Because SCEF publicly denounced de jure segregation and had such obvious links to men and women labeled as subversives, it received little foundation or union support and was relegated to the sidelines of the civil rights struggle. The fact that it continued to function at all, however, was used by white supremacist politicians as the basis for the charge that the civil rights movement was Communist dominated.

Similar distortions of truth were made possible by exaggerating the influence of Claude Williams. He took part in a 1947 World Fellowship trip to Yugoslavia along with William Melish and Gus Emery Shipler, editor of *The Churchman*, and with them he stated that religious groups were not being persecuted in this Soviet-bloc country. Boston's Archbishop Cushing labeled their publication "infamous and monstrous." In 1948 HUAC released its own report entitled "100 Things You Should Know about Communism and Religion," which tagged Williams and his People's Institute of Applied Religion as "one of the most vicious Communist organizations ever set up in this country. . . . It teaches Communist ideas, pretending that they are Christian ideas."[3]

The United States attorney general also cited the People's Institute as both subversive and Communist in letters to the Loyalty Review Board sent in June and September 1948. And the evangelist Carl McIntire published a six-page leaflet on his Christian Beacon Press bearing the title *Communist Minister, Claude C. Williams, Detroit Presbytery, Presbyterian Church, U.S.A., Questions Existence of Christ: Openly Espouses Communism, and Uses Church to Promote It*. His organization thus become useless baggage, Williams formally interred the People's Institute in a ceremony at St. Paul's Chapel in Brooklyn on July 20, 1948.[4]

The Alabaman Clifford Durr refused reappointment to the Federal Communications Commission in 1948 because he did not want to implement the loyalty investigations ordered for every federal employee by President Truman. He had also come under attack from J. Edgar Hoover for his defense of blacklisted radio commentators and because his wife, Virginia, was a local chairwoman of Henry Wallace's campaign for the presidency on the ticket of the Progressive party. Joseph Gelders, who had risen to the rank of master sergeant as an electronics instructor during the war, also was tracked down by antisubversives and forced to resign his assistant professorship at Davis, California, because he would not sign a loyalty oath. He died soon afterwards, partly as a result of the lingering injuries he had suffered at the hands of Birmingham company detectives in 1936.[5]

An event which received far more public attention than the disruption of these people's careers was the Smith Act trial of 1947 that resulted in the conviction of eleven Communist party leaders, including Benjamin Davis, who had represented Angelo Herndon fifteen years before. The Smith Act, passed in 1940, had made it a crime "to knowingly or willfully advocate, abet, advise, or teach the duty, necessity, desirability, or propriety of overthrowing any government in the United States by force and violence." The result of this prosecution was to make it effectively illegal, at least in the minds of most Americans, to be a member of the Communist party.

Don West, who had withdrawn from almost all political activity by war's end, was fired from the Oglethorpe faculty in 1948 by President Philip Weltner. This was in response to pressures applied by Atlanta editor Ralph McGill, who attacked West personally and Communists generally in his newspaper column, and by a north Georgia right-winger who claimed he had been maligned by one of West's poems. What brought the matter to a head was West's defense, at a public meeting in Macon, of a black woman named Rosa Lee Ingram who had been sentenced to die, along with her two sons, for shooting a white man she claimed had tried to rape her. In the following year Paul Crouch, a former Communist organizer in North Carolina, testified before the House Un-American Activities Committee that West had been a party member during the Burlington Ten trials. Crouch also identified West's sister, whom he had known as "Jeanette Weaver," as a correspondent for the *Daily Worker*.[6]

The meaning of the term *Communist* was by then so flexible that it could even be applied to the Fellowship of Southern Churchmen. After the Kesters' departure for Penn School, the FSC was run by Nelle Morton, a busy campus organizer. She had been born in 1905 in a Sullivan County, Tennessee, lumber camp later buried beneath South Holston Lake and educated at Flora MacDonald College in North Carolina and the Biblical Seminary in New York. She became active in the Fellowship of Socialist Christians and, later, when she joined the staff of the Presbyterian Committee on Publications in Richmond, discovered the Fellowship of Southern Churchmen. Without its support, she said, she would have left the church, where her views on race, peace, and economics were generally unpopular.[7]

The headquarters of the FSC moved to the basement of the Presbyterian church in Chapel Hill, North Carolina. Its pastor, and the FSC chairman, was the Reverend Charles M. Jones, a Tennessean and former Du Pont millworker. The office was moved later to a downtown building in order "to

230

make a greater witness in the public domain of an interracial and an interclass nature." It became a meeting place for ministers and teachers such as Warren Ashby, Neal Hughley, and J. C. Herrin and for college activists like Zan Harper, Charles McCoy, Elizabeth Taylor, Douglas Hunt, and Allard Lowenstein.[8]

Thirteen interracial college chapters were organized across the South under Morton's direction; one of these integrated the Duke University Chapel on the occasion of a speech by Reinhold Niebuhr. Their job was to protest anti-Semitic and Klan activity, and the work was financed by regular contributions from the Anti-Defamation League. Morton also operated an interracial children's camp at her father's farm in Tennessee, and the FSC sponsored work camps for black, white, Arab, and Asian students at Big Lick, at Koinonia Farm in Georgia, and in several other industrial and rural settings.[9]

One of these was held in the summer of 1947 in Columbia, North Carolina, to build a headquarters for a cannery and credit union in the black community. Among the ten students were two blacks and a Syrian. Though they kept to themselves on the farm of a black high school principal, their project was abruptly terminated. A Charlotte paper reported: "An interracial church group living in the home of a Negro in defiance of segregation customs was ordered out of Tyrell County . . . by a group of more than 300 white people who called on them and gave them 24 hours to leave town." The mob dispersed after delivering its ultimatum, and the sheriff rounded the students up from the fields where they had hidden and put them on a bus out of town. Asked to comment by the press, Morton said succinctly that "segregation is a sin and as we begin living as Christians, segregation lines will dissolve."[10]

Another student project conducted in cooperation with the Georgia Workers Education Service met a similar end. The students held a party at the GWES office in downtown Atlanta. Trying to be discreet, they entered the building one at a time and tightly shuttered the windows. But city policemen were watching the place, and, just as one of the students, Hibbard Thatcher, began to demonstrate a square dance, the lawmen broke in. They arrested the entire group for violating Atlanta's comprehensive segregation codes, which specifically prohibited interracial dancing, and hauled them to the police station. The young people were fined and released, but the press took such an interest in the case that the work camp was canceled. The project's supervisor protested that "we are merely a group who believe that if a man is a Christian or a churchman, his denomination or race doesn't matter." But such was the climate of fear that the counselor felt the need to add in the next breath: "But we certainly don't like what has been going on in Moscow."[11]

The Chapel Hill group cooperated with the Fellowship of Reconciliation and the Congress of Racial Equality in planning an interracial bus trip through the South designed to test the 1946 Supreme Court ruling that outlawed segregated seating on interstate buses and trains. The sixteen white and black participants on this "journey of reconciliation" split into teams and rode south from Washington, D.C., in April 1947. Their swing took them through Virginia, North Carolina, Tennessee, and Kentucky, and members were arrested in both Petersburg and Durham. Four demonstrators, Andrew Johnson, Bayard Rustin, Igal Roodenko, and Joseph Felmut, were arrested at the depot in Chapel Hill, and a fifth, James Peck, was beaten. Charles Jones bailed the men out and hid them in his home. But a mob followed, and a police escort was necessary to get the demonstrators safely out of town.

For their crime in Chapel Hill the four protestors served thirty days on prison road gangs. Rustin wrote a pamphlet about his experiences at the colored road camp in Roxboro in which he told of men being strung up by their wrists for three

232 days at a time while others were kept in solitary for weeks. The treatment of Rustin and the other demonstrators was less harsh than that of the common prisoner, however, because the FSC recruited students to walk beside the men on the chain gang and provide them with personal necessities. Charles Jones came under investigation by the state synod of the Presbyterian church in 1953 for his part in the bus demonstration plus the fact that he ran an integrated church. He was eventually removed from the pulpit "for the welfare of the church."[12]

Even Frank Graham, who had been appointed to the United States Senate to fill the vacancy caused by the death of J. Melville Broughton, was toppled in 1950. He was the last proponent of racial tolerance that the South would send to the Senate for nearly two decades. Graham stood for reelection in the May Democratic primary and missed winning a majority by less than a percentage point. In the runoff he faced Willis Smith, past president of the American Bar Association and chairman of the board of Duke University. Finding that he could not undermine Graham's popularity among middle-of-the-roaders, Smith dove to the right. His forces heaped abuse on Graham as a "nigger lover" and "communist," and thousands of leaflets were distributed claiming that the senator's reelection would put Negroes in the same schools, jobs, and beds as whites. Smith called Graham a socialist and alleged that he had been a member of five "communist front groups": the International Labor Defense, the American Committee for the Protection of the Foreign Born, the China Aid Council, the Medical Bureau of the North American Committee to Aid Spanish Democracy, and the Committee to Free Earl Browder. The first and last charges were patently false though Graham had once signed a petition urging Browder's release from prison shortly before President Roosevelt ordered the Communist leader freed in a pitch for national unity. Graham admitted a minor role in the other

three organizations, but his participation had ended long before any were put on the attorney general's list of subversive
groups.

In the June runoff Graham was defeated by 18,000 votes.
He left the Senate without apparent bitterness. In his farewell speech he said: "Through faith in God and love of man,
the light of liberty will, we trust, yet shine through the iron
curtain of men's minds. The warmth of human brotherhood
will yet melt away the iron curtain of men's hearts. The
peoples with their hope of freedom and peace still . . . look
up in prayer to the God of us all for one free and federated
world neighborhood of human brotherhood."[13]

By and large, the targets of both HUAC and its Senate
counterpart, the Internal Security Subcommittee, during the
early 1950s and Korean War years were suspected Communists in government or the army. They shared the arena with
Joseph McCarthy, who launched his senatorial career by wav-
ing a list purporting to contain the names of 204 Communists
in the State Department (yet who, by the time he was cen-
sored by the Senate in 1954, had failed to present evidence
leading to anyone's conviction for subversion). His chief investigator, J. B. Matthews, took on the church by writing in
the *American Mercury* that he could name 7,000 clergymen
who had been "infected by the social gospel" and were therefore supporters of the aims of Communism. He singled out
Harry F. Ward, Willard Uphaus, and three other ministers as
"top pro-Soviet propagandists" in the church. So unsupported
was this charge that Senator McCarthy was persuaded to obtain Matthews's resignation.[14]

In 1954, however, Communism in the South became a primary focus of Congress. The censure of Senator McCarthy
had then discredited the hunt for Communist government
officials, and in this year the final push to end legal segregation was launched by the Supreme Court's decision in *Brown
v. Topeka Board of Education* outlawing dual public school

234

systems. The decision forced the issue and unleashed a vitri-
olic campaign of resistance to desegregation and the expan-
sion of the rights of blacks such as had not been seen in the
region since Reconstruction.

A patriotic veneer was given to white resistance by influential politicians who charged that the growing civil rights agitation was Communist inspired. Their evidence related for
the most part to men, women, and organizations who had
reached the peak of their influence before the war. Memories
of Southern Tenant Farmers' Union organizers, other leftist
agitators, and Eleanor Roosevelt's criticism of southern man-
ners were still fresh in the minds of many whites, and southern leaders like Senator James O. Eastland played upon
them, created the myth that radicals had equivalent influence
in the 1950s, and embellished this with the notion that a
mixed bag of socialists, New Dealers, and Christian dissenters was under the influence of a central conspiring force.

The first major set of hearings on "Subversive Influences"
in the South took place in New Orleans in March 1954 under
the auspices of the Senate Internal Security Subcommittee.
Eastland presided at the sessions; in fact, he was the only
senator there. He was uniquely suited to the task of flailing
opponents of white supremacy. Son of a prominent Delta
planter, he had been named for an uncle who had been murdered by an unfaithful servant. His father had led the posse
that had captured the fleeing slayer and his wife and burned
both of them at the stake. Eastland's senatorial career was
built on his complete intransigence on the race issue.[15]

The New Orleans hearings were billed as an investigation
of the Southern Conference Educational Fund, successor to
the Southern Conference for Human Welfare. If the aim was
to embarrass the greatest number of southern liberals, SCEF
was a good target because the Southern Conference had already been cited as Communist by HUAC, and thousands of
people had been associated with it. SCEF, directed by James

Dombrowski, was headquartered in New Orleans, but it had been reduced to a small committee and a staff of two. Its most influential activity was publishing the *Southern Patriot*.

Eastland began from the premise that "the Southern Conference for Human Welfare was conceived, financed, and set up by the Communist Party in 1938 as a mass organization to promote communism throughout the Southern states." The dominant role of New Dealers in the Southern Conference was entirely overlooked. To substantiate his charge, Eastland called his chief investigator, Paul Crouch, to the stand. Crouch had been a witness at numerous hearings, and he was known to *Reader's Digest* buyers as one of America's foremost ex-Communists. His testimony was that at different times between 1925 and 1942 he had been in charge of Communist party activity in the armed forces and in the states of Florida, Utah, North Carolina, South Carolina, and Tennessee. He went on that he, Joseph Gelders, and the Communist district organizer in Birmingham, Robert Hall, had planned the Southern Conference in 1938 and that the Communist party had contributed several thousand dollars to the organization.[16]

Dombrowski was called to the stand, and he angered Eastland by refusing to produce a list of SCEF's financial contributors because, he argued, the committee's subpoena did not require it. Eastland thought otherwise and threatened to find Dombrowski in contempt, but nothing came of this. Eastland then asked the question most relevant to these proceedings: "are you now or have you even been" a member of the Communist party?

Dombrowski answered with an "emphatic no," and he continued: "in giving you the answer to a question involving my political beliefs I wish to state that I do not believe that any committee of Congress has the right to inquire into my political beliefs, and this is a very humiliating experience to me and I am doing this again for the reason . . . that I wanted to be faithful to the stewardship of people who have supported this corporation who might misunderstand the failure to do so."

After further testimony that Alton Lawrence had once, in Crouch's hearing, referred to Dombrowski as a Communist and that Crouch had heard him sing the "Internationale," the government counsel quizzed Dombrowski about whether, in his view, a Communist was just a man with certain beliefs or a part of a conspiracy. His response was: "Mr. Chairman, I will be very happy to discuss my thoughts with you about communism at the appropriate time, but I didn't come here to discuss that." Of course, communism was precisely the topic Dombrowski had been subpoenaed to discuss, but all of his answers were so graceful and uninformative that Eastland seemed almost relieved when he stepped down from the witness chair.

Dombrowski begged pardon, for example, when he corrected Special Counsel Richard Aren's reference to Modjeska Simkins, SCEF vice-president, as a "he." When asked why he permitted his name to appear with those of 279 other people on an amnesty petition for the Smith Act defendants, Dombrowski replied that he had forgotten the occasion, but "if I decided to sign it, they were in very good company." When Eastland wanted to know what, if any, groups Dombrowski belonged to that were not on the attorney general's list of subversive organizations, the witness replied: "Senator, I could have answered that a lot easier a few years ago, but lately—let's see," and he then proceeded to list the Sigma Chi fraternity, which he had helped to found, the American Legion (he had served eighteen months in the Air Force), the National Council on Religion and Higher Education, and the Methodist church. "Mr. Chairman, as you can see you haven't had very many witnesses like me," Dombrowski said. "I am willing to answer everything and answer truthfully." After more than two hours Eastland dismissed him.[17]

Virginia Durr was Eastland's next witness. The subcommittee wanted to use her to discredit her husband, Clifford Durr, who since being forced off the FCC in 1948 had been chairman of the National Lawyers' Guild and counsel for the National Farmers' Union. The Durrs had been living in Wetumpka, Alabama, where Clifford practiced law. Mrs. Durr's lawyer objected that the subcommittee was on a "fishing expedition" and said his client would not have "her brain probed by an instrumentality of the Government." On his advice Durr refused to answer any question except to give her name, her husband's name, and to state that she had never been a member of the Communist party.

Unable to proceed directly, Eastland brought Paul Crouch back to the stand to testify about his "acquaintanceship" with Virginia Durr. Crouch alleged that she had contributed an article to the Communist press, and he stated that during the war her Washington, D.C., home had been a meeting place "for the people connected with top Soviet espionage and infiltration of the United States Government." She had knowingly supported Communist cell groups, Crouch claimed, including those run by Joseph Gelders, the Reverend Malcolm Dobbs, Howard Lee, Joseph Lash, and Gilbert Parks, and she had used her influence with the Roosevelt White House to further Communist aims. Neither her brother-in-law, Hugo Black, nor the First Lady had realized that these people were "Red agents," Crouch testified, "but Mrs. Durr had full knowledge of the work." At this, Clifford Durr charged from the back of the room screaming, "You dirty dog, I'll kill you for lying about my wife!" As a marshal rushed forward to restrain him, Durr collapsed from a weak heart and was rolled from the chamber in a wheelchair. Virginia was cited for contempt but released without further interrogation.[18]

After this hectic episode the subcommittee heard from Aubrey Williams, then publisher of a mass-circulation advertising sheet called *Southern Farm and Home,* who declared that

Billboard in Nashville depicting Martin Luther King at
Highlander Folk School's 25th anniversary celebration, 1957
(*Dale Ernsberger, in the Nashville* TENNESSEAN)

Superbird.
Buick Skylark Gran Sport.

OZIER

he had never been a Communist. Alva Taylor had also been subpoenaed, but a flare-up of arteriosclerosis had prevented the eighty-three-year-old minister from leaving Nashville.

On the third and last day of this set of hearings Myles Horton, represented by Clifford Durr, was called before the subcommittee. Highlander was now being troubled constantly by the communism issue, and this had already seriously undermined its relations with organized labor. When the CIO expelled ten "Communist-dominated" unions in 1949, including Donald Henderson's Food, Tobacco and Allied Union, it also asked certain groups which it had endorsed to issue a condemnation of Communism. Highlander Folk School was one of these groups, and when a CIO Rubber Workers meeting was scheduled there in 1949, the school was ordered to declare its politics. But the Highlander executive council refused to pass a "negative" political statement condemning the left, insisting rather that it would retain its "positive" policy embracing all democratic organizations. Not satisfied, the CIO severed its relations with the school. [19]

Thus robbed of most of its union students, Highlander became for a time "the educational and organizing center" for the Farmers' Union in Tennessee and began trying to expand its relations with the new crop of black leaders emerging in the South. In the summer of 1953 Highlander held its first workshop on implementing the anticipated Supreme Court ruling on school desegregation, and the following year it chartered a Community Leadership Project on Johns Island, South Carolina, run by Septima Clark, a black schoolteacher. [20]

Seated before Senator Eastland, Horton described the program of Highlander Folk School as "educating rural and industrial leaders for democratic living and activity." The senator asked if James Dombrowski had ever been associated with the school, and Horton tried to make a statement giving his reasons for declining to answer the question. Eastland refused to hear it; the exchange between the two men became heated, and Horton was taken from the room by United States marshals. As he was pushed out the door, he cried, "You're just putting on a show here—that's all." The statement Horton had tried to read contained the declaration that "Communism has never tempted me because I believe in Democracy, a powerful concept worthy of mankind the world over—You know, if you have made any effort to find out, that I have never been a member of the Communist Party."[21]

The subcommittee's report concluded that SCEF was a Communist-front group, and the government moved directly against two SCEF organizers, Carl and Anne Braden, in the summer of 1954. Carl Braden was a reporter for the Louisville *Courier Journal*. He had purchased a home in one of Louisville's white neighborhoods as the front man for a black family; when the couple tried to take possession, the house was bombed. The Bradens, a Spanish Civil War veteran named Vernon Brown, and four other people were subsequently charged with plotting the overthrow of the government under Kentucky's version of the Smith Act. The state was aided in the case by HUAC, which provided several ex-Communist witnesses including Benjamin Gitlow, Leonard Patterson, Manning Johnson, and Matthew Cvetic. Only Vernon Brown and Carl Braden, who swore that he was not a Communist, were convicted. Braden got fifteen years and was placed under a $40,000 bond pending his appeal. He was held in solitary for six weeks and in jail for seven months before his friends could raise the bail money.

The Bradens then became the field organizers for SCEF and moved its headquarters to Louisville. The convictions of Braden and Brown were vacated in 1957 when the United States Supreme Court refused to overrule a decision rendered in Pennsylvania that state sedition laws, like the one under which the "Louisville Seven" were tried in Kentucky, had been superseded by the Smith Act.[22]

242 The government was intent on the suppression of religious radicals as well. Illinois Congressman Harold H. Velde, a successor of Martin Dies as the chairman of HUAC, was one of those who led the vendetta against Claude Williams, depicting him as a Communist masquerading as a Christian and prompting the Detroit Presbytery to try the Alabama-based pastor for heresy. At issue were Williams's belief in God and the Trinity, the meaning of his published statement that "Protestant Church religion came into being to enhance the rise of capitalism," and his links to the Communist party. The presbytery asked for specific information on these matters, and Williams's response was to charge it with operating under the orders of the "McCarthy gestapo." He affirmed his belief in the Trinity, the Virgin Birth, and salvation in Jesus, and, as for being a Communist, he wrote: "Whatever work I have done with persons who may have been members of the Communist Party, whatever convictions I have held which might have paralleled positions held by Communists, I have done this work and reached these convictions on the basis of the clear teachings of the Scriptures of the Old and New Testaments which set forth the most righteous rule of faith and practice, if correctly interpreted."

Far from satisfied, and under pressure to demonstrate its anti-Communism, the Detroit Presbytery initiated proceedings to "unfrock" Williams on January 4, 1954. Five ministers and four laymen made up the court, and it found him guilty, not of Communism, but of heresy. Williams's appeals were exhausted by December, and he was then stripped of his ordination in the Presbyterian Church, U.S.A. Worn as he was by the ordeal, he could still write to Alva Taylor: "Well laugh with me about how 'serious' my brethren take themselves— But the time of this death will pass; though deepening, is passing—even in, by and because of such deepening."[23]

The "time of this death" was deep indeed in Mississippi. The first White Citizens' Council was organized there in 1955 to preserve segregation by intimidating liberal whites and frightening blacks. In cotton-rich Holmes County the second White Citizens' Council was formed, and it made investigating Providence Farm its first order of business. Besides the farming operation, Providence included a cooperative grocery, a credit union, a purchasing cooperative, a supplemental school for black children, and a medical clinic. Years before at Rochdale Farm the co-op had paid a teacher $37.50 a month to teach local black children at the end of the four-month term provided by the state. When the corporation moved to Holmes County, which had an eight-month school term for blacks, it continued to supplement the local educational program by running a summer camp.

The medical clinic was first established by a nurse, Dorothy May Fischer, and acquired its first doctor in 1938 when David R. Minter, the son of a Presbyterian missionary, came to the farm fresh from his hospital residency. In the four years before he went to war, Minter ran a general practice and syphilis treatment center at Rochdale. When his tour of duty as MacArthur's chief malaria control officer ended, Minter returned to Providence and opened his clinic in a renovated dairy barn. He charged his patients, mostly blacks, whatever they could afford, and he treated some fifteen thousand people during his career there.[24]

On Tuesday, September 27, 1955, the Holmes County White Citizens' Council called a public meeting in the Tchula High School auditorium to discuss what was going on at Providence Farm. About six hundred people were there. Though a number of local residents had long been suspicious of the farm, a real "investigation" did not begin until the sheriff picked up two black teenagers near Tchula and charged them with making obscene remarks to a white girl at a school bus stop. One of the boys got six months at the county farm for this crime. Under the questioning of police officers the youngsters told of "mixed swimming parties" at the Providence plantation. What they referred to were occasions when the children of Minter and the manager, A. Eugene Cox, swam in the creek with black playmates, but the boys' statements seemed more incriminating when the sheriff's tape recording was played to the crowd.

State Representative J. Y. Love, the leader of the Tchula White Citizens' Council, and County Attorney Pat Barrett, who headed the chapter in nearby Lexington, chaired the meeting. Love wanted to find out if racial agitation were going on at Providence that might lead to "another Till killing." He was referring to the murder of fourteen-year-old Emmett Till in LeFlore County for which two whites had been acquitted three days before.

Both Cox and Minter bravely made an appearance at the high school to defend themselves and their work and to deny that they had permitted interracial swimming, were violating any segregation laws, or were teaching Communism. Cox even produced a letter he had solicited from HUAC stating that Providence Farm appeared on no list of subversive organizations. The sixty-year-old pastor of the First Presbyterian Church in nearby Durant, the Reverend Marsh Calloway, also spoke eloquently in their defense from the point of view of one who had once been a member of the Ku Klux Klan. This performance cost Calloway his pulpit a week later when his congregation asked him to resign because they had lost confidence in him. The questions Cox and Minter failed to answer to the crowd's satisfaction were, "Why would a doctor stick himself away in such an obscure place," and "How can the people . . . on the place live when they only put a few acres in pasture, and grow no cotton or soy beans?" By a voice vote, the citizens passed a resolution "inviting" the Cox and Minter families to leave Holmes County. "We just can't afford to have them up there teaching what they are teaching . . . ," said State Representative Edwin White, "which will lead to violence unless it is stopped."

While the local newspaper, edited by the outspoken Hazel Brannon Smith, begged for a "sober second thought," and the *Delta Democrat Times*, published in Greenville by Hodding Carter, Jr., called the citizens' ultimatum "as un-American as any bestial idea that ever came out from behind the Iron Curtain," the voices of moderation were without influence in Mississippi in 1955. Before long the dirt road leading up to Providence was blockaded by policemen and other watchful whites who interrogated anyone coming or going. Tradespeople stopped doing business with the farm, and threats mounted against the lives of the Coxes and Minters. In spite of the pressure the families made it until summertime, when the children finished school, but then David and Sue Minter packed their household goods and the clinic equipment and moved to Arizona. In August, with the credit union and other cooperative businesses shut down, Gene and Lindsey Hail Cox left, too, and moved just across the state line to a Memphis suburb known, ironically, as Whitehaven. It was the safety of his family he was worried about, said Cox, who for nine months had maintained a lonely nighttime vigil, armed and watchful, outside his farmhouse; "If I'd been a Roman Catholic priest I could have stuck it out."[25]

Two months later Cox was hired by the National Council of Churches as director of rural development programs. A handful of white and black families remained on the land that was Providence Farm, but the cooperative begun as a sanctuary for evicted sharecroppers amidst dreams of Christian and racial brotherhood was gone from Mississippi for good. It was but one of the many victims of the fierce reaction sweeping the South. As the doors of the cooperative grocery and clinic were being locked for the last time, Don West was being hounded from yet another Georgia town.

Not long after being fired from Oglethorpe, West had befriended the Reverend Charles Pratt, a Church of God of the Union Assembly minister in north Georgia. Pratt was well into his seventies, but as a younger man he had been a Harlan County coal miner, and in 1948 he had been co-chairman in Georgia of the Progressive party. In the thirty-five churches Pratt supervised in Georgia, Tennessee, and Kentucky there was hellfire and brimstone preaching, speaking in tongues, and an insistence that poor people had the responsibility to join or start a union. In 1954 Pratt invited West to move to the mountain city of Dalton, Georgia, and edit his church newspaper, *The Southerner*.

The Church of God of the Union Assembly was particularly strong among the chenille mill workers in Dalton. Determined to thwart union organizing in their plants, the Lawtex Corporation and the Belcraft Company circulated questionnaires among their employees asking them what church they belonged to. Lawtex then fired twenty-eight workers who professed to be members of the Church of God, and Belcraft discharged twenty-three. Since both of the plant managers were Jews, West had friends in the Brooklyn, New York, B'nai B'rith investigate the situation and send a letter of protest to their Dalton members. This, however, had no visible effect upon company policy.

Organizers from the Textile Workers Union (CIO) were summoned, and the workers struck the Lawtex plant after five union members were fired in September. "Effective picketing," in West's words, discouraged strikebreakers from entering the mill and caused its owner, who lived in Cambridge, Massachusetts, to ask Governor Marvin Griffin to call out the state patrol. Griffin did, and the strike was broken by troopers and the court injunctions prohibiting more than a token force on the picket line.

At the same time West was subpoenaed to appear before a Dalton grand jury that wanted to know if he was a Communist. He refused to waive his right to "take the Fifth," and such pressure was brought to bear upon the church and the union on this account that West resigned from the newspaper and left Dalton. As he was driving down Fort Mountain on his way out of town, a car tried to force him off the road. Thrusting the Reverend Mr. Pratt's .38 Smith out the window, West shot out one of the other vehicle's tires and drove on without being molested further.[26]

Convinced that he could no longer work for political or union causes without jeopardizing his friends, West retired to his family farm in Douglasville, Georgia, to grow vegetables and become a regular vendor at the state farmers' market in Atlanta. He was plowing by the river when a United States marshal walked across his field and subpoenaed him to appear in Memphis on October 28, 1957, to testify before the Senate Internal Security Subcommittee.

These hearings, conducted by Senator William E. Jenner of Indiana, were staged primarily to give Kentucky Commonwealth Attorney Scott Hamilton an opportunity to rehash the case made, but ultimately lost in the courts, against Carl Braden and SCEF. West's appearance was just a sideshow. As in the past he took the position that the government had no right to know his politics, but to friends he explained that he professed the "primitive communism" of the Christian Apostles. They "had all things in common; and they sold their possessions and goods and distributed them to all, as had any need."[27]

When asked if he had once been in charge of the Communist party in Atlanta, West replied: "Sir, I would like to say at the beginning that on any questions relative to my past political associations or affiliations, or religious beliefs or political, I will have to respectfully claim the rights of the fifth amendment of our Constitution. I might say further that I am not a member of any political organization. I am only working on the matter of running a farm, trying to make a living thereby."[28] No more could be got out of him, and the chief counsel satisfied himself by inserting in the record several documents dating back to 1938 in which West was identified as a Communist by HUAC, by Paul Crouch, and by a new agency established by the state of Georgia to fight integration, the Georgia Commission on Education.

Another round of hearings on these same topics was held in Atlanta in July 1958 by the House Un-American Activities Committee, under the chairmanship of Representative Francis E. Walter of Pennsylvania. This time West was subpoenaed while tending his wife, Constance, in a Kentucky hospital where she was recovering from an automobile accident. West made the required appearance, but the federal prosecutors did not call him to the stand. They did, however, accept testimony from a witness against him, an FBI man who said he had been an undercover agent in the Communist party. He testified that West had recruited two Harvard students, both of them known in Cambridge as Communists, to help in the Dalton strike. It was part of the Communist scheme to send "colonizers" to the South, said the agent.[29]

After hearing this unsubstantiated testimony, the government proceeded with its main business: a no-holds-barred battle with Carl Braden and Frank Wilkinson of the Emergency Civil Liberties Committee. The purpose of this committee was to defend those accused of subversion and to lobby against HUAC and similar agencies. It had been founded after the American Civil Liberties Union refused to intervene in the defense of Ethel and Julius Rosenberg, charged as Soviet spies, and though Communists gratefully accepted its support, there were prominent non-Communists in its leadership like I. F. Stone, Clark Foreman, and Albert Einstein. The attorney general had more than once cited it as a subversive organization, and HUAC was out to squelch it.

The confrontation with Braden and Wilkinson did not take long. Each man refused to cooperate, in his own way, and suffered the consequences. When asked if he was a member of the Communist party, Braden based his refusal to answer on the First Amendment's guarantee of freedom of speech.

He did not invoke the Fifth Amendment's protection against self-incrimination. Wilkinson simply stated, fifteen times, "I am refusing to answer any questions of this committee," and he, too, never "took the Fifth." Walter ruled that neither man had exercised his constitutional right to remain silent, and he found them both in contempt. For their intransigence both Braden and Wilkinson were sent to prison for a year.[30]

Willard Uphaus, Claude Williams's faithful benefactor, also faced prison at this time. He had been a constant critic of United States policy toward Russia and of the FBI's domestic spying. HUAC summoned him in 1956. Uphaus testified that he had never been a member of the Communist party but instead was a Christian. He refused, however, to obey a court order to turn over the names of people who had attended workshops at the World Fellowship Center, a camp he ran on Lake Conway in New Hampshire, and he was sentenced to one year in jail for contempt. The conviction was finally upheld by the United States Supreme Court, and Uphaus was escorted into the Merrimac County jail early in 1960. He celebrated his seventieth birthday there in November.[31]

J. B. Matthews also brought his campaign south in 1958. In testimony before the Florida Legislative Investigation Committee he presented information purporting to document extensive Communist infiltration of the NAACP. He went on to say that "Communists or communist influence were directly involved in every major race incident in the past four years since the Supreme Court 'legislation' on the subject of integration." These statements were published by the State of Georgia's intelligence-gathering agency, the Commission on Education, and they were quoted in newspapers and Citizens' Council meetings across the South.[32]

One of the great triumphs of anti-Communists in the South was their successful pursuit of the Highlander Folk School. More than most of those whose politics had developed in the 1930s, Myles Horton had remained an important figure in the civil rights movement. He accommodated himself well to the new black leadership, as was indicated by his comment in 1957 that "any white person who advises that Negroes share their leadership with white people is either naive or a compromiser. The Negroes must furnish their own leadership and the role of white people is to strengthen that leadership rather than to share it with them on an equal basis. . . . After having had twenty-five years experience I don't waste any time on an assumption which I would like to be able to make, that I'm not considered different. . . . I am satisfied to do my share indirectly. Maybe not satisfied, but I know that's the score."[33]

Highlander's main points of contact with the black movement of the 1950s were its Citizenship Education Program and its annual workshops dealing with desegregation. The Citizenship Education Program, designed to teach black people the fundamentals of American government, operated throughout the South Carolina sea islands after 1954 under the direction of Septima Clark. Songster Guy Carawan joined the project in 1959 and helped more than any other to spread the powerful anthem "We Shall Overcome." Martin Luther King, Jr.'s Southern Christian Leadership Conference finally absorbed this program and opened its own citizenship training center in McIntosh County, Georgia.[34]

One of those who attended Highlander's school desegregation workshops was Mrs. Rosa Parks of Montgomery, who came in 1955. Virginia Durr, a friend of hers, wrote to Horton that "when she came back she was so happy and felt so liberated and then as time went on she said the discrimination got worse and worse to bear *after* having, for the first time in her life, been free at Highlander." On December 1, 1955, Parks refused to move to the back of the bus and set off the historic Montgomery bus boycott. She discovered that the price of being a heroine was high, however; she lost her job as a seamstress, and her rent was raised. Virginia Durr and other

friends supported her for over a year, but Parks finally had to
move to Detroit.[35]

These activities kept Highlander in the eye of the government agencies. In February 1957 the school was notified by
the Internal Revenue Service that its tax exemption was
being revoked because it had engaged in "organized action
programs," a slap applauded by Senator Eastland. Later that
year white supremacists scored a major coup when the Georgia Education Commission planted a spy at Highlander's
twenty-fifth anniversary celebration held on Labor Day. His
report and photographs gave the civil rights movement one
of its greatest embarrassments.[36]

It was a public gathering, and Edwin Friend, posing as a
reporter but acting under orders from Governor Griffin, was
freely admitted. He mingled with the crowd, took copious
notes, and snapped pictures of whites and blacks eating,
dancing, and talking together. The most famous of his photographs captured Martin Luther King, Jr., seated near a
known Communist party member, Abner Berry. An enlarged
version was pasted to billboards all across the South over the
caption: "Martin Luther King at the Communist Training
School." The taxpayers of Georgia financed the publication of
vast numbers of glossy brochures containing Friend's report.
Called *Highlander Folk School—Communist Training School,
Monteagle, Tenn.*, the report began: "During Labor Day
Weekend, 1957, there assembled at Highlander the leaders
of every major race incident in the South." Besides King, its
list included Don West, Bayard Rustin, Rosa Parks, Fred
Routh from the Southern Regional Council, Conrad Browne
from Koinonia, and Pete Seeger.

One of the reasons Governor Griffin took an interest in
Highlander was that he wished to discredit the Atlanta-based
Southern Regional Council. Its director, George Mitchell, sat
on the Highlander board of directors. Griffin used the occasion of his exposure of Highlander to exclaim, "The leader-

ship of few units of the Communist apparatus have records of Communist affiliations which exceeded those of present and past directors of Southern Regional Council." There was no factual basis for this statement, but it made sense to large numbers of southerners who now thought that "integrationist" and "Communist" were two names for the same creature. SRC represented the moderate liberal community, and it was a rare individual who had fewer connections to the Communist party than did its officers. For easy reference Griffin printed the names of SRC's original incorporators: Atlanta editor Ralph McGill, Atlanta University President Rufus E. Clement, Methodist Bishop of Atlanta Arthur J. Moore, Fisk sociologist Charles S. Johnson, and University of North Carolina sociologist Howard W. Odum.[37]

The attorney general of Arkansas, Bruce Bennett, joined the hunt next. He was already a well-known figure for his strenuous legal efforts to prevent the desegregation of Little Rock's Central High, and when he addressed the Tennessee General Assembly in 1959 to ask it to investigate Highlander, he was treated with all the pomp due a visiting celebrity. The legislature appointed three of its own, aided by Bennett and Edwin Friend, to hold hearings in Tracy City and Nashville concerning the school. Their report recommended that Highlander be closed due to imperfections in the wording of its charter and certain alleged financial irregularities. Under the direction of Circuit Prosecutor A. F. Sloan, state agents raided Highlander on July 31, 1959, and confiscated the school's files and a small quantity of beer and liquor in Horton's home. On charges of illegally selling alcohol and other "immoral, lewd and unchaste practices," Sloan ordered the school shut down though Horton explained that the staff merely maintained a common kitty to which each person who wanted beer contributed.

The case came to trial in November 1959 in Altamont, Tennessee. Highlander's attorney, Cecil Branstetter, conducted an eloquent defense and paraded before the jury a distinguished array of educators who attested to the character and quality of the staff and the program. But the court's ruling was that Highlander had peddled beer and whiskey without a license, had been operated for Horton's personal gain, and had practiced integration in violation of Tennessee law. After two years of fruitless appeals, the entire property of Highlander, its furnishings, beds, office equipment, library, eight residences, fourteen school buildings, and 175 acres of land were auctioned off by the state for slightly more than $50,000. The old house originally donated to Horton and West by Lillian Johnson went with the rest, but it burned down mysteriously before new tenants could move in. No compensation was ever given to Highlander or to Myles Horton, whose private home had been one of the buildings confiscated. What Senator Eastland had first tried to accomplish in 1956 was now a fact: Highlander had been closed.[38]

It is ironic that the last workshop held at the school, in April 1961, had the optimistic theme, "New Frontiers for College Students." Far from hearing the revolutionary message imagined by those who had hounded the school out of existence, the ninety-three participants were told by Nashville sit-in leader C. T. Vivian that they must involve conservatives in the movement and bring a "spiritual force" to bear upon the champions of segregation. Tuskegee sociologist Lewis Jones admonished them to beware of alienating white liberals and the black middle class by becoming too militant. The leader of this group of students was also judged a moderate in comparison to other activists of that period; he was the Reverend Andrew Young of the National Council of Churches.[39]

The most vital strain of southern radicalism in the 1930s had been the rebellion of sharecroppers and farm workers. But this protest, in its organized form, either vanished in the fifties and sixties, was absorbed into the broad movement for

Bruce Bennett, attorney general of Arkansas, explains the
southern "conspiracy," with Highlander Folk School at the

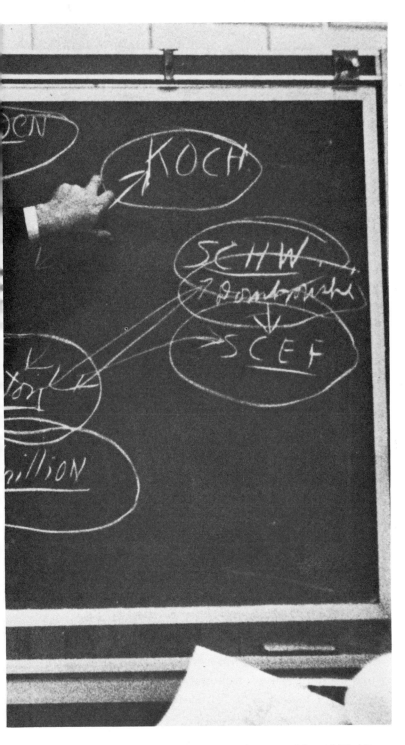

center, to the Tennessee General Assembly, 1959 (*Joe Rudis, in the Nashville* TENNESSEAN)

voting rights and legal equality, or was channeled into more acceptable forms by government-supported antipoverty agencies. When the Southern Tenant Farmers' Union, re-named the National Farm Labor Union (AFL), moved to California, in 1948 to conduct a strike at DiGiorgio Farms near Bakersfield, that marked the end of the agricultural union movement in the Deep South. The growers of the San Joaquin Valley fought just as hard as the planters of Arkansas, and they even persuaded the House Education and Labor Subcommittee to issue a report, written by Representative Richard M. Nixon, exonerating their labor practices. When the Hollywood Film Council made a movie about the strike called *Poverty in the Land of Plenty*, DiGiorgio successfully brought a $2 million libel suit against the union to quash the film.

Future strikes in California led by Hank Hasiwar and Er-nesto Galarza met with greater success. Cesar Chavez re-ceived his first taste of the labor movement in an NFLU cot-ton pickers' strike in 1949. H. L. Mitchell returned to the South as an Amalgamated Meat Cutters organizer in 1960 after his union merged with the butchers. From Lake Charles, Louisiana, he helped to organize the menhaden fish-ermen, known as "pogy boatmen," and to document the squalid living conditions on Louisiana's sugarcane plantations. Though southern plantations were still inhabited by poorly paid, educated, and housed workers, there were few fresh attempts to rekindle the union spirit of the 1930s. One of the reasons, of course, was the history of failure. But another was that there was no longer a Socialist party or a coherent pro-gressive community willing to underwrite the cost of pressing the one demand that had traditionally rallied southern farm workers: "land for the landless."[40]

The same evaporation of support caused the demise of the Fellowship of Southern Churchmen, the last organizational expression of the radical gospel idea in the region. Howard

Kester had resumed his post as FSC secretary in 1952, after a stint as the principal of the John C. Campbell Folk School in North Carolina. During his absence the FSC had continued to press the causes of organized labor, racial equality, and rural improvement under the supervision of Nelle Morton, Charles Jones, David Burgess, and Eugene Smathers. Upon his return he reaffirmed the old principles: Christians would preside at the funeral of "dead imperialism and a waning capitalism"; they must resist "ruthless Soviet imperialism and tyranny"; and they should strive for the ultimate justice of "a simple brotherhood of all men and all nations."[41] As a practical matter, however, the FSC of the 1950s conceived its purpose to be convincing the established church to promote the peaceful desegregation of southern society. Other aims were advanced by FSC members in their own communities, but the organization's focus narrowed to race and the church.

In casting aside the broader revolutionary message it had professed in the 1930s, the FSC lost much of its reason for existing. The major civil rights confrontations were taking place at the lunch counters of Greensboro and on the streets of Nashville, and converting the church on race seemed increasingly irrelevant. Also, there was little in the notion of racial brotherhood that could not finally be endorsed by more established religious bodies, and the numerous denominational social action committees that sprang up in response to the civil rights movement assumed the role that the FSC had played in lending support to ministers persecuted for standing against segregation. The FSC, therefore, passed quietly from view in 1963.

By subordinating all goals to that of black emancipation, the Fellowship of Southern Churchmen was merely following the course taken by southern progressivism in general in the decades between the end of the Second World War and the passage of the Voting Rights Act of 1965. In part this process owed to the overriding wish of black southerners to eliminate the immediate barriers to their progress. But it owed also to the government's successful campaign to equate the advocacy of socialist ideas with high treason. In effect, the Cold War and the pressures of agencies like HUAC forced the issues of economic equality and racial equality to become separate and pushed the civil rights struggle in a direction that posed no challenge to the vital elements of the American economic system.

The fact that whites and blacks shared unequally the fruits of that system remained, of course, a concern of movement leaders. Martin Luther King, Jr., made that point in an address he gave to the final large gathering of the Fellowship of Southern Churchmen just as he was beginning to rise to national prominence. "I never intend to adjust myself," he said, "to the tragic inequalities of an economic system which takes necessities from the many to give luxuries to the few."[42]

Yet rarely did King, or any other leader of the emerging black movement, call capitalism his enemy. Their struggle altered the fundamental characteristic of southern society, the second-class citizenship of blacks, but it set aside for consideration by future generations many of the historic demands of southern dissenters: "land for the landless," "full and decent employment," a halt to the invasion of carpetbag industry, the holding in common of "all natural resources and all scientific processes," and "the liberation of all workers from enslavement to the machine."[43]

Epilogue

A great many of the organizations and people discussed in these pages outlived the period studied in this volume. Some of the transitions should be mentioned.

Don West continues to preach in Holiness churches in West Virginia, and Willard Uphaus leads an interdenominational parish in Florida. Ward Rodgers has retired after twenty years' labor as an airplane machinist in California. Nelle Morton has become a noted figure in the movement for a women's theology. Eugene Smathers was elected moderator of the Presbyterian Church, U.S.A., in 1967. Eugene Cox performs volunteer duties in Memphis hospitals, and Sam Franklin directs the social action committee of his local church in Maryville, Tennessee. The Southern Conference Educational Fund still exists, though without James Dombrowski. He remains active in an organization known as the Southern Organizing Committee. Charles Jones has had a park in Chapel Hill, North Carolina, named for him. Virginia Durr continues to campaign against the death penalty in Alabama. Myles Horton leads tours of students and educators to China. The Highlander Folk School was reorganized as the Highlander Research and Educational Center. Alice Kester died in 1970. Howard Kester followed in 1977. His memorial service in Black Mountain, North Carolina, was conducted by H. L. Mitchell, who, still a socialist, retired from the labor movement in 1972, and by the Reverend Will D. Campbell, director of the Committee of Southern Churchmen, successor to the FSC. Claude Williams, after some years of living alone in a house trailer in Fungo Hollow, Alabama, died in

260   1979. At a memorial service held for him it was said: "We mourn the passage of the most insurrectionary and prophetic missionary ever born in the Southland."

Bibliographical Note

Notes

Index

Bibliographical Note

Most valuable in a rich field of resources available to students of southern protest in the 1930s are the Howard Kester Papers, a remarkable collection touching a score of important organizations and a hundred scenes of conflict, accumulated by a man who evidently never threw a letter away. Ranging from the most intimate correspondence between husband and wife to countless mimeographed "minutes" of meetings, these documents portray in a rare and lively way the changing South from the collapse of prosperity in the 1920s to the civil rights struggle of the 1950s. Kester impressed his habit of hoarding paper upon the office staff of the Southern Tenant Farmers' Union, and as a result the papers of the STFU trace in ample detail three decades of heated campaigns in Arkansas, California, and Louisiana, and nearly another decade of repose and retirement. Both of these collections have been carefully catalogued and are preserved in the Southern Historical Collection at the University of North Carolina, Chapel Hill. They are available to a larger audience in microfilmed editions placed at numerous colleges and universities, and, for the convenience of film readers who wish to examine a particular point I have made, references to these collections are identified by the microfilm reel on which the documents appear.

Other collections of documents have helped immeasurably to fill out the picture. The Fellowship of Southern Churchmen Papers color portions of the canvass. They are also located in the Southern Historical Collection, as are the Delta and Providence Farm Papers. In the North Carolina Collection at Chapel Hill is the Harriet Laura Clipping Collection, which contains newspaper fragments on diverse topics such as the "Burlington Dynamite Plot" and the CIO southern drives. The papers of a most important man, Alva Wilmot Taylor, reside almost unnoticed at the Disciples of Christ Historical

Society in Nashville. In the same city, at the State Archives, are some of the papers of the Highlander Folk School. The more complete and better organized Highlander Collection is at the State Historical Society of Wisconsin, Madison. Additional documents are on file in the archives of the Highlander Research and Educational Center in Newmarket, Tennessee. Other collections that might have given great service to the historian, the papers of Don West and Claude Williams, were lost to fires that destroyed the libraries of both men in the early 1970s.

It was my good fortune to be able to test the written evidence against the recollections and interpretations of many of the main subjects of this narrative. I was the guest of Howard Kester at his home in Black Mountain, North Carolina, on several occasions. Reading the freshly typed draft of his unpublished manuscript, "Radical Prophets, A History of the Fellowship of Southern Churchmen," originally set me to writing this book. Myles Horton, H. L. Mitchell, Don West, and Kester all consented to speak for the tape recorder whenever asked, and they each agreed to read early versions of this manuscript with an eye to preventing errors of fact, such as names, places, and dates. They have disagreed with me on several matters of interpretation, and therefore can in no way be held responsible for the final product. Benjamin Mays, Roy Wilkins, Michael Smathers, Claude Williams, Eugene Cox, Sam Franklin, Will Campbell, Hibbard Thatcher, Charles Jones, Marion and Euphemia Gordon Young, Robert Metcalfe, Dagnall F. Folger, and Nelle Morton all graciously permitted me to interview them as this book was being written. I have also made free use of interviews conducted by others, particularly H. L. Mitchell's sessions with Clay East, Ward Rodgers, Clyde Johnson, and Booker Clark, William Finger's interview with Myles Horton, and Charles H. Martin's interview with Don West.

The labors of others have added much to this history. Donald Grubbs broke ground with his examination of the politics of agriculture, *Cry from the Cotton: The Southern Tenant Farmers' Union and the New Deal* (Chapel Hill, N.C., 1971). Thomas A. Krueger's *And Promises to Keep: The Southern Conference for Human Welfare, 1938–1948* (Nashville, 1967) is the basic reference for that or-

ganization, and Highlander's rocky road has been skillfully described by Frank Adams (with Myles Horton) in *Unearthing Seeds*
of Fire: The Idea of Highlander (Winston-Salem, N.C., 1975).
H. L. Mitchell published his own autobiography in 1979; *Mean
Things Happening in This Land: The Life and Times of H.L. Mitch-
ell* (Montclair, N.J., 1979). A personal view of a fascinating institu-
tion is provided by Raymond and Charlotte Koch in *Educational
Commune: The Story of Commonwealth College* (New York, 1972).
All historians of the South must also acknowledge a debt to George
B. Tindall, *The Emergence of the New South, 1913–1945* (Baton
Rouge, La., 1967).

The following abbreviations are used in the notes:

AWT Papers	The Alva Wilmot Taylor Papers (Disciples of Christ Historical Society, Nashville)
Field Foundation Files	The files and archives of The Field Foundation (New York City)
FSC Papers	Fellowship of Southern Churchmen Papers (Southern Historical Collection, UNC, Chapel Hill)
Highlander Papers	Highlander Research and Education Center Papers, 1917–1973 (Social Action Collection of the State Historical Society of Wisconsin, Madison)
Highlander Papers (Tennessee Archives)	Highlander Folk School Collection (Tennessee State Archives, Nashville)
HK Papers	The Howard Anderson Kester Papers (Southern Historical Collection, UNC, Chapel Hill)
HREC Archives	Papers in the archives of the Highlander Research and Education Center, Newmarket, Tenn.
STFU Papers	Southern Tenant Farmers' Union Papers, 1934–1970 (Southern Historical Collection, UNC, Chapel Hill)
STFU Scrapbook	STFU Scrapbook and Newspaper Clippings, 1924–1973 (Southern Historical Collection, UNC, Chapel Hill)

Notes

Chapter I: The First Encounter: Wilder

1. Albert Barnett, "Trouble in the Tennessee Coal Fields," Dec. 4, 1932, Howard Kester, "A Brief Account of the Wilder Strike," Aug. 1, 1933, "Annual Report of Howard Kester, Southern Secretary, Annual Conference of the Fellowship of Reconciliation, October 1933," all in HK Papers, reel 1; Nashville *Tennessean*, May 5, 1933.

2. Livingston (Tenn.) *Enterprise*, Nov. 25, 1932; Nashville *Tennessean*, Nov. 18, 1932, "State Officials Probe Wilder Bombing."

3. Nashville *Tennessean*, Nov. 17, 1932, "Wilder Miners Go to Court Today in Fight for Homes," Nov. 16, 1932, "Fentress Miners Ask Court Change in Eviction Cases," Nov. 20, 1932, "Troops Reach Wilder to Preserve Peace As Guard Reports Ambush Firing," Nov. 22, 1932, "Additional Men on Way to Wilder to Guard Tracks," Nov. 24, 1932, "Strikers Dynamite Second Trestle," Nov. 25, 1932, "Violence Calls More Troops to Wilder," Nov. 27, 1932, "Fearing Trouble at Powerhouses, Guards Increased," and Nov. 26, 1932, "Wilder Strikers Called to Attend a Secret Session."

4. Barnett, "Trouble in the Tennessee Coals Fields," Dec. 4, 1932, and Jones to Albert Barnett, Dec. 12, 1932, both in HK Papers, reel 1.

5. Horton interview, Oct. 31, 1976; *Chattanooga Times*, Nov. 26, 1932, "State Police Hold Suspect at Wilder," and Nov. 27, 1932, "Boyd Releases Horton after Arrest at Mines."

6. *Knoxville News-Sentinel*, Nov. 28, 1932, "Teacher Tells Church of Arrest at Wilder"; *Evening Tennessean* (Nashville), Dec. 1, 1932, "Communications" to the editor; Don West to Howard Kester, Feb. 15, 1933, HK Papers, reel 1; *Chattanooga Times*, Nov. 27, 1932, "Boyd Releases Horton after Arrest at Mines."

7. Nashville *Tennessean*, Dec. 22, 1932, "Last of Troops Withdraw Today from Wilder Area," Dec. 31, 1932, "Mine Guard Shot from Ambush,"

Jan. 4, 1933, "Governor Erred in Withdrawing Troops," and Jan. 6, 1933, "Troops Ordered Back to Wilder Mine Strike Area."

8. Barnett, "Trouble in the Tennessee Coal Fields," Dec. 4, 1932, HK Papers, reel 1.

9. "Report of Wilder Emergency Relief Committee," Dec. 1932, ibid.; Howard Kester, "Radical Prophets: A History of the Fellowship of Southern Churchmen" (manuscript dated 1974; hereafter cited as "Radical Prophets"), p. 7, in the author's possession, available on microfilm in the collection "The Green Rising, 1910–1977: A Supplement to the Southern Tenant Farmers Union Papers," Southern Historical Collection, UNC, Chapel Hill.

10. Kester, "A Brief Account of the Wilder Strike," Aug. 1, 1933, HK Papers, reel 1.

11. "Annual Report of Howard Kester, October 1933," ibid.; Alva W. Taylor to James Myers and William Spofford, May 18, 1933, Taylor to Jerome Davis, March 18, 1933, AWT Papers, box 2, folders 8 and 7. Also see Stanley Lincoln Harbison, "The Social Gospel Career of Alva Wilmot Taylor" (Ph.D. diss., Vanderbilt University, 1975), hereafter cited as Harbison, "Taylor."

12. "Radical Prophets," p. 8; Howard Kester to the author, Sept. 17, 1976; Kester, "A Brief Account of the Wilder Strike," Aug. 1, 1933, HK Papers, reel 1; *Labor Advocate* (Nashville), Feb. 23, 1933, "Final Report of the Wilder Emergency Relief Committee."

13. Thomas to Myles Horton, Feb. 7, 1933, Highlander Papers, box 27, folder 24; Howard Kester to Horton, Feb. 22, 1933, HREC Archives, "Wilder-Kester Letters" folder; "Annual Report of Howard Kester, October 1933," HK Papers, reel 1.

14. The miners who claimed Graham's body said his skull had been smashed; the broken handle of a pistol was found nearby. A functional handgun lay beside Graham's hand, but the miner who found it, Tom Hall, said it was not Graham's and that the safety was still on. Half an hour after the slaying, a company watchman was fired upon, and the next morning nonunion workers were marched into the mines under heavy guard. See *Evening Tennessean* (Nashville), May 2, 1933; Nashville *Banner*, May 1, 1933; and Nashville *Tennessean*, May 1, 1933. See also Fran Ansley and Brenda Bell, "Strikes at Davidson and Wilder," *Southern Exposure* 1 (1974): 113–34.

15. "Radical Prophets," p. 10.

16. Myles Horton to Alva Wilmot Taylor, undated, James Myers to Roger Baldwin, May 9, 1933, AWT Papers, boxes 3 and 4.

17. "Radical Prophets," pp. 9–10; *Labor Advocate* (Nashville), May 4, 1933, "Barney Graham Killed Last Sunday"; *Livingston* (Tenn.) *Enter-*

prise, May 5, 1933, "Green Indicted as Slayer of Wilder Union Head." In regard to the prosecution of Green, Kester wrote: "Turnblazer did every damn thing he could to get out of helping in the case at all as my correspondence with him will show. My correspondence with him in regard to this matter would be a fitting chapter in the UMWA's attempt to break militant strikes" (Howard Kester to Myles Horton, Oct. 2, 1933, HREC Archives, "Wilder-Kester Letters" folder).

18. *Livingston* (Tenn.) *Enterprise*, May 19, 1933, "Wilder Feuds Flare Anew in 3 Ambushings," and June 2, 1933, "Ten Held at Jamestown in Wilder Killing."

19. Eleanor Kellogg to Alva W. Taylor, June 1, 1933, and Kellogg to "Dearest Folks," June 28, 1933, HK Papers, reel 1; Margaret S. Lehman to Taylor, April 2 and May 16, 1934, AWT Papers, box 4; Fran Ansley and Sue Thrasher, "The Ballad of Barney Graham" (an interview with Barney Graham, Jr.), *Southern Exposure* 4 (1976): 136–42.

20. Horton interview, Oct. 31, 1976.

21. Frank Adams (with Myles Horton), *Unearthing Seeds of Fire: The Idea of Highlander* (Winston-Salem, N.C., 1975), p. 34; "Radical Prophets," p. 10–11; interview with Dagnall F. Folger, July 16, 1979.

Chapter II: The Early Days

1. Clues to the Kester family origins may be found in a clipping from *The Tablet* (Millville, Pa.), Sept. 14, 1904, included in the STFU Scrapbook, reel 2, "Howard Kester Clippings and Articles, 1904–1972." See also John Stark Bellamy, "If Christ Came to Dixie: The Southern Prophetic Vision of Howard Anderson Kester, 1904–1941" (M.A. thesis, University of Virginia, 1977), pp. 1–23. The baptism story is contained in a letter from Kester to the author, May 1966.

2. Kester interview, July 27 and 28, 1976; Howard Kester to the author, May 1976.

3. See Bellamy, "If Christ Came to Dixie," pp. 24–37 for more of Kester's experiences at Lynchburg College. Kester inscribed his 1923 college annual, *The Argonaut* (found among his personal effects), "Buck Shot."

4. Kester frequently acknowledged the impact this European tour had upon him. It "helped to change my whole view toward Negro-white relations" he wrote in March 1976, in a letter to the author. In the Kester interview of April 26, 1976, he expressed his debt to Channing Tobias and William Craver for opening his eyes to the parallels between the treatment of Jews in Europe and Negroes in the United States, and in "Radical Prophets," pp. 20, 86–88, he provided more details about

his first attempts to organize interracial student groups. The leader of the European tour, Ray Legatte, prepared a lengthy travelogue, drawn from participants' diaries, in the spring of 1949, and a copy of this manuscript, entitled "The American Student Friendship Pilgrimage to Europe (YMCA)," was found among Kester's personal papers.

Kester's first preaching assignment was to the Southern Presbyterian church in Grassy Meadows, West Virginia, in the summer of 1922. His opening sermon, "If a Man Die Shall He Live Again," may be found under Sermons, HK Papers, reel 11. He discussed his experiences at Thurmond in the Kester interview of April 26, 1976.

5. *The Critograph*, 10, no. 7, "Peace Issue," (Nov. 8, 1924), HK Papers, "Writings 1924–1957, Articles," reel 11. The editors' only mistake was to underestimate the horrors of the world war to come. They wrote: "The last war was a war of tanks, machine-guns and submarines, the next war will be a war of aeroplanes loaded with gas shells. We shudder at the picture this statement conjures up: a picture of radio-controlled airships, like phantom angels of death, floating silently above sleeping cities, raining upon men, women and children poison gas so powerful that a single drop will produce instant death or loosing disease germs sufficient to contaminate whole nations."

6. A statement made at the memorial service held for Kester at Blue Ridge Assembly.

7. *The Argonaut* (Lynchburg College, Va., 1925).

8. Among the liberal student Y members were Virgil Lowder, Francis Henson, Edward King, Ada Belch, Karl Zerfoss, Kyle Smith, Arthur Moore, and Paul Deering (Kester, "Radical Prophets," pp. 21–21A; Bellamy, "If Christ Came to Dixie," p. 59).

9. The story of Carver's visit to Blue Ridge is related in "Radical Prophets," pp. 21–23, and in the Kester interview of April 27, 1976.

10. Mays to Alice Kester, June 10, 1930, HK Papers, reel 1.

11. Carver liked to refer to Kester as one of his "Lynchburg Boys," his favorites among the group that hosted him at Blue Ridge. Several of these students visited Tuskegee at one time or another; Kester, himself, made a point of visiting the school whenever he was nearby up until the pioneer agronomist's death in 1943. Carver seemed to have no particular fondness for the women of Lynchburg, however. He told Kester there were three things he disliked: bluejays, because they were robbers, Negro bishops, because they were hypocrites, and women, because they annoyed him. See Kester interview, April 27, 1976.

12. Howard Kester to Alice Harris, July 7, 1926, HK Papers, reel 1.

13. "Radical Prophets," p. 88; Kester interview, April 27, 1976; Bellamy, "If Christ Came to Dixie," p. 47.

14. The industrial secretary of the Nashville YWCA was Elizabeth Jones. She and Dagnall F. Folger later married.

15. Nashville *Evening Tennessean*, March 30, 1927, "Students Rap U.S. Policy in China." See also Nashville *Tennessean*, March 30, 1927, "Group of Students Here Attacks U.S. Policies in China."

16. Kester interview, April 27, 1976.

17. Howard Kester to Alice Kester, Nov. 30, 1928, HK Papers, reel 1.

18. Same to same, Nov. 6, 1928, ibid.

19. Howard Kester to John Stark Bellamy, Nov. 21, 1975, cited in Bellamy, "If Christ Came to Dixie," p. 79; interview with Kester by Jess Gilbert and Steve Brown, Aug. 8, 1976, unpublished.

20. Taylor, article in *Missionary Intelligencer*, March 1914, located in AWT Papers, box 11, "Printed Articles and Reports 1912–1929."

21. Taylor to——, 1932–33, AWT Papers, box 2, folder 5; Taylor, "Obstacles to Progress," in *Social Progress and Christian Ideals*, ed. William P. King (Nashville, 1931), p. 191.

22. Harbison, "Taylor," pp. 234–35.

23. West interview, May 30, 1977.

24. Don West, "Knott County, Kentucky: A Study" (B.D. thesis, Vanderbilt School of Religion, 1932), pp. 81, 56. See also Jesse Stuart, *To Teach, to Love* (Baltimore, 1973), pp. 85, 141–42.

25. Ward Hotchkiss Rodgers, "The Religion of Nationalism" (B.D. thesis, Vanderbilt School of Religion, 1932), p. 101. See also interview with Rodgers by H. L. Mitchell, April 30, 1976, H. L. Mitchell's personal papers.

26. Cedric Belfrage, *South of God* (New York, 1941), pp. 66–83. This, and the enlarged version, *A Faith to Free the People* (New York, 1944), is an extremely sympathetic biography of Claude C. Williams. I interviewed Williams at his home in Pelham, Ala., on Aug. 17 and 18, 1976, but Williams did not permit the sessions to be tape-recorded.

27. Kester interview, July 28, 1976; Williams to "Committee of Four," May 1934, HK Papers, reel 1.

28. Howard Kester, "A Study of Negro Ministers in Nashville" (B.D. thesis, Vanderbilt School of Religion, 1931); "Radical Prophets," pp. 55–56; "Minutes of the Council Meeting of the Fellowship of Reconciliation, March 14, 1931," and promotional leaflet announcing the Paine College retreat, April 27, 1931, HK Papers, reel 1.

29. Howard Kester to "Dear Friend," Aug. 15, 1931, HK Papers, reel 1.

30. Howard Kester to Alice Kester, Aug. 24, 1931, and to Walter White,

Sept. 5, 1931, ibid.; "Radical Prophets," p. 89; Nashville *Tennesseean*, April 19, 1931, "Mob Crashes Jail, Hangs Negro from Courtyard Tree."

31. "Radical Prophets," p. 84. Also see Paul E. Baker, *Negro-White Adjustment: An Interpretation and Analysis of Methods in the Interracial Movement in the United States* (New York, 1934), pp. 166–69.

32. Alva W. Taylor, *Christianity and Industry in America* (New York, 1933), p. xi.

33. Howard Kester to Alice Kester, Oct. 13, 1931, HK Papers, reel 1; Howard Kester, "The Interracial Situation," ibid., "Other Reports 1932–38," reel 11.

34. Quoted in W. A. Swanberg, *Norman Thomas: The Last Idealist* (New York, 1976), p. 136.

35. Nashville *Tennessean*, April 6, 1932, "For Congress Howard Kester."

36. Nashville *Evening Tennessean*, Nov. 8, 1932, "Final Davidson Vote."

37. Harry F. Ward, *Our Economic Morality and the Ethic of Jesus* (New York, 1929), p. 30.

38. Horton interview, Aug. 5, 1977. The claim that Joshua Haughton received the first land grant in what later became Tennessee is substantiated by *Goodspeed's General History of Tennessee* (Nashville, 1973; first published in 1887), p. 125. A good biography of Myles Horton and history of Highlander Folk School is provided by Frank Adams (with Myles Horton), *Unearthing Seeds of Fire: The Idea of Highlander* (Winston-Salem, 1975).

39. Horton interview, Aug. 5, 1977.

40. Horton was in the habit of recording some of his impressions on notecards. A few of these, which shed light on his youthful intellectual development, can be found in the Highlander Research and Education Center Archives. The dates on the cards were added by Horton in 1979. The two cards quoted here are both dated "UTS 1929."

41. "Horton Note Cards," dated "UTS 1929" and "1931 Denmark," HREC Archives. Horton discussed his graduate education and voyage to Denmark in Horton interviews, Oct. 31, 1976, and Aug. 5, 1977.

42. Niebuhr to ——, May 27, 1932, Highlander Papers, box 22, folder 1. Also see Roger N. Baldwin to Myles Horton, June 6, 1933, ibid., box 6, folder 4.

43. Lillian W. Johnson to "My dear Friends," Jan. 20, 1917, ibid., box 16, folder 18.

44. George B. Tindall, *The Emergence of the New South, 1913–1945* (Baton Rouge, La., 1967), p. 633.

45. Lillian Johnson to Myles Horton, Dec. 8, 1932, and to the editor of

the Chattanooga *Times*, Dec. 8, 1932, Highlander Papers, box 16, folder 18.

Chapter III: From Social Gospel to Radicalism

1. Kester, "A Brief Account of the Wilder Strike," Aug. 1, 1933, HK Papers, reel 1.

2. Howard Kester to Alice Kester, Oct. 2, 1933, and "Statements of U.S. Congress Against War," Oct. 1, 1933, ibid.

3. Others who took part in this investigation were Nat Ross, Alfred M. Hirsch, Jessica Henderson, Bruce Crawford, Hollace Ransdell, Barbara Alexander, and Grace Lumpkin. Arthur Raper also wrote a report of the affair entitled *The Plight of Tuscaloosa: A Case Study of Conditions in Tuscaloosa County, Alabama, 1933*, published by the Southern Commission on the Study of Lynching in Atlanta, an offshoot of the Commission on Interracial Cooperation. See also *Daily Worker*, Nov. 13, 1933; Kester interview, July 27, 1976; Howard Kester to Tess Sinovich, July 21, 1934, HK Papers, reel 1; and Kester to Myles Horton, March 27, 28, and April 10, 1933, HREC Archives, "Wilder-Kester Letters" folder.

4. Howard Kester to Alice Kester, Nov. 11, 1933, HK Papers, reel 1.

5. "Annual Report of Howard Kester, October 1933," ibid.

6. The FOR questionnaire is quoted by Donald B. Meyer, *The Protestant Search for Political Realism, 1919–1941* (Berkeley, Calif., 1961), pp. 205–6. See also *New York Times*, Dec. 19, 1933; Nevin Sayre to Alice Kester, Jan. 16, 1934, and J. B. Matthews to "Dear Friend," Jan. 1934, HK Papers, reel 1.

7. Don West and Clyde Johnson to "Dear Friend," [probably Dec. 1933], Highlander Papers, box 29, folder 21.

8. West to Rev. W. T. Scott, Dec. 29, 1939, Don West's personal papers.

9. West interview, May 30, 1977; interview with Clyde Johnson by H. L. Mitchell (with Charles H. Martin and Bob Dinwiddie), April 4, 1976, H. L. Mitchell's personal papers; Willis Sutton to West, Feb. 13 and Aug. 13, 1979, West's personal papers.

10. *New Republic* 76 (Oct. 4, 1933), p. 216.

11. West to Myles Horton, Dec. 16, 1933, Highlander Papers, box 29, folder 21; Taylor to Paul ——, Oct. 16, 1933, AWT Papers, box 2, folder 10; George Wessling and "Teacher" to *New Republic*, Oct. 31 and Nov. 1, 1933, West's personal papers.

12. Don West to Myles Horton, Feb. 24, 1936, Highlander Papers, box 29, folder 21.

13. Angelo Herndon, *Let Me Live* (New York, 1969; first published in 1937); *Daily Worker*, May 13, 1933, "Negro Bishops Back I.L.D. Fight."

14. West interview, May 30, 1977; interview with Don West by Charles H. Martin, Sept. 13, 1970, in Martin's personal papers.

15. "Liebovitz Shirt Factory Strike," Highlander Papers, box 63, folder 9.

16. Horton to Alva W. Taylor, July 15, 1933, ibid., box 27, folder 16; Aimee L. Horton, "The Highlander Folk School: A History of the Development of Its Major Programs Related to Social Movements in the South, 1932–1961" (Ph.D. diss., University of Chicago, 1971), p. 109.

17. Interview with James Dombrowski, Nov. 8, 1976; "Invitation to Conference of Younger Churchmen of the South," April 30, 1934, HK Papers, reel 1.

18. "Radical Prophets," p. 17.

19. "Findings: Conference of Younger Churchmen of the South, Monteagle, Tennessee, May 27–29, 1934," HK Papers, reel 1.

20. The Revolutionary Policy Committee, *An Appeal to the Membership of the Socialist Party*, April 1934, ibid., reel 14.

21. Howard Kester to Alice Kester, March 5, 1934, Francis A. Henson to Stuart Nelson, Oct. 18, 1934, list of those invited to Shaw Conference, October 26, 1934, Kester to Francis Henson, July 21, 1935, ibid., reel 1.

22. Kester to Elisabeth Gilman, Feb. 12, 1934, to Alice Kester, June 7, 1934, to Tess Sinovich, July 21, 1934, ibid.

23. Howard Kester, "I See America," ibid., "Writings 1924–1957—Poetry," and "We Have Come to the End of an Era," ibid., "Writings 1924–1957—Speeches," both on reel 11. See also Elisabeth Gilman to Kester, Sept. 20, 1934, "A Resume of the Chief Activities of Howard Kester, Secretary of the Committee on Economic and Racial Justice, March 1934–October 1934," and Kester to Katherine Gardner, Nov. 26, 1934, ibid., reel 1.

24. Belfrage, *South of God*, pp. 80, 86–100.

25. Ibid., pp. 115–21.

26. Robert J. Havigurst, "Introduction" to Raymond and Charlotte Koch, *Educational Commune: The Story of Commonwealth College* (New York, 1972), p. 3.

27. Belfrage, *South of God*, pp. 126–27; Bill Murrah, "Llano Cooperative Colony, Louisiana," *Southern Exposure* 1 (Winter 1974): 88–104; William Edward Zeuch, "Notes on Commonwealth College," available at the State Historical Society of Wisconsin.

28. Belfrage, *South of God*, p. 174; Kester to Norman Thomas, Oct. 30,

1934, Uphaus to Kester, May 8, 1935, and Uphaus to "Dear Friend," May 7, 1935, HK Papers, reel 1.

29. Claude Williams to Howard, Alice, and Nancy Kester, May 1934 and Jan. 15, 1935, HK Papers, reel 1.

30. Interview with Ward Rodgers by H. L. Mitchell, April 30, 1976, p. 3, H. L. Mitchell's personal papers.

31. Ward H. Rodgers, Joyce King Williams, Claude C. Williams, "A Fellow and Conference," Aug. 13, 1934, HK Papers, reel 1.

32. Belfrage, *South of God*, pp. 220–27; Mitchell interview, Aug. 16, 1976.

33. Henson to Howard Kester, Feb. 23, 1935, John Herling to Kester, Feb. 25, 1935, HK Papers, reel 1; Robert Moats Miller, *American Protestantism and Social Issues, 1919–1939* (Chapel Hill, N.C., 1958), pp. 101–2; Uphaus to Kester, Nov. 10, 1935, HK Papers, reel 2.

34. Kester to Williams, Nov. 18, 1934, Uphaus to Kester, Jan. 30, 1935, HK Papers, reel 1; Belfrage, *South of God*, pp. 216–17.

35. Belfrage, *South of God*, pp. 234–42; Mitchell interview, Aug. 16, 1976.

36. HK Papers, reel 1.

37. "Report from Second Annual Conference of Younger Churchmen by Eugene W. Sutherland, Chairman," Dec. 6, 1934, Kester's invitations to Louise McLaren, James Myers, Norman Thomas, Julius Mark, and J. Raymond Henderson, Oct.-Nov., 1934, and "Tentative Program of the Conference on Religion and the Struggle for Social Justice," Oct. 29, 1934, ibid., reel 1; James Dombrowski to Niebuhr, Dec. 8, 1934, Highlander Papers, box 22, folder 1; undated Chattanooga newspaper clipping describing the conference (at Dec. 1934), STFU Scrapbook, "Howard Kester Clippings and Articles, 1904–1972," reel 2; Kester, "Radical Prophets," pp. 26–29.

38. The most comprehensive and graphic account of the Neal lynching is contained in Howard Kester's report, *The Lynching of Claude Neal*, issued by the NAACP on Nov. 30, 1934 (HK Papers, "Writings 1924–1957, Lynchings," reel 11);. See also *Daily Times-Courier* (Marianna, Fla.), Oct. 25 and 27, 1934, and *The Floridian* (Jackson County, Fla.), Oct. 26, 1934, STFU Scrapbook, "Howard Kester Clippings and Articles, 1904–1972," reel 2.

39. Quoted in Kester, *The Lynching of Claude Neal*.

40. *Daily Times-Courier* (Marianna, Fla.), Oct. 25, 1934.

41. Ibid., Oct. 27, 1934.

42. Kester to Ansley Moore, Oct. 30, 1934, and to Frank Bullock, Nov. 18, 1934, HK Papers, reel 1; "Radical Prophets," p. 101.

43. "Radical Prophets," p. 102.

44. Dec. 3, 1934.

Chapter IV: Sharecroppers Organize

1. Interview with Rodgers by Mitchell, April 30, 1976, and Mitchell to Claude Williams, Dec. 1, 1976, both among the personal papers of H. L. Mitchell.

2. H. L. Mitchell's family history is outlined in Mitchell interview, July 20, 1976, and three interviews conducted with him in 1972 and 1973 by the Institute for Southern Studies staff, Bell I. Wiley participating, microfilm in STFU Scrapbook, reel 2. See also Mitchell's autobiography, *Mean Things Happening in This Land: The Life and Times of H. L. Mitchell, Cofounder of the Southern Tenant Farmers Union* (Montclair, N.J., 1979).

3. *New York Times*, May 7, 1933, "Thomas Demands Capitalism's End," and May 8, 1933, "Socialists to Ask Communist Link."

4. Mitchell interview, July 20, 1976.

5. Johnson to Thomas, Nov. 9, 1932, Norman Thomas Papers, New York Public Library, quoted in Mitchell, *Mean Things Happening*, pp. 38–39.

6. According to Donald H. Grubbs, "The AAA . . . first, . . . enlarged the pool of labor available for such work by cutting acreage out from under sharecroppers; second, by enriching the planters, the AAA made it more profitable for them to pay labor with cash than with a share of the crop; and finally, since the AAA required that benefits be shared with sharecroppers but not the wage laborers, it created a positive monetary inducement to change the workers' status" (*Cry from the Cotton: The Southern Tenant Farmers' Union and the New Deal* [Chapel Hill, N.C., 1971], pp. 22–23). A more colorful account of the early days of the union is Howard Kester's *Revolt among the Sharecroppers* (New York, 1969; first published in 1936).

7. Stuart Jamieson, *Labor Unionism in American Agriculture*, U.S., Department of Labor, Bureau of Labor Statistics, Bulletin no. 836 (Washington, D.C., 1945), pp. 303–5. See also Mitchell, *Mean Things Happening*, pp. 47–49, and *New York Times*, April 18, 1935, "Tenant Law Clash Roils Cotton Belt," by F. Raymond Daniell.

8. *New York Times*, April 20, 1935, "'Run Off Farms,' Tenants Declare," by F. Raymond Daniell.

9. Mitchell later acknowledged that he had hoped at first to make a paying

proposition out of the Southern Tenant Farmers' Union. J. R. Butler shared the same delusion, and he wrote into the original bylaws a provision that the general organizer, in this case himself, would be paid 25¢ for each new member signed up. Neither man then truly understood how penniless the Arkansas sharecroppers were. Even at the union's peak dues barely covered the cost of office stationery. Butler never received his 25¢ per member, and this became a long-standing source of friction between him and Mitchell, who controlled the checkbook. On the other hand, Butler initially did little to earn the money. He was absent from the field during the union's first hectic months of organizing due to his deep involvement in Arkansas Socialist party politics and the fact that he was retained by Commonwealth College to be, more or less, its "sharecropper in residence." Though Butler was not a sharecropper, he had a good understanding of farm problems, and, with his gaunt features and hair sprouting straight up from all sides of his head, he looked the part (H. L. Mitchell to Howard Kester, Aug. 3, 1935, HK Papers, reel 1).

10. "Constitution and By-laws of the STFU," STFU Papers, reel 1; Howard Kester, "Religion—Priestly and Prophetic—in the South," *Radical Religion* 1, no. 4 (Autumn 1936): 23–31.

11. Mitchell to Kester, Aug. 8, 1934, HK Papers, reel 1.

12. "I want aggressive action," Thomas told Kester when asking him to go to Arkansas, "and I don't want the ILD to horn in" (the International Labor Defense was the legal arm of the Communist Party) (Thomas to Howard Kester, Jan. 26, 30, 1935, ibid., reel 1).

At their first meeting Mitchell noticed that Kester carried a pistol in the trunk of his car and a small pouch of poison around his neck. The latter was a suicidal concoction prepared by George Washington Carver intended to spare Kester from torture if he was ever caught by a lynch mob. Kester soon stopped wearing the potion because he decided it was "foolish for a family man" (Kester interview, July 28, 1976; H. L. Mitchell to Howard Kester, Nov. 24, 1934, ibid., reel 1).

13. Interview with H. L. Mitchell by Institute for Southern Studies staff, p. 23. Also see William R. Amberson to Howard Kester, Jan. 22, 1935, Mitchell to Kester, Jan. 1935, and Mitchell to "Dear Sir," Jan. 1935, ibid., reel 1.

14. Koch, *Educational Commune*, pp. 153–57.

15. *New York Times*, April 15, 1935, "AAA Piles Misery on Share Croppers," by F. Raymond Daniell.

16. C. C. Davis to "District Agents," April 5, 1934, STFU Papers, reel 1. See also Grubbs, *Cry from the Cotton*, pp. 32–35; Calvin B. Hoover, *Human Problems in Acreage Reduction in the South*, personal report to

Henry A. Wallace and Chester C. Davis (Durham, N.C., 1934); *New York Times*, March 21, 1935, "South's Land Evils Assailed in Report."

17. *New York Times*, May 19, 1935, "Tenant Farmers Picket the AAA." Later, Cobb did object to the planters' practice of downgrading sharecroppers to day laborers; see ibid., March 9, 1937, "AAA Warns Owners of 'Cropper' Rights."

18. Grubbs, *Cry from the Cotton*, pp. 30–61. Wallace did express concern for the plight of sharecroppers. In his "Wallace Points to Dangers of Tenancy" article in the *New York Times*, March 31, 1935, he noted that "the present condition, particularly in the South, provides fertile soil for Communist and Socialist agitators." His solution was for the government to buy the large estates and sell them in parcels to tenant operators.

19. ACLU press release, Feb. 8, 1935, "Arkansas Tenant Farmers Union Speaker Attacked," Kester's report to J. David Stern, Feb. 8, 1935, STFU Papers, reel 1; Rodgers to Howard Kester and H. L. Mitchell, March 16, 1935, Rodgers to Kester, July 7, 1935, HK Papers, reel 1.

20. Taylor to Paul ——, March 15, 1935, AWT Papers, box 2, folder 13.

21. Sage to Hutchinson, June 10, 1935, HK Papers, reel 1.

22. Opal Benton to Howard Kester, March 6, 1935, J. Abner Sage, Executive Secretary of the Marked Tree Cooperative Association, to Kester, March 5, 1935, Kester's comments written in the margin of a letter from Sage to J. R. Butler, July 10, 1935, ibid., reel 1. See also *New York Times*, April 16, 1935, "Arkansas Violence Laid to Landlords," by F. Raymond Daniell.

23. Kester, *Revolt among the Sharecroppers*, pp. 50–51, 76.

24. Ibid, p. 21.

25. Interview with Clay East by H. L. Mitchell, April 13, 1975, in H. L. Mitchell's personal papers; STFU press release, March 1935, "Norman Thomas Visits the Cotton Fields," STFU Papers, reel 1; Kester, "Radical Prophets," pp. 109–10.

26. STFU press release, March 1935, "Norman Thomas Visits the Cotton Fields," STFU Papers, reel 1; Kester interview, April 29, 1976; Carpenter to Howard Kester, March 16, 1935, HK Papers, reel 1.

27. STFU press release, March 1935, "Black Terror in Arkansas," HK Papers, reel 1; affidavit of Arthur Brookings, June 1935, STFU Papers, reel 1.

28. STFU press releases, March 1935, "Black Terror in Arkansas," March 1935, "Marked Tree, Arkansas," and March 27, 1935, "Telegrams Received from Arkansas," HK Papers, reel 1.

29. Howard Kester and H. L. Mitchell to Thomas, March 27, 1935, and

the account of events, March 30 through April 2, 1935, Gilman to Kester, April 10, 1935, and Lewis to Kester, April 18, 1935, ibid., reel 1.

30. H. L. Mitchell to Howard Kester, Aug. 22, 1935, and Senior to Mitchell, Oct. 1, 1935, STFU Papers, reel 1.

31. Harry Haywood, *Black Bolshevik: Autobiography of an Afro-American Communist* (Chicago, 1978), pp. 398–402; Don West, "Page from an Organizer's Note Book" (undated), Highlander Papers, box 76, folder 14; Jamieson, *Labor Unionism in American Agriculture*, pp. 289–97; Nashville *Tennessean*, Dec. 20, 1932; "Eulogy for Ralph Gray," July 1935, STFU Papers, reel 1.

32. Interview with Johnson by H. L. Mitchell, in H. L. Mitchell's personal papers; SCU Victory Statement, July 4, 1935, STFU Papers, reel 1; Albert Jackson, "You Can Kill Me, But You Can Never Scare Me," *Labor Defender* (I.L.D.), 11, no. 10 (Oct. 1935).

33. H. L. Mitchell to Norman Thomas, Aug. 4, 1935, and to Howard Kester, Aug. 3, 1935, HK Papers, reel 1.

34. Kester interview, July 28, 1976; Howard Kester to Mr. and Mrs. Bergthold, Nov. 16, 1934, HK Papers, reel 1.

35. Thomas to H. L. Mitchell, Aug. 7, 1935, HK Papers, reel 1; H. L. Mitchell to Howard Kester, Nov. 6, 1935, Mitchell to Norman Thomas, Dec. 20, 1935, and Thomas to Mitchell, W. R. Amberson, and Kester, Dec. 27, 1935, ibid., reel 2.

36. H. L. Mitchell to J. R. Butler and Powers Hapgood, June 15, 1935, and to Jack Herling, Aug. 24, 1935, and Frank Morrison to Mitchell, Sept. 24, 1935, STFU Papers, reel 1; Mitchell to Howard Kester, July 15, Aug. 3, 1935, and Kester to Mitchell, Aug. 5, 1935, HK Papers, reel 1.

37. "Minutes of the National Executive Council of the STFU," Sept. 1, 1935, STFU Papers, reel 1; Kester, "Religion—Priestly and Prophetic—in the South," *Radical Religion* 1 (Autumn 1936): 23–31, HK Papers, reel 11.

38. "The Southern Tenant Farmers' Union," *Southern Exposure* 1 (Winter 1974): 26.

39. Howard Kester, "A Statement concerning Farm Tenancy Submitted to the Governor's Commission on Farm Tenancy" (hereafter cited as Kester, "Statement to the Governor"), p. 15, "Writings 1924–1957, Farm Tenancy," HK Papers, reel 11; statement of J. E. Cameroon, Nov. 23, 1935, STFU Papers, reel 11.

40. H. L. Mitchell to Clarence Senior, Oct. 4, 1935, Mitchell to Nathan Wiley, Nov. 21, 1935, STFU Papers, reel 1.

41. H. L. Mitchell to Howard Kester, Nov. 6, 1935, Kester to Niebuhr, Dec. 4, 1935, HK Papers, reel 2.

42. Howard Kester to H. L. Mitchell, Oct. 21, 1935, STFU Papers, reel 1.

43. "STFU Convention Proceedings—Official Report of Second Annual Convention, January 3, 4, 5, 1936, Labor Temple, Little Rock," STFU Papers, reel 1. See also "Lists of Locals," April 18, 1936, ibid., reel 2.

44. Rodgers to Howard Kester, Feb. 10, 1938, HK Papers, reel 4, and Kester, "Religion—Priestly and Prophetic—in the South," *Radical Religion* 1 (Autumn 1936): 29–30, ibid., reel 11.

Chapter V: Gaining Ground

1. H. L. Mitchell to J. E. Cameroon and Wiley Harris, Jan. 13, 1936. STFU Papers, reel 1; Howard Kester and Mitchell to union supporters, Jan. 16, 1936, and STFU press release, Jan. 18, 1936, HK Papers, reel 2; Mitchell to Norman Thomas, Feb. 21, 1936, STFU Papers, reel 1; Roger Baldwin to Governor Futrell, July 8, 1936, ibid., reel 2.

2. STFU press release, Jan. 18, 1936, HK Papers, reel 2; Kester, "Radical Prophets," pp. 106–7; Kester interview, April 29, 1976; H. L. Mitchell to Norman Thomas and James Myers, Jan. 17, 1936, HK Papers, reel 2.

3. Amberson to Howard Kester and H. L. Mitchell, Jan. 1936, HK Papers, reel 2.

4. Gardner Jackson to Howard Kester, Feb. 10, 1936, ibid. Jackson discussed the origins of the La Follette Committee in a letter to Kester (Nov. 22, 1937, ibid., reel 3), noting that the initial financing came from Ethel Clyde, daughter of the Clyde steamship lines chief, who first proposed the Cosmos Club dinner following a meeting at the Friends House in Washington where Kester spoke. H. L. Mitchell to Kester, Feb. 20, 1936, W. R. Amberson to Kester, Feb. 25, 1936, Reinhold Niebuhr and Norman Thomas to Clarence Pickett, March 2, 1936, ibid., reel 2. See also interview with Clyde Johnson by H. L. Mitchell, in H. L. Mitchell's personal papers; Gardner Jackson to Kester, Nov. 22, 1937, HK Papers, reel 3.

5. Grubbs, *Cry from the Cotton*, pp. 98–100; Thomas to Franklin D. Roosevelt, March 14, 1936, H. L. Mitchell to Roosevelt, March 18, 1936, Mitchell to Croom, April 8, 1936, Croom to Mitchell, April 28, 1936, STFU Papers, reel 1.

6. W. R. Amberson to Howard Kester, Feb. 25, 1936, HK Papers, reel 2.

7. Mitchell to Gardner Jackson, March 18, 1936, STFU Papers, reel 1.

8. Howard Kester to James Myers, March 10, 1936, HK Papers, reel 2.

9. H. L. Mitchell to J. R. Butler and Walter Moskop, March 10, 1936, STFU Papers, reel 1.

10. Sherwood Eddy to Howard Kester, March 18, 1936, HK Papers, reel 2. See also Alva W. Taylor's "News Reports" in *Christian Century*, April 22, 1936, Sept. 20, 1939, and June 5, 1936, in AWT Papers, box 5.

11. Sam Franklin interview, Sept. 17, 1976; Claud Nelson to Howard Kester, March 13, 1936, HK Papers, reel 1.

12. Eugene Cox interview, Aug. 24, 1976.

13. W. R. Amberson to Howard Kester, March 16, 1936, H. L. Mitchell to Gardner Jackson, March 16, 1936, Mitchell to Kester, March 22, 1936, HK Papers, reel 2; Mitchell to Johnson, April 20, 1936, STFU Papers, reel 2.

14. "Memo: To All Locals, STFU," March 19, 1936, and Ernie Maddox (quoting Governor Futrell) to League for Southern Labor, March 20, 1936, STFU Papers, reel 1; Kester, "Statement to the Governor," p. 16.

15. Brophy to H. L. Mitchell, March 24, 1936, STFU Papers, reel 1.

16. H. L. Mitchell to Norman Thomas, April 29, 1936, McKinney to Mitchell, April 20, 22, and 26, 1936, Roger Baldwin to Mitchell, May 13, 1936, Parchman to Mitchell, April 5, 1936, ibid., reel 2.

17. STFU press releases, May 20, 23, 1936, Blackstone to H. L. Mitchell, May 20, 1936, Eddy to Cummings, May 21, 1936, STFU Papers, reel 2. See also George Sherwood Eddy, *Eighty Adventurous Years: An Autobiography* (New York, 1955), pp. 156–58.

18. STFU press release, May 23, 1936, Isgrig to H. L. Mitchell, May 25, 1936, STFU Papers, reel 2.

19. Spradling to H. L. Mitchell, May 24, 1936, Haywood and Brown to Mitchell, May 20, 1936, ibid.

20. STFU press releases, June 2, 5, 1936, ibid.; interview with East by H. L. Mitchell, April 13, 1975, p. 17, in H. L. Mitchell's personal papers.

21. "Confidential Brief Digest of Trip to Arkansas by James Myers, June 6–10," STFU press release, June 5, 1936, H. L. Mitchell to Myles Horton and James Dombrowski, June 6, 1936, STFU Papers, reel 2. See also Koch, *Educational Commune*, pp. 148–50; interview with East by Mitchell, April 13, 1975, pp. 18–20, in H. L. Mitchell's personal papers.

22. STFU press release, June 9, 1936, STFU Papers, reel 2.

23. C. J. Spradling to H. L. Mitchell, June 8, 1936, ibid.; "Affidavit of Frank Weems," May 5, 1937, ibid., reel 4.

24. Claude Williams interview, Aug. 17–18, 1976. See also Belfrage,

South of God, pp. 280–84; Willie Sue Blagden, "Is It True What They Say about Dixie?" *Labor Defender* (ILD), 10 (Aug. 1936).

25. Thomas to Roosevelt, June 16, 1936, Glenn to H. L. Mitchell, June 23, 1936, STFU Papers, reel 2.

26. H. L. Mitchell to Sam Franklin and J. R. Butler, Sept. 3, 1936, Butler to Mitchell, Sept. 7, 1936, Thomas, "Arkansas Shame," Sept. 17, 1936, ibid., reel 3.

27. "STFU Calender, June-October 1936," ibid.; *New York Times*, Nov. 25, 1936, "Arkansas Negroes Tell of 'Slavery,'" Nov. 26, 1936, "Arkansas Officer Convicted by Jury on Slavery Charge," Nov. 29, 1936, "'Slavery' Verdict Won by 'G' Men."

28. "Minutes of the National Executive Council, STFU," Oct. 4, 1936, Mitchell to Myles Horton, Oct. 21, 1936, STFU Papers, reel 3; Horton to STFU, Feb. 12, 1937, ibid., reel 4; Mitchell, *Mean Things Happening in This Land*, p. 97.

29. "Minutes," Oct. 4, 1936, STFU Papers, reel 3; Jamieson, *Labor Unionism in American Agriculture*, pp. 292–302.

30. Henderson to H. L. Mitchell, Dec. 21, 1936, STFU Papers, reel 3.

31. H. L. Mitchell to Thomas, Sept. 3, 1936, White to Howard Kester, Dec. 3, 1936, ibid.

32. H. L. Mitchell to Jackson, Sept. 3, 1936, Jackson to Mitchell, Oct. 21, 1936, Mitchell to Norman Thomas, Nov. 17, 1936, ibid. "I never really disliked any Communist except Don Henderson, and I had a great deal of admiration for men like Leif Dahl, Lem Harris and Clyde Johnson," Mitchell wrote in *Mean Things Happening in This Land*, pp. 97–98.

33. "Minutes of Committee on Economic and Racial Justice," Nov. 21, 1936, "Minutes of the SP Southern Conference," Jan. 2, 1937, HK Papers, reel 2.

Chapter VI: Southern Radicals and National Unions

1. Horton, "Highlander Folk School," pp. 114–15; "Report on Highlander Folk School for 1935," Highlander Papers (Tennessee Archives), box 14, folder 8; Hulbert to Roger Baldwin, Feb. 19, 1935, Zilphia Horton to Baldwin, April 10, 1935, Highlander Papers, box 6, folder 4. See also Hawes to Howard Kester, April 2, 1935, HK Papers, reel 1.

2. "Minutes of the Conference of Younger Churchmen of the South," Nov. 11–13, 1936, HK Papers, reel 2; Howard Kester to Zilphia Mae Johnson,

Jan. 24, 1935, ibid., reel 1. See also Glyn Thomas, "Hear the Music Ringing," *New South* 23 (Summer 1968).

3. Ross to Howard Kester, May 18, 1935, Alice Kester to J. Harris, May 21, 1935, Mary W. Hillyer to Howard Kester, May 22, 1935, James Dombrowski to Hillyer, May 25, 1935, HK Papers, reel 1. See also Horton interview, Oct. 31, 1976; Commonwealth College *Fortnightly*, June 1, 1935; Robert Wood, "The I.L.D. in Dixie," *Labor Defender* (ILD), 11 (June 1935); and Robert Sherrill, *Gothic Politics in the Deep South* (New York, 1968), pp. 77–81.

4. Chattanooga *Times*, May 27, 1935; Sutherland to Howard Kester, June 19, 1935, HK Papers, reel 1.

5. W. T. Couch, "Pennsylvania 'Detectives' in North Carolina," *Carolina Magazine* 65 (Dec. 1935): 21–25, *Daily Tar Heel*, Jan. 16, 1935 (clipping located in the Harriet Laura Herring Clipping Collection, box 56A, Burlington Dynamite Case folder), and Walter Whitaker, *Centennial History of Alamance County, 1849-1949* (Burlington, N.C., 1949), pp. 97–103, all in the North Carolina Collection, UNC, Chapel Hill.

6. Walt Pickard, *Burlington Dynamite Plot*, International Labor Defense pamphlet (New York, 1935), copy in the North Carolina Collection, UNC, Chapel Hill.

7. *Daily Tar Heel*, Feb. 22, 1935, "Burlington Prisoners Given Whole-Hearted Support by Group Here," and Feb. 26, 1935, letter from Woodward to editors, North Carolina Collection, UNC, Chapel Hill.

8. W. T. Couch and J. O. Bailey, "Dynamite in Burlington," *Carolina Magazine*, April 1935; E. E. Erickson, "Burlington Dynamite Plot," *Labor Defender* (ILD), 11 (March 1935).

9. Don West, "Dirty Work in Burlington," *Labor Defender* (ILD), 11 (Oct. 1935).

10. John L. Anderson, "Union Misleaders Turn against the Burlington Six," *Labor Defender* (ILD), 11 (June 1935). The ILD printed stories about this case in *Labor Defender* in February, March, April, May, June, July, and October 1935.

11. Alton Lawrence to Kester, Aug. 5, 1935, Kester to Clarence Senior and Thomas, Aug. 24, 1935, HK Papers, reel 1. See also Don West, "Dirty Work in Burlington," *Labor Defender* (ILD), 11 (Oct. 1935), in which he quotes Thomas in the *Socialist Call* of Sept. 7, 1935.

12. Don West, "Page from an Organizer's Note Book," undated, in West's personal papers.

13. See Giles Cooper and Allen McElfresh, "Story of the Kentucky Workers Alliance in the 1930's," copy among Don West's personal papers.

14. *Songs for Southern Workers, 1937 Songbook of the Kentucky Workers Alliance*, prepared by Don West (Huntington, W. Va., 1973).

15. *Building a Union of Textile Workers: A Report to the Convention, Philadelphia, May 19, 1939*, p. 65, copy at UNC, Chapel Hill.

16. Greensboro *Daily News*, July 1, 1937, "Cox Denounces Lewis," and July 12, 1937, "KKK to Fight C.I.O.," Harriet Laura Herring Clipping Collection, North Carolina Collection, UNC, Chapel Hill.

17. John Wesley Kennedy, "A History of the Textile Workers Union of America, C.I.O." (Ph.D. diss., University of North Carolina, 1950), p. 66.

18. "Confidential Memorandum for the Staff," May 8, 1937, Highlander Papers (Tennessee Archives), box 11, folder 1; "Statistics on Highlander Students 1932–1939," ibid., box 10, folder 8.

19. Information about the McColl and Lumberton strikes is from three principal sources: Horton interview, May 12, 1978; Lucy Randolph Mason, *To Win These Rights—A Personal Story of the CIO in the South* (New York, 1952), esp. pp. 40–50; and interview with Myles Horton by William R. Finger, Dec. 6, 1974, Southern Historical Collection, UNC, Chapel Hill.

20. Raleigh *News and Observer*, June 20, 1937, "Labor Organizer Meets Old Enemy."

21. Interview with Myles Horton by William R. Finger, pp. 36–37, Southern Historical Collection, UNC, Chapel Hill.

22. *Building a Union of Textile Workers*, pp. 31–44, 131.

23. Howard Kester to H. L. Mitchell and J. R. Butler, Aug. 4, 1935, HK Papers, reel 1.

24. Aaron Levenstein to Sidney Hertzberg and Norman Thomas, "Report on the STFU Convention," Jan. 14–17, 1937, STFU Papers, reel 4.

25. Howard Kester to Roger Baldwin, Jan. 28, 1937, ibid.

26. A copy of the agreement is among the convention proceedings, Jan. 14–17, 1937, ibid.

27. Howard Kester to Roger Baldwin Jan. 8, 1937, HK Papers, reel 2. See also Aaron Levenstein's report, Jan. 14–17, 1937, STFU Papers, reel 4.

28. STFU press release, Jan. 17, 1937, and "Proceedings of the Muskogee Convention," p. 62, STFU Papers, reel 4. The official union count was:

	Number of locals	Enrolled membership
Texas	8	480
Mississippi	8	988
Tennessee	3	565
Missouri	20	1,373
North Carolina	1	10

Oklahoma	76	8,595
Arkansas		
Counties:		
Crittenden	36	2,487
Cross	28	2,641
Jefferson	24	1,360
Poinsett	17	1,840
St. Francis	51	4,457
Woodruff	9	421
Miscellaneous counties	47	5,610
	328	30,827

29. "Constitution and Bylaws of the STFU, revised," ibid.

30. STFU press release, Jan. 17, 1937, ibid.

31. Howard Kester and Smith, *Ceremony of the Land*, HK Papers, reel 11. Several of the biblical passages used in this ceremony were selected by Alice Kester (Alice Kester to Howard Kester, Jan. 14, 1937, ibid., reel 2).

32. Aaron Levenstein, "Report on the STFU Convention," Jan. 14–17, 1937, Claude Williams to Gardner Jackson, Jan. 23, 1937, H. L. Mitchell to Sidney Hertzberg, Feb. 1, 1937, STFU Papers, reel 4; Mitchell to the National Executive Committee of the Socialist Party, Feb. 2, 1937, HK Papers, reel 2.

33. Jackson to Members of the Executive Council, STFU, June 9, 1937, STFU Papers, reel 4.

34. H. L. Mitchell to Howard Kester, June 10, 14, 1937, Evelyn Smith to Elisabeth Gilman, May 10, 1937, William Amberson to NEC of STFU, June 15, 1937, Kester to Norman Thomas, Aug. 16, 1937, Kester to J. R. Butler, Aug. 20, 1937, HK Papers, reel 2; Thomas to Butler, June 17, 1937, Frank N. Trager to Butler, June 17, 1937, and "Minutes of NEC-STFU, June 18–20," STFU Papers, reel 4.

35. "Press Release—First National Convention of Agricultural, Cannery, and Fruit and Vegetable Packing House Unions," July 1, 1937, Donald Henderson to H. L. Mitchell, July 2, 1937, Blaine Treadway to Sam Franklin, July 8, 1937, and a preliminary draft of the UCAPAWA Constitution, dated July 9, 1937, STFU Papers, reel 5.

36. "Memorandum to CIO on UCAPAWA," July 19, 1937, and UCAPAWA memo to All Affiliated Unions, July 27, 1937, HK Papers, reel 2.

37. Norman Thomas agreed with Kester (Thomas to Howard Kester, Sept. 22, 1937, ibid., reel 3).

38. Howard Kester, "Lynching by Blow Torch, Duck Hill, Mississippi, April 13, 1937," and his notes on Hotel Claridge stationery, ibid., reel 11.

39. "Minutes of NEC, Socialist Party, May 7–9, 1937," and "Minutes of the National Action Committee Meeting Continued from July 30," ibid., reel 2.

40. James P. Cannon, *The History of American Trotskyism* (New York, 1944; based on lectures given in 1942), p. 232.

41. "Minutes of NEC, Socialist Party, June 19, 1937," "Motion by Ward Rodgers of California," Aug. 7, 1937, Roy E. Burt to Members of NEC, Aug. 11, 1937, Norman Thomas to Howard Kester, Aug. 23, Oct. 30, 1937, HK Papers, reel 2. See also "Minutes of NEC, Socialist Party, September 1–4, 1937," ibid., reel 3.

42. Norman Thomas to Howard Kester, Oct. 30, 1937, Aaron Levenstein to Kester, Sept. 8, 1937, ibid., reel 3; Cannon, *History of American Trotskyism*, p. 252.

Chapter VII: Wild Enthusiasm, Disruption, Confusion

1. H. L. Mitchell to Thomas, Roy Burt, and W. R. Amberson, Sept. 26, 1937, Kester to Thomas, Sept. 27, 1937, HK Papers, reel 3.

2. H. L. Mitchell to Sabino Rodriguez, Sept. 1, 1937, STFU Papers, reel 5; District IV UCAPAWA Constitution and By-Laws, HK Papers, reel 2.

3. Niebuhr to Howard Kester, Aug. 1937, HK Papers, reel 2; STFU press release, Sept. 30, 1937, STFU Papers, reel 5.

4. H. L. Mitchell to Norman Thomas, Roy Burt, and W. R. Amberson, Sept. 26, 1937; Mitchell to Howard Kester, Sept. 1, 1937, HK Papers, reel 3. See also Mitchell to Henderson, Sept. 30, 1937, STFU Papers, reel 5.

5. Thomas to H. L. Mitchell, Sept. 29, 1937, Howard Kester to Baldwin, Oct. 9, 1937, HK Papers, reel 3.

6. H. L. Mitchell to Donald Henderson, Oct. 6, 1937, STFU Papers, reel 5.

7. Lawrence to Alice Kester, Oct. 12, 1937, HK Papers, reel 3.

8. Norman Thomas to H. L. Mitchell, Sept. 29, 1937, ibid.

9. Affidavits of Walter Biggs, Henry Burnett and Jesse Rose, Oct. 13, 1937, STFU Papers, reel 5. J. R. Butler was also attacked in the St. Francis County courthouse when he came with Claude Williams and Howard Kester to the trial of Melvin Swinea, an organizer accused of shady business dealings. Kester wrote that Butler was "pretty bunged up" (STFU press release, Oct. 2, 1937, ibid.).

10. H. L. Mitchell to All Locals, Jan. 1, 1938, S. C. E. Taylor's survey form, Jan. 2, 1938, ibid., reel 7.

11. "Proceedings, Fourth Annual Convention STFU, Little Rock, Arkansas, February 25–27, 1938," ibid.

12. Young to Howard Kester, Feb. 28, 1938, White to Kester, March 11, 1938, HK Papers, reel 3; Young to Evelyn Smith, Feb. 9, 1938, Claude Williams to H. L. Mitchell, March 3, 1938, STFU Papers, reel 7.

13. "Record of Oklahoma STFU Meeting, January 12, 1938, Muskogee," STFU Papers, reel 7. See also Odis Sweeden to H. L. Mitchell, July 19, 1938, ibid., reel 8.

14. STFU press release (never issued), April 29, 1938, and H. L. Mitchell to Howard Kester, April 29, 1938, HK Papers, reel 4; "Minutes of International Board Meeting, April 28, 1938," STFU Papers, reel 8.

15. Howard Kester to Scotty and Gladys Cowan, April 30, 1938, to Elisabeth Gilman, May 2, 1938, H. L. Mitchell and J. R. Butler to all STFU locals, May 11, 1938, HK Papers, reel 4; Mitchell to Jackson, May 18, 1938, STFU Papers, reel 8.

16. Thomas to H. L. Mitchell, Aug. 16, 1938, HK Papers, reel 4.

17. Butler to Williams, Aug. 22, 1938, STFU Papers, reel 8.

18. Untitled and undated document, placed at August 1938, ibid.

19. J. R. Butler to Claude Williams, Aug. 22, 1938, ibid.; Hays to Howard Kester, April 21, 1936, HK Papers, reel 2.

20. H. L. Mitchell to Howard Kester, Aug. 29, 1938, J. R. Butler to Kester, Sept. 9, 1938, HK Papers, reel 4; Claude Williams to ——, Aug. 25, 1938, STFU Papers, reel 8.

21. J. R. Butler to Members of the Executive Council, STFU, July 18, 1938, E. B. McKinney to Wiley Harris, July 29, Aug. 11, 1938, STFU Papers, reel 8.

22. "Summary Minutes of NEC Meeting," Sept. 16–17, 1938, ibid., reel 9.

23. Claude Williams to J. R. Butler, Nov. 1, 1938, ibid.

24. "E. B. McKinney's statement at Cotton Plant, Arkansas, January 1, 1939," Claude Williams's personal papers; "Proceedings Fifth Annual Convention STFU, 1939," STFU Papers, reel 9.

25. "Annual Convention of the STFU," and "Proceedings Fifth Annual Convention STFU, 1939," STFU Papers, reel 9.

26. The STFU (District IV) was credited with having 146 of the 371 chartered locals in UCAPAWA and 42,000 of the international's total membership of 124,865 ("Report of Donald Henderson, General President,

287

to the Second Annual Convention of the UCAPAWA, San Francisco, California, December 12–16, 1938," ibid.).

27. H. L. Mitchell to John Herling, Feb. 10, 1939, ibid., reel 10; Claude Williams interview, May 11, 12, 1977.

28. STFU press release, Oct. 1, 1938, J. R. Butler to Roger Baldwin, Oct. 6, 1938, to H. L. Mitchell, Oct. 10, 1938, "The Southern Tenant Farmer's Union in 1938, Report to the Annual Convention by H. L. Mitchell," Owen H. Whitfield to Mitchell, Dec. 1, 1938, STFU Papers, reel 9; Murphy to Whitfield, Jan. 9, 1939, ibid., reel 10.

29. J. R. Butler to H. L. Mitchell, Jan. 9, 1939, STFU press release, Jan. 14, 1939, STFU Executive Council to John L. Lewis, undated (probably Jan. 15, 1939), Owen H. Whitfield to STFU, Jan. 10, 1939, ibid., reel 10.

30. Howard Kester to Walter Sikes, Jan. 14, 1939, H. L. Mitchell to Kester, Jan. 14, 1939, T. B. Cowan to Kester, Jan. 16, 1939, HK Papers, reel 4.

31. Priscilla Robertson to "Dear Friends," July 5, 1939, STFU Papers, reel 11; "Minutes, STFU Executive Council, January 21, 1939," "STFU Statement of Cash Receipts and Disbursements for Month of January 1939," ibid., reel 10.

32. Mitchell interview, Aug. 16, 1976.

33. Interview with Booker Clark by H. L. Mitchell, April 6, 1974, in H. L. Mitchell's personal papers.

34. Announcement of District IV UCAPAWA Convention on June 14–15, 1939, and Priscilla Robertson to "Dear Friends," July 5, 1939, STFU Papers, reel 11; Fellowship of Southern Churchmen Newsletter, April 1945, FSC Papers, box 2, folder 8; Burgess to "Dear Friends of Delmo Homes," March 25, 1946, ibid., box 3, folder 25.

35. J. R. Butler to Donald Henderson, Jan. 31, 1939, Williams to Butler, Jan. 11, 1939; —— to H. L. Mitchell, Feb. 24, 1939, STFU Papers, reel 10.

36. Owen H. Whitfield to All Locals and Members of the STFU, Feb. 24, 1939, ibid.; H. L. Mitchell to Lewis, March 1, 1939, Mitchell to Brophy, March 11, 1939, STFU press release, March 12, 1939, ibid., reel 11.

37. Harriet Young to J. R. Butler and H. L. Mitchell, March 14, 1939, ibid., reel 11.

38. Joyce Crawford to J. R. Butler and H. L. Mitchell, March 13, 1939, Mitchell to Harriet Young, March 16, 1939, ibid.

39. Donald Henderson to All STFU Locals, March 22, 1939, "Instructions to Delegates Representing STFU," April 2, 1939, STFU press release,

April 2, 1939, UCAPAWA press release, undated (filed at May 4, 1939), ibid.

40. Sweeden to J. R. Butler, Dec. 1, 1938, ibid., reel 9; Butler to Lawrence Burr, Feb. 3, 1939, Butler to Howard Kester, Feb. 18, 1939, W. M. Tanner to H. L. Mitchell, Feb. 26, 1939, ibid., reel 10; "Constitution and By-Laws of Oklahoma Tenant Farmers Union," March 1939, ibid., reel 11.

41. H. L. Mitchell to Thomas, May 5, 1939, ibid., reel 11.

42. Jackson to H. L. Mitchell, Feb. 21, 1939, ibid., reel 10; Mitchell to Lincoln Fairley, April 13, 1939, ibid., reel 11.

43. Priscilla Robertson to "Dear Friends," July 5, 1939, H. L. Mitchell to Myles Horton, June 24, 1939, ibid., reel 11. See also *STFU News*, June 1940, ibid., reel 58.

44. Hayes to H. L. Mitchell, May 9, 1939, ibid., reel 11.

45. See the "Statement of STFU to the President's Special Commission on Farm Tenancy," Jan. 4, 1937, Howard Kester's statement to the Commission in Montgomery, Jan. 6, 1937, H. L. Mitchell to Gardner Jackson, Jan. 6, 1937, ibid., reel 4. A detailed account of the FSA is given by Sidney Baldwin in *Poverty and Politics: The Rise and Decline of the Farm Security Administration* (Chapel Hill, N.C., 1968).

Chapter VIII: Progressivism Besieged

1. A careful history of the SCHW is provided by Thomas A. Krueger, *And Promises to Keep: The Southern Conference for Human Welfare, 1938–1948* (Nashville, 1967). He notes the meeting between President Roosevelt and Joseph Gelders on pp. 16–17. See also Eleanor Roosevelt's foreword to Lucy Randolph Mason's *To Win These Rights* (New York, 1952). The first chapter contains information on her family background.

2. Horton interview, Oct. 31, 1976.

3. "Report on Proceedings of the Southern Conference for Human Welfare," p. 2, Highlander Papers, box 70, folder 8.

4. Ibid., pp. 13–14; Graham to Howard Kester, Dec. 1, 1939, HK Papers, reel 5.

5. Krueger, *And Promises to Keep*, p. 38; Miller to Howard Kester, March 22, 1939, HK Papers, reel 4; Raymond Wolters, *Negroes and the Great Depression: The Problem of Economic Recovery* (Westport, Conn., 1970), pp. 353–76.

6. Francis P. Miller to Kester, Nov. 25, 1938, Kester to Miller, March 19,

1939, HK Papers, reel 4; H. L. Mitchell to Kester, Oct. 1, 1938, STFU Papers, reel 9; William F. Illig to Mitchell, Feb. 4, 1939, Mitchell to J. R. Butler, Feb. 5, 1939, ibid., reel 10.

7. Belle Barton, "Things Happen in Alabama," *Labor Defender* (ILD), 10 (Dec. 1936).

8. Lucille B. Milner to SCHW, Nov. 15, 1938, Howard Kester to Francis P. Miller, March 19, 1939, HK Papers, reel 4.

9. Howard Kester to Francis P. Miller, March 19, 1939, ibid.; Howard Lee to Willard Uphaus, May 7, 1935, H. L. Mitchell's personal papers. According to the evidence available to Thomas Krueger, Howard Lee was at this time or shortly afterwards a member of the Communist party. In 1939 several of Lee's friends, including Fellowship of Southern Churchmen leader William W. McKee, insisted hotly that Lee was neither a Communist nor a subversive (Krueger, *And Promises to Keep*, p. 79; McKee to Frank P. Graham, Dec. 18, 1939, HK Papers, reel 5).

10. Francis P. Miller to Howard Kester, March 22, 1939, HK Papers, reel 4; Graham to Kester, Dec. 1, 1939, ibid., reel 5.

11. Howard Kester to Frank P. Graham, Dec. 9, 1939, to Gilman, Dec. 31, 1939, ibid., reel 5.

12. "Statement of Principles, Fellowship of Southern Churchmen, adopted in Berea, Kentucky, 1938, Authored by T. B. Cowan, Howard Kester, Walter Sikes," ibid., reel 4. See also *Prophetic Religion* 13 (Spring 1953). the FSC held its 1937 annual meeting in Norris, Tenn. on Nov. 16–18, and for the first time performed the *Ceremony of the Prophets*, written by Howard and Alice Kester, which begged God to forgive the "sloth and cowardice" of the church. The conference also resolved to oppose the invasion of carpetbag industry seeking to "enslave and exploit" the South (see *Southern Churchmen* 1 [Dec. 1937], HK Papers, reel 12; *Ceremony of the Prophets*, ibid., reel 11).

13. FSC press release, undated (April 1938), Cowan to Howard Kester, April 27, 1938, Kester to Scotty and Gladys Cowan, Oct. 23, 1938, HK Papers, reel 4. See also *Prophetic Religion* 1 (May 1938), ibid., reel 12; Carl Herman Voss, "Churchmen Adopt Strong Positions," *Christian Century*, May 11, 1938.

14. Scotty Cowan and Howard Kester to Williams, Dec. 11, 1939, Alice Kester to Scotty and Gladys Cowan, Dec. 11, 1949, HK Papers, reel 5; Kester interview, July 28, 1976; Kester to Maxwell Hahn, Feb. 18, 1955, Field Foundation Files, "Fellowship of Southern Churchmen 1942–1953."

15. Don West to Myles Horton, Sept. 14, 1939, Highlander Papers, box 29, folder 21; West to Howard Kester, Nov. 27, Dec. 14, 1939, Kester to West, Dec. 11, 1939, Jan. 15, 1941, HK Papers, reel 5.

Chapter IX: The War Years

1. Eugene Cox interview, Aug. 24, 1976.

2. See STFU Papers, reels 17 to 22, and H. L. Mitchell interview, Aug. 17, 1976.

3. *Tenant Farmer* 1 (Aug. 15, 1941), STFU Papers, reel 58. See also STFU Papers, reel 20.

4. See STFU Papers, reels 25 to 32.

5. See Mark Naison, "Claude and Joyce Williams, Pilgrims of Justice," *Southern Exposure* 1 (Winter 1974): 38–50; and Bill Troy and Claude Williams, "People's Institute of Applied Religion," ibid., 4 (Fall 1976): 46–53. See also the "Digest: People's Institute of Applied Religion," Field Foundation Files, "People's Institute of Applied Religion."

6. Harbison, "Taylor," pp. 257–63; Taylor to Bill ——, May 16, 1936, AWT Papers, box 2, folder 16.

7. Quoted in *Economic Justice Bulletin* (National Religion and Labor Foundation), 10 (Jan. 1942).

8. See Cedric Belfrage, *A Faith to Free the People* (New York, 1944), pp. 247–95; Claude Williams to Maxwell Hahn, May 25, 1943, and "Program for a Peoples' Congress of Applied Religion, July 22–24, 1944," Field Foundation Files.

9. Howard Kester to Brad Young, Jan. 5, 1939, to Elisabeth Gilman, Jan. 5, 1939, to Niebuhr, Jan. 9, 1939, and Alice Kester to Walter Sikes, April 3, 1939, HK Papers, reel 4; Howard Kester to Fred Ensminger, Oct. 15, 1939, to CERJ, Oct. 27, 1939, ibid., reel 5; Howard Kester to Alice Kester, April 3, 1941, Alice Kester to Scotty and Gladys Cowan, April 4, 1941, ibid., reel 6.

10. NAACP press release, Jan. 16, 1942, and *That America Be Not Blamed*, Oct. 14, 1942, ibid., reel 7; FSC press release, Dec. 26, 1942, FSC Papers, box 1, folder 4; "A Program of the Conference of FSC, March 23–26, 1943," ibid., box 1, folder 5; FSC Newsletter, May 1943, HK Papers, reel 12; "Radical Prophets," p. 52.

11. Michael Smathers interview, May 16, 1977; Eugene Smathers, *The Contribution of the Church to Big Lick Community*, reprinted from *Religious Education*, Jan.–Feb. 1955, Eugene Smathers, *A Primer for Friends of the Soil*, also *I Work in the Cumberlands*, and FOS "General Statement," Smathers family papers. See also "Friends of the Soil Membership," Dec. 10, 1947, FSC Papers, box 12, folder 110.

12. S. J. Wright to Howard Kester, Dec. 19, 1944, Francis R. Cope, Jr., to Kester, June 21, 1943, Mays to Kester, Aug. 17, 1943, Alice Kester

to Family, Aug. 30, 1943, HK Papers, reel 8. The "Journal of Rural Exploration, July 1935" (ibid., reel 9) provides a history of Penn School.

13. Penn School, 1944 Salary Schedule ("Penn School Reports"), ibid., reel 9; Kester interview, July 27, 1976; Charles S. Johnson, *Into the Main Stream: A Survey of Best Practices in Race Relations in the South* (Chapel Hill, N.C., 1947), pp. 181–82; G. H. Aull to Howard Kester, Oct. 16, 1944, Kester to Trustees, May 9, 1944, to Ethel Moors, July 11, 1944, HK Papers, reel 8; "Radical Prophets," p. 30.

14. See U.S. Department of the Interior, *Negro Education: A Study of the Private and Higher Schools for Colored People in the United States* (Washington, D.C., 1917).

15. Alice Kester to Miss Merriam, Sept. 25, 1945, HK Papers, reel 9.

16. "Minutes of the Summer Meeting of the Trustees of Penn School, June 11, 1946," "Meeting of the Committee on the Future Development of Penn School, November 21, 1946," untitled report, Jan. 7, 1947, ibid.

17. Elizabeth Jacoway Burns, "The Industrial Education Myth: Character Building at Penn School, 1900–1948" (Ph.D. diss. University of North Carolina, Chapel Hill, 1974), p. 531; Grace B. House to Howard Kester, March 17, 1948, W. E. Cadbury to Dr. George H. Aull, Feb. 20, 1948, "Penn School Board Annual Meeting, March 31, 1948," Beaufort County Schools to Penn, May 26, 1948, Mrs. Courtney Siceloff to Alice Kester, Aug. 23, 1951, HK Papers, reel 9. See also Kester interview, July 27, 1976.

18. West to Myles Horton, Sept. 14, 1939, Highlander Papers, box 29, folder 21; West, *"Blessed Are the Peace Makers,"* ibid., box 76, folder 14.

19. Don West to Taylor, July 25, 1941, AWT Papers, box 4.

20. Don West, "Education for Victory" (excerpts from a speech given March 19, 1943), Highlander Papers, box 29, folder 21.

21. *Amalgamated Clothing Worker*, April 10, 1946, "Georgia Minister Brings Stirring Message to Striking Andalusians," ibid., box 76, folder 14; Don West to Horton, Feb. 25, April 5, 1946, ibid., box 29, folder 21; West interview May 30, 1977.

22. Dombrowski to Virginia Durr, July 3, 1941, Highlander Papers, box 11, folder 1; Lucy Randolph Mason to Eleanor Roosevelt, Jan. 13, 1942, ibid., box 24, folder 17.

23. Lee to Kester, Jan. 15, 1940, Graham to Kester, Feb. 13, 1940, Kester to Graham, Feb. 17, 1940, to McDowell, Feb. 17, 1940, McDowell to Kester, April 2, 1940, HK Papers, reel 5.

24. Krueger, *And Promises to Keep*, pp. 60–64.

25. Ibid., pp. 76–82, 87–88.

26. Roger Baldwin to Clark Foreman, May 19, 1942, Highlander Papers, box 6, folder 4; "Program for Southern Conference for Human Welfare, April 19–21, 1942," and "SCHW Outstanding Achievements in 1942," Field Foundation Files.

27. Alva W. Taylor, "News Report," *Christian Century*, April 24, 1946, AWT Papers, box 5; Krueger, *And Promises to Keep*, pp. 150–51; Dombrowski interview, Nov. 8, 1976.

28. Virginia Durr to James Dombrowski, March 11, 1941, Highlander Papers, box 11, folder 1.

29. Malvina C. Thompson to James Dombrowski, April 23, Oct. 25, 1940, Dombrowski to Mrs. Franklin D. Roosevelt, April 26, 1940, Blair to Mrs. Roosevelt, Sept. 26, 1940, ibid., box 24, folder 17; Durr to Dombrowski, ante March 11, 1941, and leaflet ("Mrs. Roosevelt Continues to Support Highlander"), Feb. 1, 1941, ibid., box 11, folder 1.

30. James Dombrowski to Eleanor Roosevelt, Jan. 14, 1942, ibid., box 24, folder 17; Dombrowski to Durr, July 3, 1941, ibid., box 11, folder 1.

31. "Resolution Launching the Southern Regional Council, August 4, 1943," and "The South of the Future: A Statement of Policy and Aims of the Southern Regional Council, December 12, 1951," in Susan Martin Weltner, "George Sinclair Mitchell: Gradualism and the Changing South" (Special Scholars thesis, University of Virginia, 1979).

Chapter X: Revolution Denied

1. August Raymond Ogden, *The Dies Committee: A Study of the Special House Committee for the Investigation of Un-American Activities, 1938–1944* (Washington, D.C., 1945), pp. 52–57; U.S., Congress, Senate, Committee of the Judiciary, *Communism in the Mid-South: Hearings before the Subcommittee to Investigate the Administration of the Internal Security Act and Other Internal Security Laws*, 85th Cong., 1st sess., p. 27 (hereafter cited as *Mid-South Hearings*).

2. Taylor to Editor of the Nashville *Tennessean*, June 19, 1947, to Barnett, May 6, 1948, AWT Papers, box 2, folders 38 and 41. See also Anne Braden, *House Un-American Activities Committee: Bulwark of Segregation* (New Orleans, 1964), p. 24; Krueger, *And Promises to Keep*, p. 191.

3. Cedric Belfrage, *The American Inquisition, 1945–1960* (Indianapolis and New York, 1973), p. 78.

4. Carl McIntire, *Communist Minister . . .* (Collingswood, N.J.), in Claude Williams's personal papers; Bill Troy and Claude Williams, "The

People's Institute of Applied Religion," *Southern Exposure*, 4 (Fall 1976): 46–53.

5. Krueger, *And Promises to Keep*, p. 4; "Cliff Durr: My Early Years with the FCC," interview by Allen Tullos and Candace Waid, *Southern Exposure*, 2 (Winter 1975): 14–22.

6. West was also estranged in this period from the Communist party district organizer in Atlanta, Homer Chase, whom he called "a little Stalin, if there ever was one" (interview with Don West by Charles H. Martin, Sept. 13, 1970, in Martin's personal papers); *Mid-South Hearings*, p. 209; Atlanta *Daily World*, Oct. 27, 1946, "Liberal Poet Object of Suit."

7. Nelle Morton interview, Sept. 10, 1978.

8. Charles Jones interview, July 26, 1977; Nelle Morton to Howard Kester, March 30, 1974, in personal papers of Howard Kester.

9. Dave Burgess to Nelle Morton, March 5, 1945, FSC *Newsletter*, June and Aug. 1945, Morton to Rev. Edward Brown, Sept. 18, 1945, to Alexander Miller, Sept. 28, 1945, FSC Papers, box 2.

10. Raleigh *News and Observer*, Aug. 19, 1947; Charlotte *News*, Aug. 20, 1947. Also see "Report of the Workshop on Cooperative Living, Tyrell C. Training School," FSC Papers, box 2, folder 11; and Nelle Morton's correspondence, April through Nov. 1947, HK Papers, reels 6 and 7.

11. Hibbard Thatcher interview, Oct. 6, 1976; Atlanta *Journal*, July 18, 1948; Atlanta *Constitution*, July 17, 1948. See also Greig and Pegi Ritchie to Cornelia Lively, Aug. 13, 1948, "A Summary of the Incident of July 16th by James A. Mackay," and "Brief Account of July 16, 1948," HK Papers, reel 7.

12. George Houser and Bayard Rustin, *We Challenged Jim Crow: A Report on the Journey of Reconciliation, April 9–23, 1947*, FOR/CORE pamphlet. See also FSC press release, April 18, 1947, and Bayard Rustin, "A Condensation of a Report on Camp 508 (Colored)," FSC Papers, boxes 4 and 18; Charles Jones interview, July 26, 1977; and Nelle Morton to Howard Kester, March 30, 1974, in Howard Kester's personal papers.

13. Taylor McMillan, *Who Beat Frank Graham*, Political Studies Program Research Report, no. 1 (Chapel Hill, N.C., May 20, 1959), "Champion of Democracy—Senator Frank P. Graham," campaign literature, and Frank P. Graham's farewell statement, Sept. 22, 1950, North Carolina Collection, UNC, Chapel Hill.

14. J. B. Matthews, "The Reds in Our Churches," *American Mercury* 77 (July 1953): 3–13.

15. *The Commonwealth* (Greenwood, Miss.), Feb. 13, 1904, "John Holbert and Wife Are Burned at the Stake," in the James O. Eastland Sub-

ject File, no. 1, Mississippi Department of Archives and History, Jackson. The report of Eastland's murder was carried in other newspapers, including the *Asheville* (N.C.) *Daily Citizen*, Feb. 3, 1904.

16. U.S., Congress, Senate, Committee of the Judiciary, *Southern Conference Educational Fund, Inc.: Hearings before the Subcommittee to Investigate the Administration of the Internal Security Act and Other Internal Security Laws*, 83d Cong., 2d sess., March 18, 19, 20, 1954, pp. v, 14 (hereafter cited as *SCEF Hearings*).

17. Ibid., pp. 42–71.

18. Ibid., pp. 84–93; Nashville *Tennessean*, March 21, 1954; *New York Times*, March 21, 1954.

19. Horton to Highlander Executive Council Members, Sept. 1949, Highlander Papers, box 41, folder 2.

20. Horton, "Highlander Folk School," pp. 242–86.

21. *SCEF Hearings*, pp. 150–51; "Statement of Myles Horton," Highlander Papers (Tennessee Archives), box 1, folder 4.

22. Belfrage, *American Inquisition*, pp. 229–30, 249, 278, 284.

23. William F. Hoot to Claude C. Williams, May 25, June 22, 1953, Williams to Presbytery of Detroit, Aug. 30, 1953, Detroit *News*, Jan. 5, 1954, "Trial to Unfrock 'Red' Pastor Opens," and Jan. 14, 1954, "Pastor Waits Ruling after Trial," in Claude Williams's personal papers.

24. Eugene Cox interview, Aug. 24, 1976; Minter to the author, Nov. 22, 1976.

25. Memphis *Commercial Appeal*, Oct. 7, 1955, New Orleans *Times-Picayune*, Oct. 2, 1955, *Delta Democrat Times*, Sept. 30, 1955, Gene and Lindsey Hail Cox to Friends, April 1957, and assorted clippings, in personal papers of Eugene Cox. See also Eugene Cox interview, April 24, 1976.

26. See *The Southerner: A Voice of the People* (Dalton, Ga.), 1 (Dec. 1955); Don West to Alva W. Taylor, Jan. 2, 25, 1955, AWT Papers, box 4; Don West interview, May 30, 1977.

27. Acts 2:44–45.

28. *Mid-South Hearings*, pp. 25–31; see also interview with Don West by Charles H. Martin, Sept. 13, 1970, in Martin's personal papers.

29. U.S. Congress, House, Committee on Un-American Activities, *Communist Inflitration and Activities in the South: Hearings*, 85th Cong., 2d sess., July 29, 30, and 31, 1958, p. 2627, testimony of Armando Penha.

30. Ibid., pp. 2667–2687, testimony of Carl Braden and Frank Wilkinson.

31. Willard Uphaus, *Commitment* (New York, 1963); Eric Bentley, ed.,

Thirty Years of Treason: Excerpts from Hearings before the House Committee on Un-American Activities, 1938–1968 (New York, 1971), pp. 728–70; Myles Horton to Richard Nixon, July 29, 1960, Highlander Papers, box 28, folder 19.

32. Georgia Commission on Education, *Communism and the NAACP* (Atlanta, 1958), Highlander Papers (Tennessee Archives), box 16, folder 6; Braden, *House Un-American Activities Committee*, p. 26.

33. Horton to Virginia Durr, Sept. 25, 1957, Highlander Papers, box 11, folder 1.

34. Adams, *Unearthing Seeds of Fire*, pp. 153–55; Horton, "Highlander Folk School," pp. 242–95.

35. Durr to Myles and Zilphia Horton, Jan. 30, 1956, to Myles Horton, Feb. 18, 1956, Highlander Papers, box 11, folder 1.

36. Internal Revenue Service to Highlander, Feb. 20, 1957, Chattanooga *News Free-Press*, Sept. 7, 1957, "Highlander Folk School Loses Tax Deductible Status, Eastland Agrees," Highlander Papers (Tennessee Archives), box 8.

37. *Highlander Folk School—Communist Training School, Monteagle, Tenn.*, Georgia Commission on Education pamphlet, ibid., box 8.

38. See John Egerton, "The Trial of Highlander Folk School," *Southern Exposure* 6 (Winter 1978): 82–89.

39. Horton, "Highlander Folk School," pp. 306–9.

40. The campaigns of the NFLU in California may be followed in the STFU Papers, reels 33 through 43, and Ernesto Galarza, *Farm Workers and Agribusiness in California, 1947–1960* (Notre Dame, Ind., 1977). There is much to document this period in the life of H. L. Mitchell in the STFU Papers, reels 44 through 57.

41. Kester, "How Shall We Clothe Him?" *Prophetic Religion* 12(1952): 14, ibid., reel 12.

42. "Proceedings of the Conference on Christian Faith and Human Relations, Nashville, Tennessee, April 23, 24, 25, 1957," p. 32, HK Papers, reel 8.

43. "Statement of Principles, Fellowship of Southern Churchmen, Adopted in Berea, Kentucky, 1938, Authored by T. B. Cowan, Howard Kester, Walter Sikes," ibid., reel 4; *Southern Churchmen* 1 (Dec. 1937), ibid., reel 12.

Index

INDEX

INDEX

INDEX

INDEX

INDEX